Critical Acclaim for *Solaris® System Administrator's Guide*

"A solid book, with all the important system administration tasks clearly explained."

—Bill Joy, Vice President, Research and Development
Sun Microsystems, Inc.

"The *Solaris® System Administrator's Guide* began as a collection of internal notes used by Sun's own administrators. It represents helpful hints and detailed references on system administration tasks that have been tried and tested by some of the toughest UNIX taskmasters in the world."

—Ed Zander, President
SunSoft, Inc.

"This small book is a perfect mix of quick-and-easy tasks and timely reference material. A must for novices and experts."

—Steve Hanlon, Product Marketing Manager
SunSoft, Inc.

"...[I] was having a problem with my workstation, so I used the *Solaris® System Administrator's Guide* and it got me up and running in no time at all! It's a very handy desktop reference."

—Bob McInroy, Manager, Developer Marketing Programs
SunSoft, Inc.

"Our system administrators are using the *Solaris® System Administrator's Guide* internally to make the transition to Solaris 2.0 and find it a helpful reference for anyone to have next to the workstation. Especially helpful is the thorough index that allows you to clue into the task at hand. The guide is useful because it is not only compact, but is also a clearly written reference."

—Bill Prouty, Chair, Sun Solaris 2.0
Internal Migration Committee, SunSoft, Inc.

Solaris® System Administrator's Guide

SunSoft Press

Solaris® System Administrator's Guide

Janice Winsor

Ziff-Davis Press
Emeryville, California

Development Editor	Melinda Levine
Copy Editor	Ellen Falk
Technical Reviewers	Pat Shriver, Robin Greynolds
Project Coordinator	Bill Cassel
Proofreader	Vanessa Miller
Cover Design	Carrie English and Ken Roberts
Book Design	Laura Lamar/MAX, San Francisco
Technical Illustration	Cherie Plumlee Computer Graphics & Illustration
Word Processing	Howard Blechman and Cat Haglund
Page Layout	Sarah Tucker and Bruce Lundquist
Indexer	Valerie Robbins

This book was produced on a Macintosh IIfx, with the following applications: FrameMaker,® Microsoft® Word, MacLink®*Plus*, Aldus® FreeHand,™ Adobe Photoshop,™ and Collage Plus™

Ziff-Davis Press
5903 Christie Avenue
Emeryville, CA 94608
1-800-688-0448

ISBN 1-56276-080-7
Manufactured in the United States of America
10 9 8 7 6 5 4

CONTENTS AT A GLANCE

TABLE OF CONTENTS

ACKNOWLEDGMENTS

MANY PEOPLE CONTRIBUTED TO THE DESIGN, WRITING, AND PRODUCtion of this book. SunSoft would particularly like to acknowledge the following people for their contributions:

Connie Howard and Bridget Burke, SunSoft Publications managers, for their support and encouragement.

Randy Enger, SunSoft Engineering Manager, for help in gaining early access to the Solaris 2.1 administration tools. Special thanks are also due to Gordon Kass, Solaris 2.1 Product Manager, and Steve Hanlon, SunSoft Marketing.

Patrick Moffitt, SunOS Ambassador, for providing background information about the Service Access Facility. Patrick Moffitt and Cindy Swearingen, Technical Education Services, for providing a modem procedure that worked.

Rick Ramsey, SunSoft Technical Writer, for source information about NIS+, and for many discussions about good technical writing.

Keith Palmby, SunSoft Technical Writer, for source information about user environments.

Charla Mustard-Foote, SunSoft Technical Writer, for providing source information and the conversion table for Appendix A, and for calmly helping make software available for screen shots.

Bruce Sesnovich, SunSoft Technical Writer, for providing background information about the Service Access Facility and modem procedures.

Tom Amiro, SunSoft Technical Writer, for providing background information about administering user accounts and printers, and for early access to information about the Solaris 2.1 administration tools. Tom also deserves thanks for help in making software available for screen shots.

John Pew, Writing Consultant, for providing information and filters for converting raster files to gif format.

Bill Edwards, Dave Miner, Jeff Parker, Chuck Kollars, Ken Kane, and Paul Sawyer, SunSoft Engineers in Billerica, MA, deserve thanks for reviewing information about NIS+ security, Administration Tool security, Database Manager, and User Manager.

Sam Cramer, SunSoft Engineer, for help with file system information. Bill Shannon, SunSoft Distinguished Engineer, for help with backup and restore information.

Pat Shriver, SunSoft Engineer, Robin Greynolds, SunSoft System Administrator, and Craig Mohrman, SunSoft Engineer, for technical review.

Karin Ellison, SunSoft Press, for parenting this book and for extraordinary assistance, including providing a Solaris 2.0 system for use on this project.

Thanks are also due to Melinda Levine, our editor at Ziff-Davis Press, and to Cheryl Holzaepfel, Managing Editor, for being so easy to work with.

The author would like to thank her husband for his love and patience.

And lastly, thanks to the engineers, writers, and marketing folks at SunSoft who helped with the SunSoft version of this book.

INTRODUCTION

THIS BOOK—TEN CHAPTERS, TWO APPENDICES, AND ONE GLOSSARY LONG—is for beginning system administrators, system administrators new to the Solaris® 2.*x* environment, or any user who wants a task-oriented quick-reference guide to basic administrative commands.

A Quick Tour of the Contents

Chapter 1, "Introducing Solaris System Administration," describes basic administration tasks, superuser status, and how to communicate with users, start up and shut down systems, and monitor processes. It also introduces some frequently used commands and the Administration Tool new to the Solaris 2.*x* environment.

Chapter 2, "Using Basic OS Commands," describes basic commands for finding user information and environment information for creating and editing files, combining commands and redirecting output, displaying manual pages, and locating disk information.

Chapter 3, "Administering Devices," describes how to use tapes and diskettes to store and retrieve files, and how to administer disks. It also introduces the Service Access Facility and provides instructions for setting up port monitors for printers and modems.

Chapter 4, "Administering File Systems," describes the types of file systems provided in the Solaris 2.*x* environment, describes the default file system, the virtual file system table, and the file system administrative commands. It shows you how to make file systems available and how to back up and restore file systems.

Chapter 5, "Administering Network Services," describes commands used to check on remote system status, log in to remote systems, and transfer files between systems. It also describes how to use the Administration Tool to make changes to NIS+ databases once NIS+ is up and running.

Chapter 6, "Administering Printing," introduces the LP print service, which is completely different from the print service of the SunOS™ 4.*x* system software. It describes how to set up printing services and how to use the printing commands.

Chapter 7, "Administering User Accounts and Groups," describes how to add and remove user accounts and how to set up new group accounts.

Chapter 8, "Understanding Shells," describes some commands common to all shells and provides basic information about the Bourne, C, and Korn shells.

Chapter 9, "Administering Systems," describes commands used to display system-specific information, configure additional swap space without reformatting a disk, and create a local mail alias.

Chapter 10, "Recognizing File Access Problems," provides information on how to recognize problems with search paths and with permissions and ownership.

Appendix A, "Major Differences: SunOS 4.*x* versus SunOS 5.*x* Operating Systems," briefly describes key differences between SunOS 4.*x* and SunOS 5.*x* system software and provides a table of SunOS 4.*x* commands with the SunOS 5.*x* equivalents.

Appendix B, "New Administration Tools with Solaris 2.1," introduces the Printer Manager and User Account Manager, which are new tools available with Administration Tool.

The Glossary contains basic system administration terms and definitions.

Important: Read This Before You Begin

Because we assume that the root path will include the /sbin, /usr/sbin, /usr/bin, and /etc directories, the steps show the commands in these directories without absolute path names. Steps that use commands in other, less common directories show the absolute path in the example.

The examples in this book are for a basic SunOS 5.*x* software installation without the Binary Compatibility Package installed and without /usr/ucb in the path.

CAUTION! *If /usr/ucb is included in a search path, it should always be at the end. Commands like ps or df are duplicated in /usr/ucb with different formats and options from those of SunOS 5.*x *commands.*

This book does not contain all the information you need to administer systems. Refer to the complete system administration documentation for comprehensive information. See Appendix A for discussion of the differences between the Solaris 1.0 and Solaris 2.*x* environments.

Because the SunOS 5.*x* system software provides the Bourne (default), Korn, and C shells, examples in this book show prompts for each of the shells. The default C shell prompt is *<system-name>*%. The default Bourne and Korn shell prompt is $. The default root prompt for all shells is a pound sign (#). In examples that affect more than one system, the C shell prompt (which shows the system name) is used to make it clearer when you change from one system to another.

Conventions Used in This Book

Commands In the steps and the examples, the commands to be entered are in bold type. For example: "Type **su** and press Return." When following steps, press Return only when instructed to do so, even if the text in the step breaks at the end of a line.

Variables Variables are enclosed in angle brackets and are in an italic typeface. When following steps, replace the variable with the appropriate information. For example, to print a file, the step instructs you to "type **lp** *<filename>* and press Return." To substitute the file named "quest" for the *<filename>* variable, type **lp quest** and press Return. Note that you do not use the angle brackets when you type the actual file name.

Mouse-Button Terminology This book describes mouse buttons by function. The default mapping of mouse buttons on a three-button mouse is:

- SELECT is Left
- ADJUST is Middle
- MENU is Right

The SELECT mouse button is used to select unselected objects and activate controls. The ADJUST mouse button is used to adjust a selected group of objects, either adding to the group or deselecting part of the group. The MENU mouse button is used to display and choose from menus.

Storage-Medium Terminology In this book, we distinguish between three different types of media storage terminology in this way:

- *Disc* is used for an optical disc or CD-ROM.
- *Disk* is used for a hard-disk storage device.
- *Diskette* is used for a floppy diskette storage device. (Note: Sometimes, screen messages use the term *floppy*.)

CHAPTER

Introducing Solaris System Administration

Defining the System Administrator's Job

Understanding Superuser Status

Communicating with Users

Starting Up and Shutting Down Systems

Monitoring Processes

Reviewing Essential Administration Tools

Winchester Mystery House [in San Jose, California] . . . was designed to baffle the evil spirits that haunted Sarah Winchester, eccentric heiress to the Winchester Arms fortune and mistress of the house. With 160 rooms and 2,000 doors, 13 bathrooms, 10,000 windows, 47 fireplaces, blind closets, secret passageways and 40 staircases, the house is so complex that even the owner and servants needed maps to find their way.

—AAA, *California/Nevada TourBook*, 1991

Sarah Winchester, listening to the advice of psychics, believed that if she kept adding rooms to the house, she would not die and be subject to the influences of spirits who had been killed with the Winchester rifles manufactured by her husband.

The UNIX® operating system is much like the Winchester Mystery House without, we hope, the evil spirits. The original operating system has been continually enhanced and expanded. There are many ways to get about, and, like the owner and the servants in the Winchester house, system administrators frequently need a map to help them get from place to place.

To add to the complexity, there are many versions of the UNIX operating system based on either Berkeley (or BSD) UNIX or AT&T's System V. This book serves as a map to some of the most frequently used "rooms" of the SunOS 5.*x* system software, which is an enhanced implementation of UNIX System V, Release 4 (usually referred to as SVR4). The book also provides comparative information to help you learn the differences between the SunOS 4.*x* versions (the Berkeley UNIX operating system) and the SunOS 5.*x* version (the SVR4 operating system).

Defining the System Administrator's Job

The system administrator's job is to keep the software (and perhaps hardware) functioning for a stand-alone system or for a set of systems on a network so that others can use them.

Typical duties of system administrators vary, depending on the number of systems supported and how the duties are divided up. It is not uncommon for system administrators to be experts in administering one or more areas and be inexperienced in others. Some administrators specialize in network administration; others in user accounts; and still others in areas such as printing.

Here's a list of typical system administration duties that are described in part or in full in this book:

- Administering devices
    - Using tape cartridges
    - Formatting diskettes

    - Monitoring disk use
    - Understanding the Service Access Facility
    - Setting up a bidirectional modem
- Administering file systems
    - Mounting and unmounting file systems
    - Backing up and restoring files and file systems
- Administering network services
    - Finding network information
    - Transferring files between systems
    - Administering NIS+ databases
- Administering printing
    - Setting up a print client and print server
    - Using printing commands
- Administering users and groups
    - Adding users
    - Removing users
    - Changing user information
    - Creating new group accounts
- Understanding shells
    - Using Generic shell commands
    - Using Bourne shell commands
    - Using C shell commands
    - Using Korn shell commands
- Administering systems
    - Finding system information
    - Creating local mail aliases
    - Configuring additional swap space
    - Administering the system date and time

- Recognizing file access problems
    - Problems with search paths
    - Problems with permission and ownership
    - Problems with network access

The organization of this book matches the tasks listed above. To accomplish these tasks, you need to know when and how to:

- Gain full access to all file systems and resources
- Communicate with users
- Shut down and start up systems
- Monitor processes

However, information about the following system administration tasks is beyond the scope of this book: installing system software, installing third-party software, setting up and administering network services, setting up and administering mail services, adding and removing hardware, administering security and accounting, and monitoring system and network performance.

The rest of the sections in this chapter, which describe how to accomplish the system administrator's tasks, will introduce some basic commands and administrative tools.

Understanding Superuser Status

The *superuser* is a privileged user with unrestricted access to all files and commands. The superuser has a special UID (user ID) of 0. The user name for this account is *root*. Note that the terms *root* and *superuser* have the same meaning and are used interchangeably in this book. You must be root to perform many system administration tasks, such as mounting and unmounting file systems, changing ownership or permissions for a file or directory you do not own, backing up and restoring file systems, creating device files, and shutting down the system.

You can become superuser in two ways:

- When logged in as another user, by typing the **su** (switch user) command with no arguments, and then typing the root password
- From a login prompt, by typing **root** and then typing the root password

When you have superuser privileges, the shell provides a special # (pound sign) prompt to remind you that you have extra access to the system. The system keeps a log that records each time the su command is used and who uses it. You can keep track of who is using the superuser account by consulting the log file /var/adm/sulog.

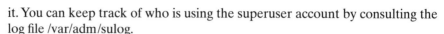

Only become superuser when it is required. You should avoid doing routine work as superuser. Occasionally, you may need to log out of your user account and log in again as root. When a task requires you to log in as root, you will be instructed to do so. You should switch user (su) to root, perform the required tasks, and exit superuser status when the tasks are complete.

Because unauthorized access to root can be a serious security breach, always add a password to the root account. For enhanced security, change the root password frequently.

Note. The default shell for root is the Bourne shell. See Chapter 8 for more information.

Becoming Superuser (su)

Become superuser only when you need to perform a task that requires root permissions. Here's how to become superuser:

1. At the shell prompt ($ or %), type **su** and press Return. You are prompted for the superuser (root) password, if one has been set up.
2. Type the superuser password and press Return. If you enter the password correctly, you have superuser (root) access to the system and the root prompt (#) is displayed:

```
oak% su
Password:
#
```

If you want to use root's environment variables, type **su -** and press Return.

Exiting Superuser Status

To exit superuser status, simply type **exit** and press Return. The shell prompt is redisplayed.

```
# exit
oak%
```

Logging In as Root

To log in as root, you must be at a login prompt:

1. At a login prompt, type **root** and press Return. You are prompted for the root password.

2. Type the root password and press Return. If you enter the password correctly, you have superuser (root) access to the system and the root prompt (#) is displayed:

```
login: root
Password:
#
```

Communicating with Users

An important part of your job as a system administrator is communicating with users to let them know that a task you are performing will affect their ability to use a system. Always let users know when you are about to perform a task that will affect them, such as rebooting a system, installing new software, or changing the environment in some way.

You can communicate with users by personal visit or phone, but the most common way is by using the system to:

- Display a system-specific message at login using the message of the day.
- Send a message directly to an individual user's terminal using the write command.
- Send a message to all users on a system using the wall command.
- Send a message to all users on a network using the rwall command.
- Send a message to an individual or a group of users by electronic mail.

Displaying System-Specific Messages at Login

Each time a user logs into a system, the message of the day in the file /etc/motd is displayed. The message is not displayed to users who are already logged in and are using the system. Use motd to give users information specific to the system which someone logging in would want to know. This information might include which operating system release is installed, changes to system software, the name of the newly installed (or deleted) third-party software, or a list of scheduled downtimes.

Be sure to keep the motd file current. If the motd displays outdated messages, users may begin to ignore all the messages, thereby missing out on critical information when it is presented. Keep the message short: If the message is longer than a screenful of information, users won't be able to read the beginning.

Root should own the /etc/motd file and be the only user who has write permission to it.

```
oak% ls -l /etc/motd
-rw-r--r--   1 root     sys       49 Jan  1  1970 /etc/motd
oak%
```

NOTE. *When the system software is installed, several files, including /etc/motd, have a time stamp of "Jan 1 1970." This date is the beginning of UNIX time. When you edit these files, the time stamp is updated.*

Creating a Message of the Day

Follow these steps to create a message of the day:

1. Become superuser.
2. Use an editor such as vi to edit the /etc/motd file.
3. Delete any obsolete messages and type the new one.
4. Save the changes. The message is changed and is displayed the next time a user logs into the system.

Sending a Message to an Individual User

You can send a message to the terminal of an individual user using the write command. When using a windowing system such as OpenWindows, each window is considered a separate login. If the user is logged in more than once, the message is directed to the console window.

Typing a Short Message to an Individual User

Use these steps to send a short, one-time message to an individual user:

1. Type **write <*username*>** and press Return. The <*username*> is the login name of the user.
2. Type the message you want to send.
3. When the message is complete, press Control-D. The message is displayed in the user's console window.

   Here is an example of a message a system administrator might type:

```
oak% write ignatz@elm
I'll come by at 12:00 to look at your problem.
oak%
```

This is how the message would display in the user's console window:

```
Message from fred@oak on ttyp1 at 11:20 ...
I'll come by at 12:00 to look at your problem.
EOF
```

Sending a Message from a File to an Individual User

If you have a longer message that you want to send to a number of users, use these steps to create the message in a file and then use the file name as an argument to the write command:

1. Create a file containing the text of the message you want to send.
2. Type **write *<username>* < *<filename>*** and press Return.

In this example, the system administrator uses the cat command to create a file containing a short message:

```
oak% cat > message
I'll come by at 12:00 to look at your problem.
oak% write ignatz@elm < message
write: ignatz logged in more than once ... writing to
console
oak%
```

If the user is logged into more than one window, the message is displayed in the console window. This is how the message displays in the user's console window:

```
Message from fred@oak on ttyp1 at 11:20 ...
I'll come by at 12:00 to look at your problem.
EOF
```

As you can see, the user doesn't see any difference in the output created from a typed message and the message included from a file. The user can initiate a dialogue by using the write command to respond, but the dialogue is not truly interactive. There are two write paths open, one in each direction. See the write(1) manual page for more information.

Sending a Message to All Users on a System or Network

You can use the wall (write all) command to simultaneously send a message to every user on a system. You can use the rwall (remote write all) command to simultaneously send a message to every user on a network.

To send a message to all users on a system:

1. Type **wall** and press Return.

2. Type the message you want to send.
3. When the message is complete, press Control-D. The message is displayed in the console window of each user on the system.

   This is an example of a message a system administrator might type:

```
oak% wall
System will be rebooted at 12:00.
oak%
```

   This is how the message would display in the users' console windows:

```
Broadcast message from root on console ...
System will be rebooted at 12:00.
EOF
```

NOTE. *Use the rwall command carefully, because it consumes extensive system and network resources.*

To send a message to all users on a network:

1. Type **rwall -n** ***<netgroup>*** and press Return.
2. Type the message you want to send.
3. When the message is complete, press Control-D. The message is displayed in the console window of each user on the system.

This is a message the system administrator might type to send to all members of the netgroup Eng:

```
oak% rwall -n Eng
System oak will be rebooted at 12:00.
oak%
```

This is how the message would display in the users' console windows:

```
Broadcast message from root on console ...
System will be rebooted at 12:00.
```

You can also use the rwall command to send a message to all users on a system by typing **rwall** ***<hostname>***.

Sending a Message by Electronic Mail

E-mail is an effective way to communicate some system administration informational messages. However, this book does not describe how to use electronic mail. See the mail(1), mailtool(1), and mailx(1) manual pages for information about the mail programs.

Starting Up and Shutting Down Systems

Starting up and shutting down systems is an integral part of performing system administration tasks. This section describes procedures for routinely starting up and shutting down systems. If a system does not start up gracefully, see your system documentation for information on how to diagnose booting problems.

The SunOS 5.*x* system software is designed to be left running continuously so that the electronic mail and network software can work correctly. You must, however, halt or shut down a system when:

- Turning off system power
- Installing a new release of the operating system
- Anticipating a power outage
- Adding hardware to the system
- Performing maintenance on a file system

Note. The *init state* (also called *run level*) determines what programs are started or initialized when a system is booted.

Choosing an Init State

The SunOS system software has eight init states; the default init state for each system is specified in the /etc/inittab file. The default init state for the SunOS 5.*x* system software is run level 3. Table 1.1 shows the seven available run levels and the state of the system at each level.

Table 1.1 System Init States

Init State	Function
0	Power-down state
1, S, s	System administrator state (single-user)
2	Multiuser state (resources not exported)
3	Multiuser state (resources exported)
4	Alternative multiuser state (currently unused)
5	Software reboot state (unused)
6	Reboot

The /sbin/init program is responsible for keeping the system running correctly and is the command you use to change init states. You can also use the init states (with the -i option) as arguments to the shutdown command. There are four types of system states:

- Power-down (run level 0)
- Single-user (run levels 1 and s or S)
- Multiuser (run levels 2 and 3)
- Reboot (run levels 5 and 6)

When preparing to do a system administration task, you need to determine which init state is appropriate for the system and the task at hand.

Finding the Run Level for a System

New with SVR4.

To find the run level for a system, type **who -r** and press Return. The run level, date and time, process termination status, process id, and process exit status are displayed.

In this example, the system named drusilla is at the default multiuser run level (3), the date and time are Feb 6 15:46, the process termination status is 3, the process id is 0, and process exit status is S:

```
drusilla% who -r
   .      run-level 3  Feb 6 15:46    3     0 S
drusilla%
```

The next sections describe how you might use each init state.

Using Power-Down State, Run Level 0

Use this level to shut down the system so that it is safe to turn off the power.

Using System Administrator State, Run Level 1

Use this level when performing administrative tasks that require you to be the only user on the system. Root and /usr are the only file systems mounted, and you can access only minimum kernel utilities. The terminal from which you issue this command becomes the console. No other users are logged in.

Note. A *daemon* is a special type of program that, once activated, starts itself and carries out a specific task without any need for user input. Daemons typically are used to handle jobs that have been queued, such as printing, mail, and communication.

Using Multiuser State, Run Level 2

Use this level for normal operations. Multiple users can access the system and the entire file system. All daemons are running except for NFS server, syslog, and remote file sharing.

Using Remote Resource-Sharing State, Run Level 3

Use this level for normal operations with NFS resource-sharing available.

Using Alternative Multiuser State, Run Level 4

This level currently is unavailable.

Using Interactive Reboot State, Run Level 5

Use this level when you want to be prompted for a device other than the default boot devices. You can also change to this level using the reboot -a command.

Using Reboot State, Run Level 6

Use this level to shut down the system to run level 0, and then reboot to multiuser level (or to whatever level is the default in the inittab file).

Using Single-User State, Run Level s or S

Use this level to run as a single user with all file systems mounted and accessible.

Changing Run Levels

New with SVR4.

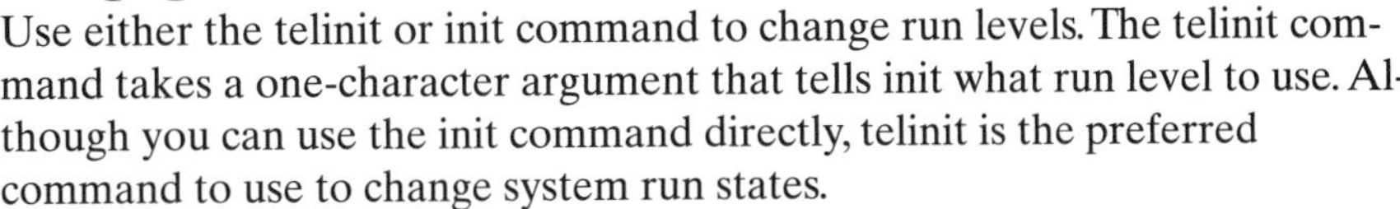

Use either the telinit or init command to change run levels. The telinit command takes a one-character argument that tells init what run level to use. Although you can use the init command directly, telinit is the preferred command to use to change system run states.

1. Become superuser.
2. Type **telinit <*n*>** and press Return. Replace the variable <*n*> with the number of the init state you want to use.

   To shut down the system:

   ```
   oak% su
   Password:
   # telinit 0
   ```

   To change to single-user state:

   ```
   oak% su
   Password:
   # telinit 1
   ```

   To change to multiuser state, no NFS server daemons:

   ```
   oak% su
   Password:
   # telinit 2
   ```

   To change to multiuser state, with NFS server daemons:

   ```
   oak% su
   Password:
   # telinit 3
   ```

To shut down and reboot a system:

```
oak% su
Password:
# telinit 6
```

Choosing Which Shutdown Command to Use

When preparing to do a system administration task, you need to determine which shutdown command is appropriate for the system and the task at hand. The next sections describe how you might use each of the available shutdown commands:

- /usr/sbin/shutdown
- /etc/telinit and /sbin/init
- /usr/sbin/halt
- /usr/sbin/reboot

These commands, respectively, initiate shutdown procedures, kill all running processes, write out any new data to the disk, and shut down the SunOS 5.*x* system software to the appropriate run level.

shutdown

Use the shutdown command when shutting down a system with multiple users. The shutdown command sends a warning message to all users who are logged in, waits for 60 seconds (the default), and then shuts down the system to single-user state. You can choose a different default wait time.

telinit and init

New with SVR4.

Use the telinit or init command to shut down a single-user system or to change its run level. The init command changes the run level of the system. The telinit command tells init what run level you want. You can use the commands interchangeably, although telinit is the preferred command. You can use telinit to place the system in power-down state (init 0) or into single-user state (init 1).

NOTE. *Use telinit/init and shutdown as the preferred method of changing system state. These programs are the most reliable way to shut down a system because they use a number of rc scripts to kill running processes.*

halt

Use the halt command when the system must be stopped immediately and it is acceptable not to warn any current users. The halt command shuts down the system without any delay and does not warn any other users on the system.

The halt command does not run the rc shutdown scripts properly and is not the preferred method for shutting down a system.

reboot

Use the reboot command to shut down a system that does not have multiple users to bring it back into multiuser state. The command reboot does not warn users on the system, does not run the rc scripts properly, and is not the preferred method for shutting down a system.

Booting a System

If a system is powered off, turning it on starts the multiuser boot sequence. The following procedures tell you how to boot in different states from the ok PROM prompt. If the PROM prompt is >, type **n** to display the ok prompt, and then follow the appropriate steps.

NOTE. *The PROM prompt description is for SPARC® systems.*

Booting in Multiuser State

To boot in multiuser state, at the ok PROM prompt, type **boot** and press Return. The automatic boot procedure starts on the default drive, displaying a series of start-up messages. The system is brought up in multiuser state.

Booting in Single-User State

To boot in single-user state, at the ok PROM prompt, type **boot -s** and press Return. The system boots to single-user state and prompts you for the root password:

```
ok boot -s

INIT: SINGLE USER MODE
Type Ctrl-d to proceed with normal start-up,
(or give root password for system maintenance)
```

Type the root password and press Return.

NOTE. *To continue the process and bring the system up in multiuser state, press Control-D.*

Booting Interactively

You may boot interactively if you want to make a temporary change to the system file or the kernel. In this way, you can test your changes and recover easily if you have any problems.

1. At the ok PROM prompt, type **boot -a** and press Return. The boot program prompts you interactively.

2. Press Return to use the default /kernel/unix kernel, or type the name of the kernel to use for booting.
3. Press Return to use the default /etc/system file, or type the name of the system file and press Return.
4. Press Return to use the default modules directory path, or type the default path for the modules directory and press Return.
5. Press Return to use the default root file system. Type **ufs** for local disk booting or **nfs** for diskless clients.
6. Press Return to use the default physical name of the root device, or type the device name.
7. Press Return to use the swapfs default swap file system type. (Note that swapfs is the only permitted swap file system type.)

In the following example, the default choices (shown in square brackets []) were accepted by pressing Return:

```
ok boot -a
(Hardware configuration messages)
rebooting from -a
Boot device: /sbus/esp@0,800000/sd@0,0 File and args: -a
Enter <filename> [/kernel/unix]:
(Copyright notice)
Name of system file [/etc/system]:
Name of default directory for modules [<null string>]:
root filesystem type [ufs]
Enter physical name of root device
[/sbus@1,f8000000/esp@0,800000/sd@0,0:a]:
Swap filesystem type [swapfs]
Configuring network interfaces:  le0
Hostname: cinderella
(fsck messages)
The system is coming up. Please wait.
(More messages)
cinderella login:
```

Looking at the Boot Messages

The most recent boot messages are stored in the /var/adm/messages file. To see these messages after you have booted the system, type **/usr/sbin/dmesg** and press Return. The boot messages are displayed. Or, type **more /var/adm/messages** and press Return.

```
drusilla% /usr/sbin/dmesg
```

```
Jan 13 11:22
SunOS Release 5.0 Version [UNIX(R) System V Release 4.0]
system file (etc/system) error:  readline error on line 1
root nexus = Sun 4_60
mem = 16384K (0x1000000)
avail mem = 14688256
Ethernet address = 8:0:20:7:83:17
sbus0 at obio 0xf8000000
dma0 at SBus slot 0 0x400000
esp0 at SBus slot 0 0x800000 SBus level 3 (sparc ipl 3)
sd1 at esp0 target 1 lun 0
/sbus@1,f8000000/esp@0,800000/sd@1,0 (sd1):
      <Quantum ProDrive 105S cyl 974 alt 2 hd 6 sec 35>
sd3 at esp0 target 3 lun 0
/sbus@1,f8000000/esp@0,800000/sd@3,0 (sd3):
      <Quantum ProDrive 105S cyl 974 alt 2 hd 6 sec 35>
root on /sbus@1,f8000000/esp@0,800000/sd@3,0:a fstype ufs
swap on swapfs fstype swapfs size 13484K
le0 at SBus slot 0 0xc00000 SBus level 4 (sparc ipl 5)
zs0 at obio 0xf1000000 sparc ipl 12
zs1 at obio 0xf0000000 sparc ipl 12
dump on /dev/dsk/c0t3d0s1 size 32748K
Dec 24 12:30:01 sendmail[82]: alias database out of date
Dec 24 12:30:01 sendmail[82]: AA00082: message-
id=<9112242030.AA00082@drusilla.Eng.Sun.COM>
Dec 24 12:30:01 sendmail[82]: AA00082: from=root,
size=592, class=0, received from local
Dec 24 12:30:02 sendmail[91]: AA00082: to=cork@cannonball,
delay=00:00:01, stat=Sent
Dec 24 12:30:58 sendmail[153]: network daemon starting
Dec 31 15:20:24 rlogind[743]: pcktread : suspect zero len
fd0 at obio 0xf7200000 sparc ipl 11
cgsix0 at SBus slot 1 0x0 SBus level 5 (sparc ipl 7)
cgsix0: screen 1152x900, single buffered, 1M mappable, rev 1
drusilla%
```

Booting after Adding New Hardware

New with SVR4.

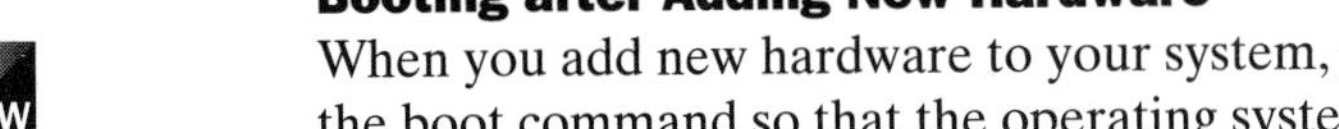

When you add new hardware to your system, you must use the -r option to the boot command so that the operating system knows to look for new device drivers and incorporate them as part of the boot process:

1. Load the new device driver following the instructions included with the hardware.

2. Shut down your system and install the new hardware.

3. Type **boot -r** and press Return. A reconfiguration script is run to load all the device drivers listed in the modules directories and to create the corresponding hardware nodes.

Aborting a Booting Process

Occasionally, you may need to abort the booting process. The specific abort key sequence depends on your keyboard type. For example, you might press Stop-A or L1-A. On tty terminals, press the Break key.

To abort the booting process, type the abort key sequence for your system. When you abort the boot process, the monitor displays the ok PROM prompt:

```
ok
```

Type **boot** and press Return to restart the boot process, or type **help** and press Return to display a list of help options. If your terminal shows the > monitor prompt, type **n** to get the ok prompt.

Shutting Down a System

The following sections describe how to use the shutdown and init commands to shut down a system.

Shutting Down a Multiuser System

Before shutting down a multiuser system, inform the other users on the system and give them time to complete critical procedures.

1. Type **who** and press Return. A list of all logged-in users is displayed.

2. Type **ps -ef** and press Return. A list of system activities is displayed. If the activity is acceptable for running shutdown, go to the next step.

3. Become superuser.

4. Type **cd /** and press Return. You must be in the root directory to run the shutdown command.

5. Type **shutdown** and press Return. You are asked to confirm that you want to shut down the system.

6. Type **y**. A message is broadcast to all users. After a 60-second wait, the system is shut down to single-user state and you are prompted for the root password.

7. Type the root password. The system is in single-user state and you can perform any maintenance task.

8. Press Control-D to return to the default run system level.

```
# cd /
# shutdown
Shutdown started Fri Aug 6 10:50:35 EDT 1993

Broadcast message from root (console) on earth Fri Aug 9
10:59:35.
THE SYSTEM IS BEING SHUT DOWN NOW ! ! !
LOG OFF NOW OR RISK YOUR FILES BEING DAMAGED
Do you want to continue?  (y or n):  y

The system is down.
Changing to init state s - please wait.

INIT: New run level S
INIT: SINGLE USER MODE
Type Ctrl-d to proceed with normal start-up,
(or give root password for system maintenance):
```

Shutting Down a System: Alternative Ways

If you want to change the default actions of the shutdown command, choose one of the tasks in the following six sections.

Shutting Down a System without Confirmation To shut down a system without confirmation, follow these steps:

1. Become superuser.
2. Type **cd /** and press Return. You must be in the root directory to run the shutdown command.
3. Type **shutdown -y** and press Return. The shutdown proceeds without asking you to type *y* to confirm it.

Changing the Shutdown Grace Period To change the shutdown grace period, follow these steps:

1. Become superuser.
2. Type **cd /** and press Return. You must be in the root directory to run the shutdown command.
3. Type **shutdown -g<*nnn*>** and press Return. The grace period is changed to the number of seconds you specify.

The following example changes the grace period to 120 seconds:

```
# cd /
# shutdown -g120
```

Shutting Down and Rebooting a Multiuser System To shut down and reboot a multiuser system, follow these steps:

1. Become superuser.
2. Type **cd /** and press Return. You must be in the root directory to run the shutdown command.
3. Type **shutdown -i6** and press Return. A message is broadcast to all users and the rc6 script is executed; the system is shut down to power-down state, and then brought back up to multiuser state.

Shutting Down a Single-User System To shut down a single-user system, type **telinit 0** (or **init 0**) and press Return. The init command runs scripts that bring the system down cleanly. No warning messages are broadcast.

Shutting Down and Rebooting a Single-User System To shut down and reboot a single-user system, type **telinit 6** (or **init 6**) and press Return. Information is written to the disk, all active processes are killed, and the system is brought to a power-down state. The system is then rebooted to the default level (usually multiuser).

Shutting Down a System in a Hurry To shut a system down in a hurry, type **uadmin 2 0** and press Return. Information is written to the disk and the system is brought to power-down state, displaying the PROM prompt.

Monitoring Processes

The programs that are running on a system at any one time are called *processes.* You can monitor the status of processes, control how much CPU time a process gets, and suspend or halt the execution of a process. The ps (process status) command is your main tool for obtaining information about processes. You can use the ps command in combination with the grep command to focus your search for specific information.

You can determine which processes are running (or not running) and get detailed information about an individual process, such as:

- PID (process ID)
- UID (user ID)

- Priority
- Control terminal
- Memory use
- CPU time
- Current status

The ps command takes a snapshot of system activity at the time you type the command. If you are monitoring system activity by time, be aware that the results are already slightly out-of-date by the time you read them. Table 1.2 shows the most frequently used options for the ps command. See the ps(1) manual page for a complete list of options.

Table 1.2 Most Frequently Used Options for the ps Command

Option	Description
–e	Report on all processes.
–f	Show the owner of the process, by name instead of by UID, in the first column. This option turns off –1, –t, –s, and –r and turns on –a.
–l	Generate a long report, which includes all fields except STIME.

What the ps Command Reports

When you type **ps -e** and press Return, you get a report that looks like this:

```
oak% /usr/bin/ps -e
PID          TTY          TIME         COMD
0            ?            0:02         sched
1            ?            0:01         init
2            ?            0:00         pageout
192          ?            0:00         sac
79           ?            0:10         inetd
75           ?            0:01         in.route
136          ?            0:04         automoun
143          ?            0:01         cron
123          ?            0:01         statd
104          ?            0:01         rpcbind
106          ?            0:01         rpc.rwal
108          ?            0:01         rpc.ruse
```

```
110        ?          0:01       rpc.spra
113        ?          0:01       ypbind
115        ?          0:00       keyserv
117        ?          0:01       kerbd
127        ?          0:02       lockd
251        pts/0      0:00       ps
165        ?          0:00       sendmail
193        ?          0:01       ttymon
174        ?          0:03       syslogd
156        ?          0:01       lpsched
209        ?          0:02       in.rlogi
211        pts/0      0:03       csh
164        ?          0:00       lpNet
oak%
```

The columns are:

- **PID:** Process identification number.
- **TTY:** The terminal from which the process (or its parent) started. If the process has no controlling terminal, this column contains a question mark (?). Processes with question marks usually are system processes.
- **TIME:** The cumulative amount of CPU time used by the process.
- **COMD:** The name of the command that generated the process. Note that for the ps -e command only the first eight characters of the file name are displayed.

When you type **ps -el** and press Return, you get a listing that looks like this:

```
oak% /usr/bin/ps -el
 F S   UID   PID  PPID  C PRI NI     ADDR     SZ    WCHAN TTY      TIME COMD
19 T     0     0     0 80   0 SY f010f1c8      0            ?      0:02 sched
 8 S     0     1     0251   1 20 ff1ad800     48 ff1ad9c4 ?      0:01 init
19 S     0     2     0  0   0 SY ff1ad000      0 ff1ad07d ?      0:00 pageout
 8 S     0   192     1 49   1 20 ff1f7000    238 ff2de348 ?      0:00 sac
 8 S     0    79     1 80   1 20 ff232800    291 f010f1a4 ?      0:10 inetd
 8 S     0    75     1 80   1 20 ff249000    258 f010f1a4 ?      0:01 in.route
 8 S     0   136     1 80   1 20 ff2c3000    327 f010f1a4 ?      0:04 automoun
 8 S     0   143     1149   1 20 ff293000    287 ff2de448 ?      0:01 cron
 8 S     0   123     1 80   1 20 ff28e000    270 f010f1a4 ?      0:01 statd
 8 S     0   104     1 80   1 20 ff25a000    301 f010f1a4 ?      0:01 rpcbind
 8 S     0   106     1 77   1 20 ff258800    272 f010f1a4 ?      0:01 rpc.rwal
 8 S     0   108     1 80   1 20 ff260800    272 f010f1a4 ?      0:01 rpc.ruse
 8 S     0   110     1 78   1 20 ff266800    272 f010f1a4 ?      0:01 rpc.spra
(More information, not shown here)
```

Table 1.3 describes the fields in the long listing report.

Table 1.3 Summary of Fields in a ps -el Report

Field	Description	
F	Hexadecimal flags, which, added together, indicate the process's current state as follows:	
	00	The process has terminated. Its place in the process table is free.
	01	The process is a system process and is always in memory.
	02	The process is being traced by its parent.
	04	The process is being traced by its parent and has been stopped.
	08	The process cannot be awakened by a signal.
	10	The process is currently in memory and is locked until an event completes.
	20	The process cannot be swapped.
S	The current state of the process, as shown by one of the following letters:	
	O	Currently running on the processor.
	S	Sleeping; waiting for an I/O event to complete.
	R	Ready to run.
	I	Idle; process is being created.
	Z	Zombie. The process has terminated and the parent is not waiting, but the dead process is still in the process table.
	T	Stopped because parent is tracing the process.
	X	Waiting for more memory.
UID	The user ID of the owner of the process.	
PID	The process identification number.	
PPID	The parent process's identification number.	
C	The process's CPU use (that is, an estimate of the percentage of CPU time used by the process).	
PRI	The process's scheduling priority. Higher numbers mean lower priority.	
NI	The process's nice number, which contributes to its scheduling priority. Making a process "nicer" means lowering its priority so it does not use up as much CPU time.	

Table 1.3 **Summary of Fields in a ps -el Report (Continued)**

Field	Description
SZ	The amount of virtual memory required by the process. This is a good indication of the demand the process puts on system memory.
TTY	The terminal from which the process (or its parent) started, or a question mark to indicate there is no controlling terminal (which usually indicates a system process).
TIME	The total amount of CPU time used by the process since it began.
COMD	The command that generated the process.

Using the ps Report

When you need to check on which processes or daemons are running, use the ps -e option. If you need more detailed information about a process, use the ps -el options. See the ps(1) manual page for a complete list of options. With experience, you will be able to know how the report should look and to judge what is out of the ordinary.

Here are some guidelines on how to spot potential problems:

- Look for many identical jobs owned by the same user. This may result from someone running a script that starts a lot of background jobs without waiting for any of the jobs to terminate. Talk to the user to find out if that's the case. If necessary, use the kill command to terminate some of the processes. See the following section for more information on killing a process.
- Look at the TIME field for processes that have accumulated a large amount of CPU time. Such processes might be in an endless loop.
- Look at the C field to find unimportant processes that consume a large percentage of CPU time. If you do not think a process warrants so much attention, use the priocntl command to lower its priority. See the priocntl(1) manual page for more information.
- Look at the SZ field for processes that consume too large a percentage of memory. If a process is a memory hog, kill the process. If many processes are using lots of memory, the system may need more memory.
- Watch for a runaway process that progressively uses more and more CPU time. You can check this by using the -f option to see the start time (STIME) of the process and by watching the TIME field for the accumulation of CPU time.

Killing Processes

Sometimes you need to eliminate a process entirely. Use the kill command to do this. The syntax of the kill command is kill -<*signal*> <*PID*>, where <*signal*> is a number or a name.

CAUTION! *Kill a process only if you cannot get it to quit in the usual way.*

Sometimes processes do not die when you use the kill command. The three most common cases are:

- The process is waiting for a device, such as a tape drive, to complete an operation before exiting.
- The process is waiting for resources unavailable because of NFS problems. To kill such a process, type **kill -QUIT <*PID*>**.
- The process is a zombie, as shown by the message <defunct> in the ps report. A zombie process is one that has had all of its resources freed, but has not received an acknowledgment from a parent process, receipt of which would ordinarily remove its entry from the process table. The next time a system is booted, zombie processes are cleared. Zombies do not affect system performance, and you do not need to remove them.

To kill a process:

1. Become superuser. You must be superuser to kill a process that you do not own.
2. Type **ps -e** and press Return. A list of the processes is displayed. Use the PID (process ID) number in the first column as input to the next step. If you know which process is causing the problem, you can type **ps -e | grep <*process-name*>** and press Return to focus your search.
3. Type **kill <*PID*>** and press Return. When you type **kill** with no arguments, signal 15 is sent.
4. Type **ps -e** and press Return. Check to see if the process has terminated. If it's still there, go to Step 5.
5. Type **kill -9 <*PID*>** and press Return. The process should be terminated. Type **man -s5 signal** and press Return to see a description of the signals used by kill.

For example, if OpenWindows is frozen on the system oak, you must log in remotely and kill the process from another system:

```
elm% rlogin oak
Password:
```

```
oak% ps -e | grep openwin
PID TTY      TIME COMD
2212 pts/0   0:00 openwin
2213 pts/1    0:00 grep openwin
oak% su
Password:
oak# kill 2212
oak# exit
oak% logout
elm%
```

Reviewing Essential Administration Tools

The SunOS 5.*x* system software provides you with two kinds of administration tools:

- The usual collection of operating system commands
- An Administration Tool with a graphical user interface

Frequently Used Commands

The sections below briefly introduce basic SunOS 5.*x* commands that you are likely to use regularly as part of routine system administration; they are grouped by tasks. See "Basic OS Commands" in Chapter 2 for more frequently used commands. See Appendix A for a list of SunOS 4.*x* commands and their SunOS 5.*x* equivalents.

Getting Around in the File System

SunOS 5.*x* system software has a hierarchical file system. When administering systems, you need to know where you are in the file hierarchy and how to change to a different directory.

Finding Where You Are in the File System To find out where you are in the file system hierarchy, type **pwd** and press Return. The print working directory command displays the current directory.

```
oak& pwd
/etc
oak%
```

Changing Directories To change directories, type **cd** ***<pathname>*** and press Return. The change directory command puts you in the directory name you type.

```
oak% cd /usr
oak% pwd
/usr
oak%
```

If you type **cd** and press Return without typing a path name, you are returned to the login home directory.

Finding Information about Files

Using the ls command, you can list the contents of a directory and display permissions, links, ownership, group, size (in bytes), modification date and time, and file name for files. Many user problems related to accessing files can be traced to problems with incorrect permissions or ownership. See Chapter 10, "Recognizing File Access Problems," for more information.

Displaying File Information

To display information about an individual file, type **ls -l** ***<filename>*** and press Return. Permissions, links, owner, group, file size in bytes, modification date and time, and the file name are displayed.

```
oak% ls -l /etc/passwd
-r--r--r--   1 root     sys          659 Feb 24 17:28 /etc/passwd
oak%
```

To see a complete list for all the files in the directory, type **ls -l** and press Return. See the ls manual page for a complete list of options.

Finding a File

To find a file by searching from the home directory, type **find $HOME -name** ***<filename>*** **-print** and press Return. The $HOME variable starts the search with the home directory. The -name option looks for the name specified in the *<filename>* variable. The -print option displays the results of the find. If the named file is not found, the prompt is redisplayed.

This example shows the results of a find looking for core files:

```
oak% find $HOME -name core -print
/home/ignatz/core
oak%
```

Table 1.4 shows some of the options to the find command that you can use to focus your searches.

Table 1.4 Options to the find Command

Option	Description
-fstype <*type*>	Finds files of the file system type you specify (typically, ufs or nfs).
-prune	Limits the search to the specified directory.
-nouser	Finds files that belong to a user not in the /etc/passwd database.
-nogroup	Finds files that belong to a group not in the /etc/group database.
-atime <*n*>	Finds files that have been accessed within the last <*n*> days.
-mtime <*n*>	Finds files that have been modified within the last <*n*> days.
-ctime <*n*>	Finds files that have been changed within the last <*n*> days. Changes can include changing its attribute such as the number of links, its owner, or its group.
-Xdev	Restrict search to one filesystem.

See the find(1) manual page for a complete list of options.

Finding the Type of a File

Sometimes you need to determine the type of a file. To find the type of a file, type **file <*filename*>** and press Return. The output of the command makes an educated guess about the type of the file.

For example, if a user is trying to execute an ASCII file that does not have execute permissions, or execute an empty file, displaying the file type will tell you whether or not the system recognizes the file as a command.

In this example, the file is empty:

```
anastasia% file junk
junk: empty file
anastasia%
```

In this example, the file is an ASCII text file:

```
anastasia% file junk
junk: ascii text
anastasia%
```

In this example, the file is a text file with executable permissions, so the file command reports that the file contains commands and is text:

```
anastasia% chmod 777 junk
anastasia% file junk
```

```
junk: commands text
anastasia%
```

NOTE. *You can, of course, determine if the command has execute permissions using the ls -l command.*

To show the file type for all files in a directory, type **file** * and press Return. The files are listed in alphabetical order followed by the file type.

```
$ file *

coterie:     directory
course:      ascii text
dead.letter  ascii text
ksyms        English text
people:      directory
personal:    directory
showrev:     ascii text
status:      directory
text:        directory
todo:        ascii text
$
```

Finding Information in Files

You can use the grep and egrep commands to search files and command output for specific information.

Searching Files for Text Strings To search files for a specific text string, type **grep** ***<search-string>*** ***<filenames>*** and press Return. Lines in the files containing the string are displayed.

In this example, the passwd file is searched for lines containing csh:

```
oak% grep csh /etc/passwd
ignatz::6693:10:Iggy Ignatz 64607:/home/ignatz:/bin/csh
fred::14072:10:Fred Lux:/home/fred:/bin/csh
oak%
```

You can search more than one file by specifying a series of file names separated by spaces, or by using metacharacters together with (or in place of) the file name.

To print out lines that do not contain the specified string, type **grep -v** ***<search-string>*** ***<filename>*** and press Return. Lines in the file that do not contain the string are displayed.

Searching Input for Lines with a Given Pattern You can use the grep command with pipes in combination with many administrative commands. For example, if you want to find all of a user's current processes, pipe the output of the ps command to grep and search for the user name, type **ps -e | grep <*name*>**, and press Return. The listing for the name you specify is displayed.

For example, to find the OpenWindows process:

```
oak% ps -e | grep openwin
PID TTY      TIME COMD
2212 pts/0    0:00 openwin
oak%
```

Looking at Files

You undoubtedly will spend lots of time looking at the content of files. When you need to look at the entire file, use the more command. When the information you need is at the end of the file (for example, in a log file), use the tail command to display the last ten lines of the file. When important information is at the beginning of the file, use the head command to display the first ten lines of the file.

Viewing a File

To view a file, type **more <*filename*>** and press Return. The file is displayed one screen at a time. Press the Spacebar to view the next screen.

To search for a specific string in a file you are viewing with more, type **/<*search-string*>** and press Return. The text scrolls to display the place in the file that contains the text you type as the <*search-string*> variable and displays the search string and the message "... skipping" at the top of the window. If there is no match, the message "Pattern not found" is displayed at the bottom of the window and the text does not scroll.

For example, to find the words *Local aliases* in the /etc/mail/aliases file, type **/Local aliases** and press Return.

```
/Local aliases
...skipping

########################
# Local aliases below #
########################
```

NOTE. *You must use exact capitalization in the search string for the more command. If you type* /local aliases *in the previous example, the pattern is not found.*

To search for the next occurrence of the search string, type **n**. To quit more, type **q**. The shell prompt is redisplayed.

Another way to quit more, if Control-C is set as your shell kill character, is to press Control-C. The shell prompt is redisplayed.

To display the shell intr character, type **stty -a** and press Return. A list of the stty settings is displayed. In this example, ^C is the shell kill character.

```
cinderella% stty -a
speed 9600 baud;
rows = 35; columns = 80; ypixels = 9; xpixels = 0;
eucw 1:0:0:0, scrw 1:0:0:0
intr = ^c; quit = ^|; erase = ^?; kill = ^u;
eof = ^d; eol = <undef>; eol2 = <undef>; swtch = <undef>;
start = ^q; stop = ^s; susp = ^z; dsusp = ^y;
rprnt = ^r; flush = ^o; werase = ^w; lnext = ^v;
parenb -parodd cs7 -cstopb hupcl cread -clocal -loblk -crtscts -parext
-ignbrk btkint ignpar -parmrk -inpck istrip -inlcr -igncr icrnl -iuclc
ixon -ixany -ixoff imaxbel
isig icanon -xcase echo echoe echok -echonl -noflsh
-tostop echoctl -echoprt echoke -defecho -flusho -pendin iexten
opost -olcuc onlcr -ocrnl -onocr -onlret -ofill -ofdel
```

Looking at the End of a File

To look at the end of a file, type **tail <*filename*>** and press Return. The last ten lines of the file (by default) are displayed.

This example shows the tail of the /etc/lp/Systems file:

```
oak% /usr/bin/tail /etc/lp/Systems
#
#       Kepler:x:-:s5:-:n:10:-:-:SVR4.0 OS
#       fubar:x:-:bsd:10:n:-:-:BSD OS
#       Galileo:x:-:s5:-:30:10:-:-:
##########

billboard:x:-:bsd:-:n:10:-:-:
homeboy1:x:-:s5:-:n:10:-:-:
regal:x:-:s5:-:n:10:-:-:
mrplod:x:-:s5:-:n:10:-:-:
oak%
```

By default, the head and tail commands display 10 lines. You can change the number of lines displayed by using the -n option. Substitute the number of lines you want to display for the letter *n*. For example, to display the last 20 lines of a file, type **tail -20 <*filename*>** and press Return.

NOTE. *Tail shows a maximum of 4096 bytes (about 400 lines).*

Looking at the Beginning of a File

To look at the beginning of a file, type **head <*filename*>** and press Return. The first ten lines of the file are displayed.

This example shows the head of the /etc/passwd file:

```
oak% /usr/bin/head /etc/passwd
root:x:0:1:0000-Admin(0000):/:/sbin/sh
daemon:x:1:1:0000-Admin(0000):/:
bin:x:2:2:0000-Admin(0000):/usr/bin:
sys:x:3:3:0000-Admin(0000):/:
adm:x:4:4:0000-Admin(0000):/var/adm:
lp:x:71:8:0000-lp(0000):/usr/spool/lp:
smtp:x:0:0:mail daemon user:/:
uucp:x:5:5:0000-uucp(0000):/usr/lib/uucp:
nuucp:x:9:9:0000-
uucp(0000):/var/spool/uucppublic:/usr/lib/uucp/uucico
listen:x:37:4:Network Admin:/usr/net/nls:
oak%
```

Changing File Ownership or Permissions

Many user problems can be traced to file ownership or permissions problems. Use the ls command to check the permissions and ownership on a file. If you need to change one or both, use the chown, chmod, and chgrp commands.

Changing File Ownership You must own a file or directory (or have root permission) to be able to change its owner.

1. Type **ls -l** **<*filename*>** and press Return. The owner of the file is displayed in the third column.
2. Become superuser.
3. Type **chown** **<*new-owner*>** **<*filename*>** and press Return. Ownership is assigned to the new owner you specify.

```
oak% ls -l quest
-rw-r--r--   1 fred    staff     6023 Aug  5 12:06 quest
oak% su
Password:
# chown ignatz quest
# ls -l quest
-rw-r--r--   1 ignatz    staff     6023 Aug  5 12:06 quest
#
```

See Chapter 10, "Recognizing File Access Problems," for more information.

Changing File Permissions Table 1.5 shows the octal values for setting file permissions. You use these numbers in sets of three to set permissions for owner, group, and other. For example, the value 644 sets read/write permissions for owner and read-only permissions for group and other.

Table 1.5 Octal Values for File Permissions

Value	Description
0	No permissions
1	Execute-only
2	Write-only
3	Write, execute
4	Read-only
5	Read, execute
6	Read, write
7	Read, write, execute

1. Type **ls -l <*filename*>** and press Return. The long listing shows the current permissions for the file.
2. Type **chmod <*nnn*> <*filename*>** and press Return. Permissions are changed using the numbers you specify.

NOTE. *You can change permissions on groups of files, or on all files in a directory using metacharacters such as (*?) in place of file names or in combination with them.*

This example changes the permissions of a file from 666 (read/write, read/write, read/write) to 644 (read/write, read-only, read-only):

```
oak% ls -l quest
-rw-rw-rw-   1 ignatz   staff    6023 Aug  5 12:06 quest
oak% chmod 644 quest
oak% ls -l
-rw-r--r--   1 ignatz   staff    6023 Aug  5 12:06 quest
oak%
```

Changing File Group Ownership

To change the group ownership of a file, type **chgrp <*gid*> <*filename*>** and press Return. The group ID for the file you specify is changed.

```
$ ls -lg junk
-rw-r--r-- 1 other 0 Oct 31 14:49 junk
$ chgrp 10 junk
```

```
$ ls -lg junk
-rw-r--r-- 1 staff 0 Oct 31 14:49 junk
$
```

Group IDs are defined in the Group database or the local /etc/group file. See Chapter 7 for more information about groups.

Setting or Displaying the System Environment

The shell maintains an environment with a set of specifications that it gets from the shell initialization files. Users can also modify the shell environment for a session by issuing commands directly to the shell. The shell receives its information about the environment from environment variables. The SunOS 5.*x* system software provides several default environment variables:

- **PS1:** Defines the shell prompt. The default prompt for the Bourne and Korn shells is $. The default prompt for the C shell is %. The default prompt for root in either shell is #. Users can specify a different shell prompt in the .profile, .login, or .cshrc files.
- **HOME:** Defines the absolute path to the user's home directory. The default value for HOME is automatically defined and set to the login directory specified in the /etc/passwd file as part of the login process. The shell subsequently uses this information to determine the directory to change to when you type the cd command without an argument.
- **LOGNAME:** Defines the user's login name. The default value for LOGNAME is automatically defined and set to the login name specified in the /etc/passwd file as part of the login process.
- **PATH:** Lists, in order, the directories that the shell searches to find the program to run when the user types a command. If the directory is not in the search path, users must type the complete pathname of a command. The default PATH is automatically defined and set as specified in .profile (Bourne or Korn shell), or .cshrc (C shell) as part of the login process. The order of the search path is very important. When identically named commands exist in different locations, the first command found with that name is used. For example, suppose that PATH is defined (in Bourne and Korn shell syntax) as PATH=/bin:/usr/bin:/usr/sbin:$HOME/bin and a file named sample resides in both /usr/bin and /home/jean/bin. If the user types the command sample without specifying its full path name, the version found in /usr/bin is used.

  Other environment variables include:

- **LPDEST:** Sets the user's default printer.
- **OPENWINHOME:** Sets the path to the OpenWindows™ executables.

- **DESKSET:** Sets the path to the DeskSet™ executables.
- **LANG:** Sets the local language. Appropriate values are Japanese, German, French, Swedish, and Italian.
- **HZ:** Sets history for Bourne and Korn shells.
- **TZ:** Sets timezone.
- **SHELL:** Sets the default shell used by make, vi, and other tools.
- **MAIL:** Tells the shell where to look for new mail.
- **MANSECTS:** Sets the available sections of manual pages.

Users and system administrators can define additional variables for their own use. When you define an environment variable from a shell command, the variable remains in effect while you remain in the shell. When you exit the shell, the environment variable is not retained. Store "permanent" environment variables in the .profile, .login, or .cshrc file. The syntax for defining environment variables depends on the shell.

Defining Bourne and Korn Shell Environment Variables

To define an environment variable for the Bourne and Korn shells, type **<*VARIABLE*>=<*value*>;export <*VARIABLE*>** and press Return.

```
$ PS1=oak$;export PS1
$
```

Defining C Shell Environment Variables

To define an environment variable for the C shell, type **setenv <*VARIABLE*> <*value*>** and press Return.

```
% setenv DISPLAY rogue:0
%
```

Displaying Environment Variable Settings

To display a list of the current environment variable settings, type **env** and press Return.

```
$ env
HOME=/home/irving
HZ=100
LOGNAME=irving
MAIL=/var/mail/irving
MANSECTS=\1:1m:1c:1f:1s:1b:2:\3:3c:3i:3n:3m:3k:3g:3e:3x11:3
xt:3w:3b:9:4:5:7:8
PATH=/usr/bin
SHELL=/bin/sh
TERM=sun
```

```
TZ=EST5EDT
$
```

Using the PATH Variable

The PATH environment variable is very important. When the user executes a command using the full path name, the shell finds the command using that path name. However, when the user specifies only a command name, the shell searches the directories for the command in the order specified by the PATH variable. If the command is found in one of the directories, the shell executes it.

A default su PATH (/sbin:/usr/sbin:/usr/bin:/etc) is set by the system, but most users modify it to add additional command directories. Many user problems related to setting up the environment and accessing the right version of a command or a tool can be traced to incorrectly defined paths.

Including **.** in the path to search the current directory is a potential security problem. If security is an issue at your site, do not include **.** as part of a user's path. Never use **.** as part of the root path.

Setting the Path for Bourne and Korn Shells

The path for the Bourne and Korn shells is specified in the user's $HOME/.profile file in this way:

```
PATH=/usr/bin:/$HOME/bin:.
```

Setting the Path for the C Shell

The path for the C shell is specified in the user's $HOME/.cshrc file (with the set path environment variable) in this way:

```
set path = (/usr/bin $home/bin.)
```

See the appropriate manual pages for an in-depth description of these commands and Chapter 10, "Recognizing File Access Problems," for more information about troubleshooting problems with paths.

Using the Administration Tool

The Administration Tool is an OpenWindows tool with a graphical user interface that you use to administer host systems and the 17 databases in the /etc directory. You use the Administration Tool to administer users and groups, and to administer NIS+ databases and local /etc files. The next section describes how to use the Administration Tool to find information.

Using the Administration Tool to Find Information

When using the Administration Tool to view NIS+ databases, you must be a member of the sysadmin UNIX group (GID 14) and run Administration Tool using your own UID, not as root. Before you can make any changes, you also need to create and delete permissions on the NIS+ databases. See Chapter 5 for information on how to set up Administration Tool security. Anyone with root permissions on a local system can use Administration Tool to modify, create, or delete information in the local /etc files for that system.

1. Start OpenWindows (if necessary) by typing **openwin** and pressing Return.
2. Start the Administration Tool by typing **admintool&** and pressing Return. The Administration Tool window is displayed, as shown in Figure 1.1.

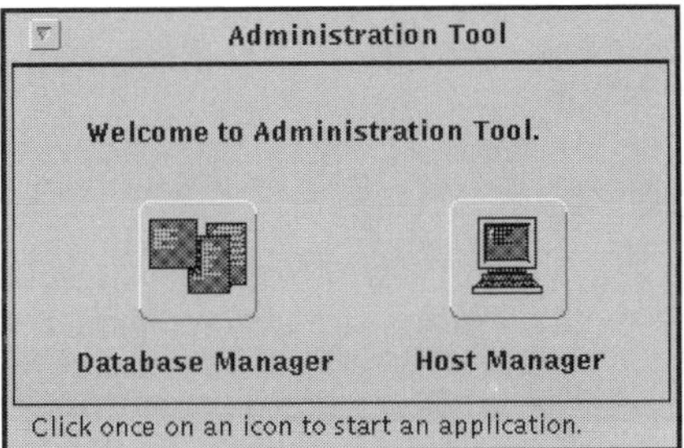

Figure 1.1
The Administration Tool window

3. Move the pointer onto the Database Manager icon and click the SELECT mouse button. The Load Database window is displayed, as shown in Figure 1.2.

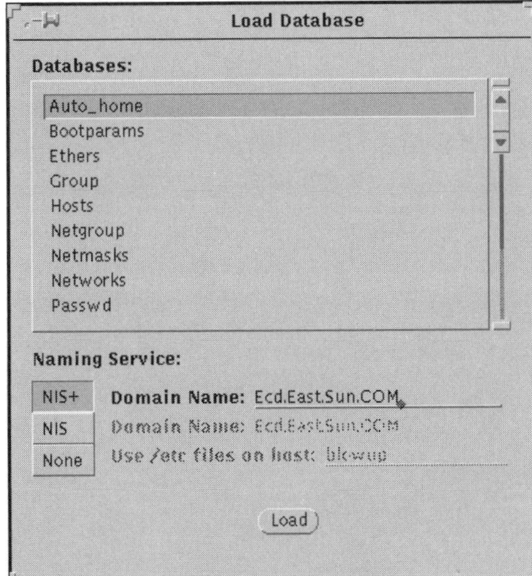

Figure 1.2
The Load Database window

4. Click SELECT on the name of a database. The database is highlighted, as shown in Figure 1.3.

Figure 1.3
Highlighted database

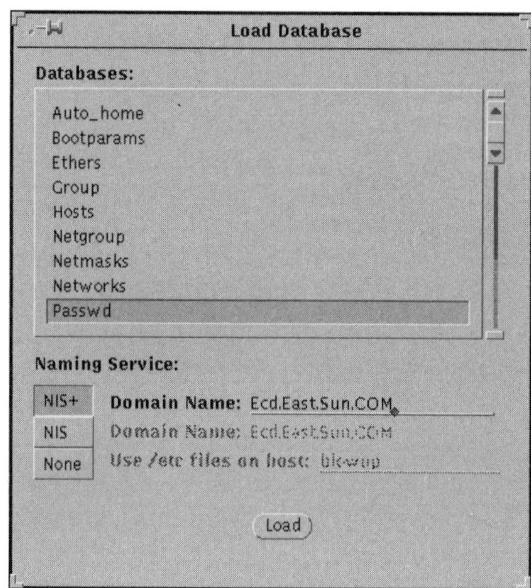

5. Choose the naming service (NIS, NIS+, or None) by clicking SELECT.

NOTE. *You can search for and display information in the NIS maps, but you cannot modify them with the Database Manager because NIS is read-only. Refer to the SunOS 4.*x *documentation for information about administering NIS.*

6. Click SELECT on the Load button. The window containing the database you selected is displayed. In this example, Figure 1.4 shows the Database Manager—Passwd Database window.
7. Each database has File, View, and Edit menu buttons at the top of the window. To search for an entry, choose one of the items from the View menu, shown in Figure 1.5.
8. To find an entry, choose Find from the View menu. The Find window is displayed (see Figure 1.6). Type the text in the text field, then click SELECT on the Find button. The database scrolls to display the information.
9. Resize the window if you need to display complete lines.

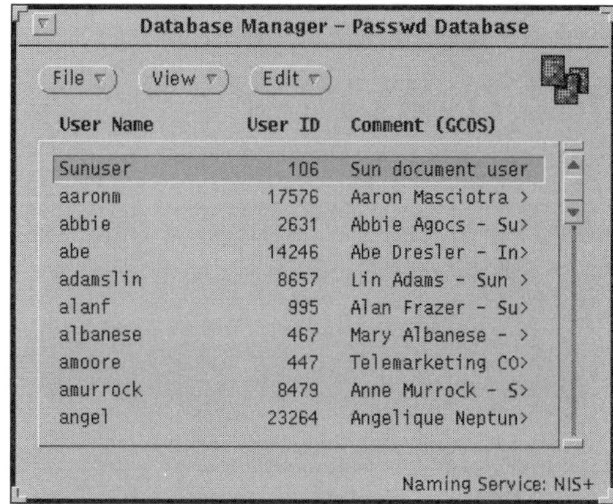

Figure 1.4
The Passwd Database window

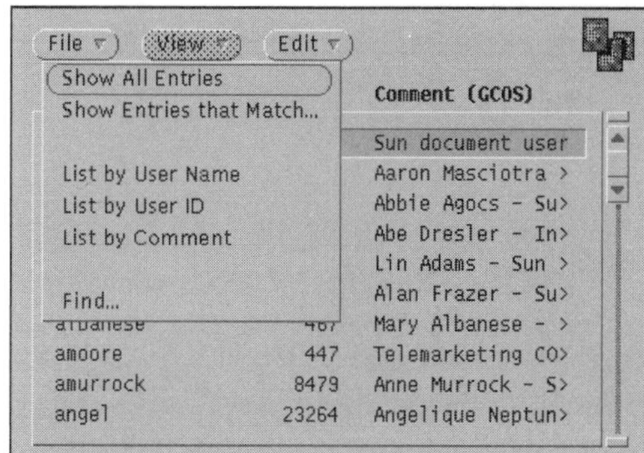

Figure 1.5
The View menu

Figure 1.6
The Find window

CHAPTER

Using Basic OS Commands

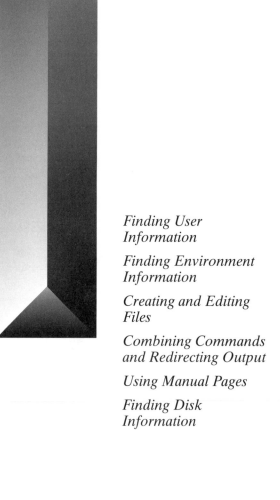

Finding User Information

Finding Environment Information

Creating and Editing Files

Combining Commands and Redirecting Output

Using Manual Pages

Finding Disk Information

THIS CHAPTER EXPLAINS SOME BASIC OPERATING SYSTEM COMMANDS that help you find information about users and the system environment. It also describes several ways to create and edit files, combine commands and redirect output, display manual pages, and locate basic disk information.

Finding User Information

When administering systems, you often need to find out who is using the system and what they are doing. This section describes the commands—who, finger, rusers -l, whodo, id—that you can use to find information about users.

Determining Who Is Logged onto a System (who, finger, rusers -l, whodo)

You can use any one of four commands (who, finger, rusers -l, or whodo) to find out who is logged onto a system. Each command gives you different additional information.

Using the who Command

The who command displays a list of the users logged onto a system, with the login TTY port and the date and time. When a user is logged on remotely, the remote system name for that user is also displayed. To use the who command, type **who** and press Return.

In this example, irving is logged on remotely (as shown by the system name), and ignatz is logged in locally to the system oak.

```
oak% who
irving pts/1   Oct 31 14:33 (elm)
ignatz console Oct 31 12:22
oak%
```

Using the finger Command

The finger command displays a list of the login names of users logged onto a system, along with the user's complete name (from the Information field of their /etc/password entry), the TTY port, the day of the week, the login time, and the remote system name if the user is logged in remotely. To use the finger command, type **finger** and press Return.

In this example, user winsor is logged on remotely from castle.

```
oak% rlogin drusilla
drusilla% finger
```

```
Login  Name           TTY    Idle When       Where
winsor Janice Winsor pts/Ø 11   Thu Ø9:59 castle
drusilla%
```

Using the rusers -l Command

The rusers -l (remote users, login) command displays a list of login names of users who are logged in on remote systems, along with the name of the system a user is logged into, the TTY port, the month, date, login time, and idle time. If the host is not idle, no time is displayed in the last field. To use the rusers -l command, type **rusers -l** and press Return.

```
cinderella% rusers -l
Sending broadcast for rusersd protocol version 3...
Sending broadcast for rusersd protocol version 2...
jah      caps:console            Mar  3 13:Ø3   22:Ø3
amber    facehole:console        Mar  2 Ø7:4Ø
sebree   ondine:console          Mar  2 1Ø:35      14
tut      cairo:console           Mar  2 1Ø:48
jrt      cairo:ttyp5             Mar  2 16:2Ø   47:54 (gap)
ramseyis mowthelawn:console      Mar  2 16:33      28
ramseyis mowthelawn:ttyp6        Mar  3 14:2Ø   25:14
(:Ø.Ø)
(More logins not shown)
cinderella%
```

Using the whodo Command

New with SVR4.

The whodo command displays the date, time, and system name. For each user logged in, device name, UID, and login time are shown, followed by a list of active processes associated with the UID. The list includes the device name, PID, CPU minutes and seconds used, and process name.

To find out who is logged in and doing what, type **whodo** and press Return.

```
oak% whodo
Tue Mar 12 15:48:Ø3 1992
SunOs

ttyØ9    mcn        8:51
ttyØ9   28158    Ø:29 sh

tty52    bdr       15:23
tty52   21688    Ø:Ø5 sh
tty52   22788    Ø:Ø1 whodo
tty52   22Ø17    Ø:Ø3 vi
tty52   22549    Ø:Ø1 sh
```

Finding User UID and GID Settings (id)

Use the id command to display the user ID and group ID number for a user who is logged in. This information can be helpful for troubleshooting problems when users cannot access files they think they own, or when users want to find out which group they belong to. To use the id command, have the user log in, then type **id** and press Return. If the uid or gid does not match those for the troublesome file, you may need to change the ownership or group on the file or add the user to the appropriate group. See Chapter 5 for more information.

```
anastasia% id
uid=6693(winsor) gid=10(staff)
anastasia% su
Password:
# id
uid=0(root) gid=1(other)
#
```

Finding Environment Information

Each shell maintains an environment with a set of specifications that it gets from the user's initialization files (.profile for the Bourne and Korn shells or .cshrc and .login for the C shell) or from environment variables set interactively from a shell. These environment variables can specify information such as the user's home directory, login name, default printer, location for Email messages, and path for accessing the OpenWindows environment. This section describes how to find environment variable settings (env). See Chapter 8 for more information.

To find a user's environment variable settings, type **env** and press Return. A list of the environment variables and their settings is displayed. See Chapter 1 for a list of the default environment variables and for information on how to set them.

```
oak% env
HOME=/
PATH=.:/home/ignatz:/usr/bin:
/home/ignatz/bin:/bin:/home/bin: /etc:/usr/etc
LOGNAME=ignatz
HZ=100
TZ=PST8PDT
TERM=sun
SHELL=/bin/csh
MAIL=/var/mail/ignatz
PWD=/
```

```
MANSECTS=\1:1m:1c:1f:1s:1b:2:\3:3
c:3i:3n:3m:3k:3g:3e:3x11:3xt:3w: 3b :9:4:5:7:8
oak%
```

Creating and Editing Files

This section describes how to create and edit files using these commands: cat, touch, cp, mv, Text Editor, and vi.

Using the cat Command

Use the cat command to create short files or to append a small amount of text to an existing file. Follow these steps to create files using the cat command:

1. Type **cat >** ***<filename>*** and press Return.
2. Type the text into the new file.
3. Press Return.
4. Press Control-D.

The text is saved and the shell prompt is redisplayed.

Follow these steps to append text to an existing file:

1. Type **cat >>** ***<filename>*** and press Return.
2. Type the text to be appended to the file.
3. Press Return.
4. Press Control-D.

The text is saved and the shell prompt is redisplayed.

Using the touch Command

The touch command sets the access and modification times for each file to the current time. If a file does not exist, an empty one is created. You can use the touch command to create an empty file to check permissions and ownership or to create a file to which you will add text at a later time.

To create an empty file, type **touch** ***<filename>*** and press Return. A new empty file is created. If the file exists, then its modification time is updated to the current date and time.

```
oak% ls -l junk
junk:  No such file or directory
```

```
oak% touch junk
oak% ls -l junk
-rw-r--r--  1 irving     staff 0 Sep 11 15:06 junk
oak%
```

Copying (cp) or Renaming (mv) an Existing File

You can create a new file by copying or renaming an existing file.

To copy an existing file, type **cp** ***<old-filename> <new-filename>*** and press Return. You have made a copy of the file, retaining the original one.

```
oak% cp quest oldquest
oak%
```

To move (and rename) an existing file, type **mv** ***<old-filename> <new-filename>*** and press Return. You have changed the name of the file and removed the old one.

```
oak% mv quest /tmp/quest.old
oak%
```

Using Text Editor

You can use the OpenWindows Text Editor to create and edit files. You may, however, have problems using the Text Editor to edit files that have root permissions.

To start Text Editor from the OpenWindows workspace from the Workspace menu, choose Programs. Then choose Text Editor from the Programs menu. To start Text Editor from a command line, type **textedit &** and press Return. A Text Editor window is displayed. Use the Cut, Copy, Paste, and Undo keys from the keyboard to make editing changes.

Using vi

The visual editor, vi, is commonly used by system administrators to edit text files. Whole books have been written about using vi. This section provides only a quick-reference table of some of the most commonly used editing commands.

To start vi, type **vi** ***<filename>*** and press Return. If the file does not exist, a new file is opened. The new file is created when you save changes made to it. If the file exists, the beginning of the file is displayed.

Table 2.1 shows a few of the many vi editing commands.

Table 2.1 Some Basic vi Commands

Task	Command
How to save/quit a file	
Quit without saving changes	:q!
Write changes	:w
Write changes and quit	:wq
Write changes and quit	ZZ
How to move around in a file	
Move cursor one character left	h
Move cursor one character right	l
Move cursor up one line	k
Move cursor down one line	j
Go to end of the file	G
How to add text	
Insert text (insert mode)	i ***text*** Esc
Append text at cursor location	a ***text*** Esc
Append text at end of the line	A ***text*** Esc
How to exit to command mode	Esc
How to make changes to a file	
Delete line	dd
Delete character	x
Delete word	dw
Open new line above	O ***text*** Esc
Open new line below	o ***text*** Esc
Yank/Copy line	Y
Put before	P
Put after	p

Combining Commands and Redirecting Output

The SunOS 5.0 system software lets you combine commands in several ways. This section describes three ways you can combine commands.

Typing Several Commands on the Same Command Line

You can type more than one command on a single command line by typing a semicolon (;) between the commands.

For example, you can change to a directory and list the commands by typing **cd /usr/bin;ls** and pressing Return. Another example is setting an environment variable for the Bourne shell and then exporting the variable:

```
PATH=.:/usr/bin:$HOME/bin;export PATH
```

Redirecting Output (<>)

Unless you indicate otherwise, commands normally display their results on the screen. You can, however, redirect the output of a command using the redirect symbols < and >. For example, to save the output to a file instead of displaying it on the screen, use the > redirect symbol to tell the shell to put the contents in a file. In this example, the output of the date command is redirected to a new file called sample.file:

```
$ date > sample.file
$
```

Here are the contents of sample.file:

```
$ more sample.file
Tue May 26 13:26:59 PDT 1992
$
```

You can also redirect input in the other direction. For example, to mail the contents of a file to user ignatz@oak, type **mail ignatz@oak < report.file** and press Return. The file called report.file is sent by electronic mail to ignatz@oak.

Combining Commands (|)

You can use the pipe (|) operator to connect two or more commands using the output from one command as the input to the next one. This section provides only two examples of the many ways you can combine commands in a pipeline.

To print the cat(1) manual page, type **man cat | lp** and press Return. The manual page is not displayed on the screen. Instead, the output is sent to the lp command, which prints it on the default printer.

You can search the process list for a particular command piping the output of ps -e to the grep command. The output is displayed on the screen. For example, to display process information for OpenWindows:

```
cinderella% ps -e | grep openwin
   260 ?        0:00 openwin
cinderella%
```

If you want to print the information, you can add an additional pipe command (| lp) to the end of the sequence and send it to the printer:

```
anastasia% ps -e | grep openwin | lp
request id is castle-51 (request id is castle-51 (standard
input)
)
anastasia%
```

Using Manual Pages

Manual pages are on-line technical references for each SunOS 5.*x* command. Manual pages are grouped into sections, with similar types of commands within the same section. For example, most user commands are in section (1), and system administration commands are in section (1M). Manual pages may be installed on a local system, or NFS mounted from a server. This section tells you how to display manual pages and how to find out the section numbers for an individual command.

Displaying a Manual Page (man)

To display a manual page, type **man *<command-name>*** and press Return. The manual page is displayed.

```
cinderella% man grep

grep(1)    USER COMMANDS   grep(1)

NAME
  grep - search a file for a pattern

SYNOPSIS
     grep   [   -bchilnsvw    ] limited-regular-expression    [
(More information not shown in this example)
```

Finding the Section Number for a Manual Page (whatis, man)

New with SVR4.

Some commands are listed in more than one section. You can find the section number(s) for a manual page using the whatis command.

NOTE. *The whatis command only works if you have used the catman command to set up your manual pages. To use the catman command to set up manual pages, become superuser and type* **catman <n>** *and press Return, where <n> is the number of the section you want to set up.*

Follow these steps to find the section number for a manual page:

1. Type **whatis *<command-name>*** and press Return. The first line of the manual page for the command is displayed. Use the section number to display the manual page in the next step.
2. Type **man -s*<section-number>* *<command-name>*** and press Return. The manual page is displayed.

```
oak% whatis chown
chown   chown (1)    - change owner of file
chown   chown (1b)   - change owner
chown   chown (1m)   - change owner
chown   chown (2)    - change owner and group of a file
oak% man -s2 chown
chown(2)                SYSTEM CALLS                chown(2)

NAME
 chown, lchown, fchown - change owner and group of a file

SYNOPSIS
 #include <unistd.h>
 #include <sys/types.h>

int chown(const char *path, uid_t owner, gid_t group);

int lchown(const char *path, uid_t owner, gid_t group);

int fchown(int fildes, uid_towner, gid_t group);

DESCRIPTION
chown() sets the owner ID and group ID of the file
specified by path or referenced by the open file
descriptor fields to owner and group respectively. If
owner or group is specified as -1, chown() does not change
```

```
the corresponding ID of the file.
(More text not shown here)
```

Finding Disk Information

Use the commands in the following sections to find disk use, and to tell if a file system is local (ufs) or remote (NFS).

Displaying Used Disk Space in Kilobytes and Percentage of Capacity (df -k)

The output from the df command, when used without arguments, is changed with the SunOS 5.*x* system software. Use the -k option to df to display disk information in the table format used with SunOS 4.*x* system software. Type **df -k** and press Return. The file system, total kilobytes, used kilobytes, available kilobytes, percentage of capacity used, and mount point for local disk partitions are displayed.

```
cinderella% df -k
dev/dsk/c0t0d0s0       30383    19926    7427      73%    /
/dev/dsk/c0t0d0s6      189683   66503    104220    39%    /usr
/proc                  0        0        0          0%    /proc
fd                     0        0        0          0%    /dev/fd
swap                   44268    12       44256      0%    /tmp
/dev/dsk/c0t0d0s7      331953   116133   182630    39%    /opt
/dev/dsk/c0t3d0s7      189858   24293    146585    14%    /export/home
cinderella:(pid146)    0        0        0          0%    /net
cinderella:(pid146)    0        0        0          0%    /home
cinderella:(pid146)    2448597  2055423  148315    93%    /usr/dist
cinderella:(pid146)    763573   574664   112552    84%    /usr/svr4
cinderella:(pid146)    818627   540672   196093    73%    /usr/netinstall
cinderella:(pid146)    0        0        0          0%    /nse
ud5-52a:/export/dist   2448597  2055423  148315    93%    /tmp_mnt/usr/dist
cinderella%
```

Determining If File Systems Are Local or NFS Mounted (df)

To find out if file systems are local or NFS mounted, type **df *<filesystem>*** and press Return. Disk formatting information (including disk location or mount point) for the file system you specify is displayed.

In this example, the file system is NFS mounted:

```
oak% df /home/ignatz
bigriver:/export/home/ignatz
    538980  399435  85647   82%    /tmp_mnt/home/ignatz
oak%
```

In this example, the file system is on a local disk:

```
# df /
/dev/dsk/cØtØdØsØ  3Ø383   11885  15468    43%    /
#
```

Finding All Mounted File Systems of a Specific Type (df -F)

If you want to display all of the mounted file systems of one file system type, use the -F option followed by the file system type. The most common file system types are ufs for local file systems and NFS for network file systems. To find all mounted file systems of a specific type, type **df -F** ***<filesystem-type>*** and press Return.

In this example, the mounted NFS file systems are displayed:

```
cinderella% df -F nfs
/net  (cinderella:(pid153)):       Ø blocks        -1 files
/usr/dist cinderella:(pid153)):    1276248 blocks  -1 files
/home  (cinderella:(pid153)):      Ø blocks        -1 files
/usr/man     (oak:/export/man):    272934 blocks   -1 files
cinderella%
```

In this example, the mounted ufs (local) file systems are displayed:

```
cinderella% df -F ufs
/  (/dev/dsk/cØtØdØsØ): 36992   blocks   13558 files
/usr  (/dev/dsk/cØtØdØs6):  274346 blocks   944Ø3 files
/export/home/cinderella (/dev/dsk/cØt3dØs7):37967Ø blocks     96Ø46 files
cinderella%
```

In this example, information about the mounted tmpfs file system is displayed:

```
cinderella% df -F tmpfs
/tmp              (swap             ):   88528 blocks    3156 files
cinderella%
```

NOTE. *You cannot use the df command to display swapfs file systems because they are never mounted.*

CHAPTER

Administering Devices

THIS CHAPTER DESCRIBES HOW TO USE TAPES AND DISKETTES TO COPY FILES. See Chapter 4 for information about how to back up and restore complete file systems. Chapter 4 also explains disk device names and commands used for administering disks, introduces the Service Access Facility (SAF)—which you must use to administer terminals, modems, and other network devices with the SunOS 5.*x* system software—provides steps for setting up port monitors for print servers and print clients, and provides steps for adding a bidirectional Hayes-compatible modem to a system. See Chapter 6 for information about administering printers.

Using Tapes

This section describes tape device–naming conventions, useful commands for streaming tape cartridges, and how to use both the tar and cpio commands to archive and retrieve files from tapes.

The tar and cpio commands can be used to copy files and file systems to tape. The command you choose depends on how much flexibility and precision you require for the copy.

Use tar to copy files and directory subtrees to a single tape. Note that the SunOS 5.*x* tar command can archive special files (block and character devices, fifos), but the SunOS 4.*x* tar command cannot extract them. The cpio command provides better portability.

Use cpio to copy arbitrary sets of files, special files, or file systems that require multiple tape volumes, or use it when you want to copy files from SunOS 5.*x* systems to SunOS 4.*x* systems. The cpio command packs data onto tape more efficiently than tar and skips over any bad spots in a tape when restoring. The cpio command also provides options for writing files with different header formats (tar, ustar, crc, odc, bar) for portability between systems of different types.

Because tar and cpio use the raw device, you do not need to format or make a file system on tapes before you use them. The tape drive and device name you use depend on the hardware and configuration for each system.

Tape Device-Naming Conventions

Tape drive-naming conventions use a logical—not a physical—device name. Tape drives fall into two categories according to controller type:

- Xylogics 472 for 1/2-inch rack-mounted (top-loaded) reel-to-reel drives (maximum four units per controller)
- SCSI for 1/4-inch cartridge, 1/2-inch front-loaded reel-to-reel, and 4mm or 8mm helical scan drives (maximum eight units per controller)

Within the /dev/rmt subdirectory is a single set of tape device files that support different output densities. In general, you specify a tape drive device as shown in Figure 3.1.

Figure 3.1
Tape drive device names

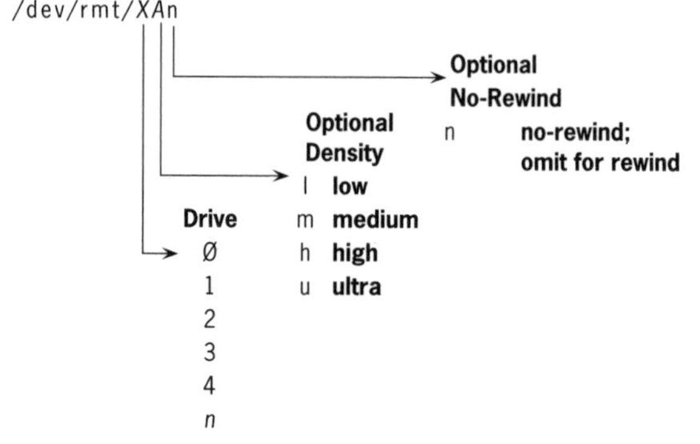

The next three sections describe drive numbers, the optional density choices, and the optional no-rewind.

Specifying the Drive Number Using the Default Density

Normally, you specify a tape drive by its logical unit number, which is a number from 0 to *n*. If you do not specify a density, the drive writes at its "preferred" density, which is usually the highest density the tape supports.

To specify the first drive, use:

```
/dev/rmt/Ø
```

To specify the second drive, use:

```
/dev/rmt/1
```

NOTE. *Most device names start their numbering sequence with zero (0). Consequently, when you talk about the first disk or target, its number is 0, not 1.*

Specifying Different Densities for a Tape Drive

You may want to transport a tape to a system whose tape drive supports only a certain density. In that case, specify a device name that writes at the desired density. Use this convention:

```
/dev/rmt/<XA>
```

The unit and density characters are shown in Table 3.1. For example, to specify a raw magnetic tape device on the first (0) drive with medium density, use:

```
/dev/rmt/0m
```

Table 3.1 Unit and Density Characters in Tape Device Names

Device Name	**= /dev/rmt/<*XA*>**
<X>	Tape drive number (digit) from 0 to *n*, regardless of controller type
<A>	Density (character), depending on controller and drive type
null	Default,preferred (highest) density
l	Low
m	Medium
h	High
u	Ultra

Specifying the No-Rewind Option

After the command is executed, the tape is automatically rewound unless you specify the no-rewind option as part of the device name. To specify no rewinding, type **n** at the end of the device name.

For example, to specify a raw magnetic tape device on the first (0) drive with medium density, use:

```
/dev/rmt/0mn
```

Understanding Device Abbreviations for Different Tape Controllers and Media

You can have both SCSI and non-SCSI tape drives on the same system. A SCSI controller can have a maximum of eight SCSI tape drives, and a non-SCSI controller can have a maximum of four tape drives. For each drive number (*X*), the density character depends on the controller and drive type as described in the following paragraphs.

Table 3.2 shows the device abbreviations for different tape controllers/units and media. Note that the first character in the device abbreviation for drive number does not have to be 0 as shown, but could be 1, 2, or 3, and so on, depending on how many tape drives are attached to the system.

Table 3.2 Device Abbreviations for Tape Controllers/Units and Media

Controller	Drive Unit	Size	Type	Format	Tracks	Device Abbreviation
Xylogics 472	Fujitsu M2444	1/2-inch	Reel	1600 bpi	9	/dev/rmt/0m
		1/2-inch	Reel	6250 bpi	9	/dev/rmt/0h
SCSI front-loaded	HP	1/2-inch	Reel	800 bpi	9	/dev/rmt/0m
				6250 bpi	9	/dev/rmt/0h
SCSI	Sysgen	1/4-inch	Cartridge	QIC-11	4	/dev/rmt/0l
				QIC-24	4	/dev/rmt/0m
				QIC-11	9	/dev/rmt/0l
				QIC-24	9	/dev/rmt/0m
	Emulex MT-02	1/4-inch	Cartridge	QIC-11	4	/dev/rmt/0l
				QIC-24	4	/dev/rmt/0m
				QIC-11	9	/dev/rmt/0l
				QIC-24	9	/dev/rmt/0m
	Archive QIC-150	1/4-inch	Cartridge	QIC-150	18	/dev/rmt/0h
	Wangtek QIC-150	1/4-inch	Cartridge	QIC-150	18	/dev/rmt/0h
	Desktop Backup Pack	1/4-inch	Cartridge	QIC-150	18	/dev/rmt/0h

Using Rack-Mounted Non-SCSI 1/2-Inch Reel Drives

For 1/2-inch rack-mounted tape drives with either a Tapemaster or Xylogics 472 controller, substitute the density from Table 3.3 for the *A* variable in the device name (/dev/rmt/*XA*).

If you omit the density character, the tape is usually written at its highest density, not compressed.

Using SCSI 1/4-Inch Cartridge and 1/2-Inch Front-Loaded Reel Drives

For SCSI 1/4-inch cartridge and 1/2-inch front-loaded reel drives, substitute the density from Table 3.4 for the *A* variable in the device name (/dev/rmt/*XA*).

Table 3.3 **Designating Density for Rack-Mounted ½-Inch Tape Drives**

Character	Density
null	Default "preferred" (highest) density (usually 6250 bpi uncompressed)
l	800 bpi
m	1600 bpi
h	6250 bpi
u	6250 bpi compressed

Table 3.4 **Designating Format or Density for SCSI Tape Drives**

Character	Density, ¼-Inch Cartridge	Density, ½-Inch Front-Loaded Reel-to-Reel
null	Default, preferred (highest) density	Default, preferred (highest) density
l	QIC-11 format	800 bpi
m	QIC-24 format	1600 bpi
h	QIC-150	6250 bpi
u	Reserved	Reserved

For ¼-inch cartridges, density is specified by the format in which the data is written: the QIC format. The QIC-11 and QIC-24 formats write approximately 1000 bytes per inch on each track. The density for QIC-150 is somewhat higher. The preferred density for a 60Mb ¼-inch cartridge drive is QIC-24 and for a 150Mb ¼-inch cartridge drive is QIC-150.

A 150Mb drive can write only QIC-150; it cannot be switched to write QIC-24 or QIC-11. Format selection is only useful for drives that can write both QIC-24 and QIC-11.

Specifying Helical Scan Drives

Helical scan drives (for example, Exabyte 8mm or Wang/DAT 4mm) are a special case of SCSI drives. They write only at the preferred density. Consequently, you always specify them using only the drive number, for example, /dev/rmt/0.

Useful Commands for Streaming Tapes

The sections below contain a few commands for use with streaming tapes.

Retensioning a Magnetic Tape

If errors occur when reading a tape, retension the tape, clean the tape drive, and then try again. Type **mt -f /dev/rmt/<*n*> retension** and press Return. The tape in the tape drive you specify is retensioned.

In this example, the tape in drive /dev/rmt/1 is retensioned:

```
oak% mt -f /dev/rmt/1 retension
oak%
```

Rewinding a Magnetic Tape

To rewind a magnetic tape, type **mt -f /dev/rmt/<*n*> rewind** and press Return. The tape in the tape drive you specify by the device number *n* is rewound.

In this example, the tape in drive /dev/rmt/1 is rewound:

```
oak% mt -f /dev/rmt/1 rewind
oak%
```

Showing the Status of a Magnetic Tape Drive

To show the status of a magnetic tape drive, type **mt -f /dev/rmt/<*n*> status** and press Return. Status for the tape drive you specify is displayed.

In this example, there is no tape in drive /dev/rmt/1:

```
oak% mt -f /dev/rmt/1 status
/dev/rmt/1: no tape loaded or drive offline
oak%
```

In this example, status is shown for the tape in drive /dev/rmt/1:

```
oak% mt -f /dev/rmt/1 status
Archive QIC-150 tape drive:
   sense key(0x6)= unit attention   residual= 0   retries= 0
   file no= 0   block no= 0
oak%
```

The tar Command

The following sections describe how to use the tar command to copy files to a tape, list the files, append the files, and retrieve the files.

Copying Files to a Tape (tar)

Follow these steps to copy files to a tape:

1. Change to the directory that contains the file you want to copy.
2. Insert a write-enabled tape into the tape drive.

CAUTION! *Copying files to a tape using the c option to tar destroys any files already on the tape. If you want to preserve the files already on the tape, use the r option described in "Appending Files to a Tape (tar)" below.*

3. Type **tar cvf /dev/rmt/<*n*> <*filename*> <*filename*> <*filename*> ...** and press Return. The c (copy) option copies the files you specify, the v (verbose) option displays information about the files as they are copied, and the f (files) option followed by the tape device name specifies where the tar files are to be written. The file names you specify are copied to the tape, overwriting any existing files on the tape.

NOTE. *You can use metacharacters (? and *) as part of the file names you specify. For example, to copy all documents with a .doc suffix, type* ***.doc** *as the file name argument. If you specify a directory name as the file name, the directory and all of its subdirectories are recursively copied to the tape.*

4. Remove the tape from the drive and write the names of the files on the tape label.

   In this example, two files are copied to a tape in tape drive 0:

```
oak% cd /home/winsor
oak% ls evaluation*
evaluation.doc    evaluation.doc.backup
oak% tar cvf /dev/rmt/0 evaluation*
a evaluation.doc 86 blocks
a evaluation.doc.backup 84 blocks
oak%
```

Listing the Files on a Tape (tar)

Follow these steps to list the files on a tape:

1. Insert a tape into the tape drive.
2. Type **tar tvf /dev/rmt/<*n*>** and press Return. The t (table) option lists the files you specify, the v (verbose) option displays complete information about the files as they are listed in a form similar to the ls -l command, and the f (files) option followed by the tape device name specifies the device where the tar files are located.

In this example, the table of contents for the tape in drive 0 contains two files:

```
oak% tar tvf /dev/rmt/0
rw-rw-rw-6693/10  44032 Apr 23 14:54 1991 evaluation.doc
rw-rw-rw-6693/10  43008 Apr 23 14:47 1991 evaluation.doc.backup
oak%
```

Reading from left to right, the first column shows the permissions for the file; the second column shows the UID and GID file ownership; the third column shows the number of characters (bytes) in the file; the fourth, fifth, sixth, and seventh columns contain the month, day, date, and year the file was last modified, and the final column contains the name of the file.

Appending Files to a Tape (tar)

Follow these steps to append files without overwriting files already on the tape:

1. Change to the directory that contains the file you want to copy.
2. Insert a tape that is not write-protected into the tape drive.
3. Type **tar rvf /dev/rmt/<*n*> <*filename*> <*filename*> <*filename*> ...** and press Return. The file names you specify are appended to the files already on the tape in the drive you specify.

NOTE. *You can use metacharacters (? and *) as part of the file names you specify. For example, to copy all documents with a .doc suffix, type* ***.doc** *as the file name argument.*

4. Remove the tape from the drive and write the names of the files on the tape label.

   In this example, one file is appended to the files already on the tape in drive 0:

```
oak% cd /home/winsor
oak% tar cvf /dev/rmt/0 junk
a junk 1 blocks
oak% tar rvf /dev/rmt/0
rw-rw-rw-6693/10  44032 Apr 23 14:54 1991 evaluation.doc
rw-rw-rw-6693/10  43008 Apr 23 14:47 1991 evaluation.doc.backup
rw-rw-rw-6693/10     18 Dec 10 11:36 1991 junk
oak%
```

You can put more than one set of tar files on a tape if you use the n (no-rewind) option as part of the tape device name. For example, type **tar cvf /dev/rmt/<*n*>n <*filename*>**. The tape is not rewound after the files are copied, and the next time you use the tape, the files are written at the end of the previous set of files.

Retrieving Files from a Tape (tar)

Follow these steps to retrieve files from a tape:

1. Change to the directory where you want to put the files.
2. Insert the tape into the tape drive.

3. Type **tar xvf /dev/rmt/<*n*>** and press Return. All of the files on the tape in the drive you specify are copied to the current directory.

   In this example, all files are copied from the tape in drive 0:

```
oak% cd /home/winsor/Evaluations
oak% tar xvf /dev/rmt/0
x evaluation.doc, 44032 bytes, 86 tape blocks
x evaluation.doc.backup, 43008 bytes, 84 tape blocks
oak%
```

To retrieve individual files from a tape, type **tar xvf /dev/rmt/<*n*> <*filename*> <*filename*> <*filename*> ...** and press Return. The file names you specify are extracted from the tape and placed in the current working directory. In this example, files with the prefix "evaluation" are copied from the tape in drive 0:

```
oak% cd /home/winsor/Evaluations
oak% tar xvf /dev/rmt/0 evaluation*
x evaluation.doc, 44032 bytes, 86 tape blocks
x evaluation.doc.backup, 43008 bytes, 84 tape blocks
oak%
```

Follow these steps to retrieve directories and subdirectories recursively from a tape:

1. Change to the parent directory where you want to copy the files. If the directory already exists, be sure you are in the parent directory, and that it is OK to overwrite the contents of the directory before you copy the files from the tape. For example, to restore the contents of a directory named Book that is in /home/winsor/Book, you would change to /home/winsor and type tar xvf /dev/rmt/<*n*> Book and press Return. If you are in the directory /home/winsor/Book, the files will be restored as /home/winsor/Book/Book.

2. Type tar xvf /dev/rmt/<*n*> <*directory-name*> and press Return. The directory and all of its subdirectories are recursively copied from the tape.

NOTE. *The names of the files extracted from the tape exactly match the names of the files stored on the archive. If you have any doubts about the names or paths of the files, first list the files on the tape. See "Listing the Files on a Tape (tar)" above for instructions and the tar(1) manual page for more information.*

The cpio Command

When you use the cpio command to create an archive, it takes a list of files or path names from standard input and writes to standard output. The output is almost always redirected to a file or to a device. The following sections describe how to use the cpio command to copy files to a cartridge tape, list the files, retrieve all files, and retrieve a subset of the files from a cartridge tape.

Copying All Files in a Directory to a Tape (cpio)

Follow these steps to copy all files in a directory to a tape:

1. Insert a write-enabled tape into the tape drive.
2. Type **ls | cpio -oc > /dev/rmt/<*n*>** and press Return. The o option copies the files out. The c option writes header information in ASCII character form for portability. All of the files in the directory are copied to the tape in the drive you specify, overwriting any existing files on the tape, and the total number of blocks copied is displayed.
3. Remove the tape from the drive and write the names of the files on the tape label.

In this example, all of the files in the directory /home/winsor/TOI are copied to the tape in tape drive 0:

```
oak% cd /home/winsor/TOI
oak% ls | cpio -oc > /dev/rmt/0
31 blocks
oak%
```

Listing the Files on a Tape (cpio)

To list files on a tape:

1. Insert a tape into the tape drive.
2. Type **cpio -civt < /dev/rmt/<*n*>** and press Return. The i option reads in the contents of the tape. The v option displays the output in a format similar to the output from the ls -l command. The t option lists the table of contents for the files on the tape in the tape drive you specify.

NOTE. *Listing the table of contents takes as long as it does to read the archive file because the cpio command must process the entire archive.*

In this example, the table of contents for the tape in drive 0 contains four files:

```
oak% cpio -civt < /dev/rmt/0
100666 winsor   3895  Feb 24 15:13:02 1992  Boot.chapter
100666 winsor   3895  Feb 24 15:13:23 1992  Directory.chapter
100666 winsor   6491  Feb 24 15:13:52 1992  Install.chapter
100666 winsor   1299  Feb 24 15:14:00 1992  Intro.chapter
31 blocks
oak%
```

The first column shows permissions in octal form; the second column shows the owner of the file; the third column displays the number of characters (bytes) in the file; the fourth, fifth, sixth, and seventh columns show the month, date, time, and year the file was last modified; and the final column shows the name of the file.

Retrieving All Files from a Tape (cpio)

If the archive was created using relative path names, the input files are built as a directory within the current directory. If, however, the archive was created with absolute path names, the same absolute paths are used to re-create the file.

CAUTION! *Using absolute path names can be dangerous because you can overwrite the original files.*

Follow these steps to retrieve all files from a tape:

1. Change to the directory where you want to put the files.
2. Insert the tape into the tape drive.
3. Type **cpio -icv < /dev/rmt/<*n*>** and press Return.

All of the files on the tape in the drive you specify are copied to the current directory.

In this example, all files are copied from the tape in drive 0:

```
oak% cpio -icv < /dev/rmt/0
Boot.chapter
Directory.chapter
Install.chapter
Intro.chapter
31 blocks
oak%
```

Retrieving a Subset of Files from a Tape (cpio)

You can retrieve a subset of the files from the archive by specifying a pattern to match using shell wild-card characters enclosed in quotes after the options.

1. Change to the directory where you want to put the files.
2. Insert the tape into the tape drive.
3. Type **cpio -icv "*<*file*>" < /dev/rmt/<*n*>** and press Return. All of the files that match the pattern are copied to the current directory. You can specify multiple patterns, but each must be enclosed in quotes.

In this example, all files that end in the suffix *chapter* are copied from the tape in drive 0:

```
oak% cd /home/winsor/Book
oak% cpio -icv "*chapter" < /dev/rmt/0
Boot.chapter
Directory.chapter
Install.chapter
Intro.chapter
31 blocks
oak%
```

See the cpio(1) manual page for more information.

Using Diskettes

Use double-sided (DS), high-density (HD) 3.5-inch diskettes. Before you can copy ufs files or file systems to diskette, you must format the diskette. Use the tar command to copy ufs files to a single formatted diskette. Use cpio if you need to copy ufs files to multiple formatted diskettes. The cpio command recognizes end of media and prompts you to insert the next volume.

You also can make a DOS file system on a diskette. To use a DOS formatted diskette, you mount the diskette as a pcfs file system and use basic OS commands such as cp and mv to archive and retrieve files from the diskette.

Diskette Device Names

The device name for the diskette drive is changed with the SunOS 5.*x* system software. The device name for the diskette drive is /dev/diskette. The raw device file for a diskette is /dev/rdiskette.

Diskettes for ufs File Systems

The following sections describe how to format diskettes for use with ufs file systems, and describe how to copy files using the tar and cpio commands. They also describe how to retrieve files that were created using the SunOS 4.*x* bar command.

Formatting a ufs Diskette

Follow these steps to format a diskette for use with SunOS 5.*x* ufs file systems:

1. Check the diskette to make sure that it is not write-protected.
2. Put the diskette in the drive.

CAUTION! *Reformatting destroys any files already on the diskette.*

3. Type **fdformat** and press Return. The message "Press return to start formatting floppy" is displayed.

4. Press Return. While the diskette is being formatted, a series of dots (...) is displayed. When formatting is complete, the prompt is redisplayed.

```
oak% fdformat
Press return to start formatting floppy.
........................................................................
oak%
```

Removing a Diskette from the Drive

Use the eject command to remove a diskette from the disk drive. You can also use the eject command to remove a CD-ROM disc from a CD-ROM drive. The default for the eject command is /dev/diskette when you type it with no arguments. To remove a diskette from the diskette drive, type **eject** and press Return. The diskette is ejected.

```
$ eject
$
```

NOTE. *If the drive jams, you can eject a diskette manually by sticking a straightened wire paper clip into the pinhole under the diskette slot.*

To eject a CD-ROM disc from a CD-ROM drive, type **eject cdrom** and press Return.

Copying ufs Files to a Single Formatted Diskette

This section provides steps for using the tar command to copy files to a single formatted diskette. Note that the tar command does not require the raw device name, /dev/rdiskette. You can use either device name. The examples in this book use the raw device name.

1. Change to the directory that contains the file(s) you want to copy.

2. Insert a write-enabled formatted diskette into the drive.

CAUTION! *Copying files to a formatted diskette using the c option destroys any files already on the diskette. If you want to preserve the files already on the diskette, use the r option described in "Appending Files to a Formatted Diskette (tar)" below.*

3. Type **tar cvf /dev/rdiskette** ***<filename> <filename> <filename>*** **...** and press Return. The file names you specify are copied to the diskette, overwriting any existing files on the diskette.

NOTE. *You can use metacharacters (? and *) as part of the file names you specify. For example, to copy all documents with a .doc suffix, type* ***.doc** *as the file name argument.*

4. Type **eject** and press Return to remove the diskette from the drive. The diskette is ejected from the drive.

5. Write the names of the files on the diskette label.

   In this example, two files are copied to a diskette:

```
oak% cd /home/winsor
oak% ls evaluation*
evaluation.doc    evaluation.doc.backup
oak% tar cvf /dev/rdiskette evaluation*
a evaluation.doc 86 blocks
a evaluation.doc.backup 84 blocks
oak% eject
oak%
```

Listing the Files on a Diskette (tar)

Follow these steps to list files that were copied using the tar command:

1. Insert a diskette into the drive.

2. Type **tar tvf /dev/rdiskette** and press Return. The t option lists the table of contents for the files on the diskette.

   In this example, the table of contents for the diskette contains two files:

```
oak% tar tvf /dev/rdiskette
rw-rw-rw-6693/10  44032 Apr 23 14:54 1991 evaluation.doc
rw-rw-rw-6693/10  43008 Apr 23 14:47 1991 evaluation.doc.backup
oak%
```

See the tar(1) manual page for more information.

If you need a multiple-volume interchange utility, use cpio. The tar command is only a single-volume utility.

Appending Files to a Formatted Diskette (tar)

When you copy tar files to a formatted diskette, any files already on the diskette are overwritten. If you want to keep the files already on the diskette and add other files, follow these steps:

1. Change to the directory that contains the file you want to copy.

2. Insert a write-enabled formatted diskette protected into the drive.

3. Type **tar rvf /dev/rdiskette *<filename> <filename> <filename>* ...** and press Return. The file names you specify are appended to the files already on the diskette.

NOTE. *You can use metacharacters (? and *) as part of the file names you specify. For example, to copy all documents with a .doc suffix, type* ***.doc** *as the file name argument.*

4. Type **eject** and press Return to remove the diskette from the drive. The diskette is ejected from the drive.

5. Write the names of the additional files on the diskette label.

   In this example, one file is appended to the files already on the diskette:

```
oak% cd /home/winsor
oak% tar rvf /dev/rdiskette junk
a junk 1 blocks
oak% tar tvf /dev/rdiskette
rw-rw-rw-6693/10  44032 Apr 23 14:54 1991 evaluation.doc
rw-rw-rw-6693/10  43008 Apr 23 14:47 1991 evaluation.doc.backup
rw-rw-rw-6693/10     18 Dec 10 11:36 1991 junk
oak% eject
oak%
```

Retrieving Files from a Diskette (tar)

Follow these steps to retrieve files from a diskette:

1. Change to the directory where you want to put the files.

2. Insert the diskette into the drive.

3. Type **tar xvf /dev/rdiskette** and press Return. All of the files on the diskette are copied to the current directory.

4. Type **eject** and press Return to remove the diskette from the drive. The diskette is ejected from the drive.

   In this example, all files are copied from the diskette:

```
oak% cd /home/winsor/Evaluations
oak% tar xvf /dev/rdiskette
x evaluation.doc, 44032 bytes, 86 tape blocks
x evaluation.doc.backup, 43008 bytes, 84 tape blocks
oak% eject
oak%
```

To retrieve individual files from a diskette, type **tar xvf /dev/rdiskette *<filename> <filename> <filename>* ...** and press Return. The file names you specify are extracted from the diskette and placed in the current working directory. In this example, all files with the prefix evaluation are copied from the diskette:

```
oak% cd /home/winsor/Evaluations
oak% tar xvf /dev/rdiskette
x evaluation.doc, 44032 bytes, 86 tape blocks
x evaluation.doc.backup, 43008 bytes, 84 tape blocks
oak% eject
oak%
```

Retrieving bar Files from Diskettes (cpio)

The SunOS 4.*x* bar command is not provided with the SunOS 5.*x* system software. You can retrieve files from diskettes that were archived using the SunOS 4.*x* bar command by using the -H bar option to cpio.

NOTE. *You can use the -H bar option with -i to retrieve files only. You cannot create files with the bar header option. It is good practice to list the contents of an archive before extracting them.*

1. Change to the directory where you want to put the files.
2. Insert the diskette that contains bar files into the drive.
3. Type **cpio -ivH bar < /dev/diskette** and press Return. All the files on the diskette are copied to the current directory.
4. Type **eject** and press Return to remove the diskette from the drive.

Multiple Diskettes for Archiving Files (cpio)

If you are copying large files or file systems onto diskettes, you will want to be prompted to replace a full diskette with another formatted diskette. The cpio command provides this capability. The cpio options you use are the same as you would use to copy files to tape, except you would specify /dev/rdiskette as the device instead of the tape device name. See "The cpio Command" above for information on how to use cpio.

Making a ufs File System on a Diskette (newfs /dev/rdiskette)

If you want to mount a ufs diskette, you must make a file system on it first.

1. Format the diskette.
2. Become superuser.
3. Type **newfs /dev/rdiskette** and press Return.

A ufs file system is created on the diskette.

```
oak% fdformat
Press return to start formatting floppy.
.......................................................................
oak% su
Password:
# newfs /dev/rdiskette
#
```

Diskettes for pcfs (DOS) File Systems

You can format diskettes with the pcfs file system for use with DOS systems. The following sections describe how to format a DOS diskette, and how to mount the diskette for use with the SunOS 5.*x* system software. See Chapter 4 for a description of the pcfs file system.

Formatting a Diskette with a pcfs (DOS) File System

Follow these steps to format a diskette with the pcfs file system:

1. Put a diskette in the drive.

CAUTION! *Reformatting destroys any files already on the diskette.*

2. Type **fdformat -d** and press Return. The message "Press return to start formatting floppy" is displayed.

3. Press Return. While the diskette is being formatted, a series of dots (...) is displayed. When formatting is complete, the prompt is redisplayed.

```
oak% fdformat -d
Press return to start formatting floppy.
.......................................................................
oak%
```

Mounting a pcfs Diskette

You can mount a pcfs diskette that was formatted using the fdformat -d command, or a DOS diskette that was formatted on a DOS system. When you mount a pcfs file system, you can create, read, write, and delete files in the file system using SunOS file utilities, subject to DOS naming conventions. See the pcfs(7) manual page for more information about the format and features of the pcfs file system.

To mount a pcfs file system from a diskette:

1. Insert the pcfs diskette in the drive.

2. Become superuser.

3. Type **mount -F pcfs /dev/diskette <*mount-point*>** and press Return. The file system is mounted on the <*mount-point*> you specify.

You can mount a pcfs file system with different mount options (for example, -o rw). See the mount_pcfs(1M) manual page for a description of the options that can be included in the list.

If you use pcfs diskettes frequently, you may want to add this entry to your /etc/vfstab file:

```
/dev/diskette   -    /pcfs    pcfs    -    no    rw
```

Create a directory named /pcfs to use as the mount point for the diskette. With the mount point and the entry in the /etc/vfstab file, you can mount a pcfs diskette by becoming superuser and typing **mount /pcfs** and pressing Return. Once the diskette is mounted, you can use any of the SunOS file utilities such as cp or mv to copy files to and from the diskette.

Unmounting a pcfs Diskette

When you are done with the pcfs diskette, you must unmount it before you can eject it. To unmount the diskette, type **umount <*mount-point*>** and press Return. To eject the diskette, type **eject** and press Return.

Administering Disks

The following sections describe the SunOS 5.*x* disk naming conventions, commands for finding disk information (du, prtvtoc), and how to repair or replace a bad disk.

Disk-Naming Conventions

New with SVR4.

The SunOS 5.*x* disk-naming conventions are different from the SunOS 4.*x* disk-naming conventions. This section describes the new disk-naming conventions; these are based on logical (not physical) device names. SunOS 5.*x* disks have both block and raw (character) device files. The device name is the same, regardless of whether the command requires the block or raw device file.

Instead of adding an r to the beginning of the disk device name (the naming convention in the SunOS 4.*x* system software), each type of device file has its own subdirectory in /dev: /dev/dsk (the block interface) or /dev/rdsk (the raw interface).

Some commands, such as mount, use the block interface device name from the /dev/dsk directory to specify the disk device. Other commands, such as newfs, require the raw interface device name from the /dev/rdsk directory to specify the disk device.

The device name you use to identify a specific disk with either type of interface depends on the controller type: bus-oriented (SCSI or IPI) or direct.

Using Disks with Bus Controllers

Figure 3.2 shows the device naming convention for disks with bus controllers.

Figure 3.2
Naming convention for disks with bus controllers

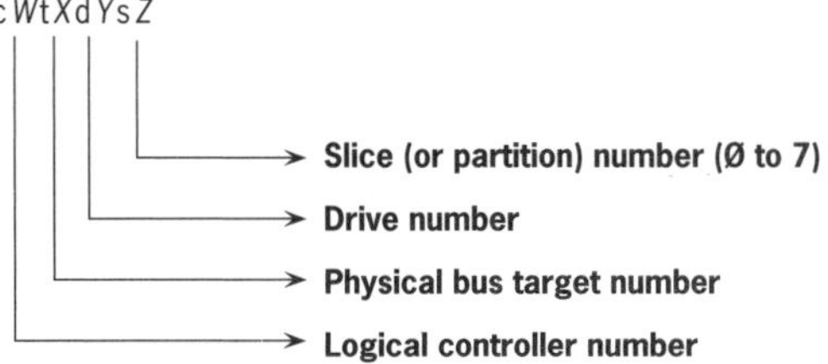

To specify a slice (partition) on a disk with a bus controller (either SCSI or IPI), use a device name with these conventions: /dev/dsk/c*W*t*X*d*Y*s*Z* (the block interface) or /dev/rdsk/c*W*t*X*d*Y*s*Z* (the raw interface).

NOTE. *SunOS 5.*x *disk device names use the term* slice *(and the letter* s *in the device name) to refer to the slice number.* Slice *is simply another name for a disk partition.*

Here are some guidelines for determining the values for the device file name:

- If you have only one controller on your system, *W* is always 0.
- For SCSI controllers, *X* is the target address set by the switch on the back of the unit.
- *Y* is the number of the drive attached to the target. If the disk has an embedded controller, *Y* is always 0.
- *Z* is the slice (partition) number, a number from 0 to 7. To specify the entire disk, use slice 2. Table 3.5 shows conventional assignments of slice (partition) numbers for the disk on which root is found.

Table 3.6 shows some examples of raw device names for disks with bus-oriented controllers.

Using Disks with Direct Controllers

Disks with direct controllers do not have a target entry as part of the device name. To specify a slice (partition) on a disk with a direct controller, use a device name with these conventions: /dev/dsk/c*X*d*Y*s*Z* (the block interface) or /dev/rdsk/c*X*d*Y*s*Z* (the raw interface).

Table 3.5 Customary Assignments of Slices for Disk with Root

Slice	File System	Use
0	root	Operating system
1	swap	Virtual memory space
2	-	Entire disk
3–5		Available for use according to your administrative policy
6	/usr	Executable programs, program libraries, and documentation

Table 3.6 Examples of Device Names for Disks with Bus-Oriented Controllers

Device Name	Description
/dev/rdsk/c0t0d0s0	Raw interface to the first slice (root) on the first disk at the first SCSI target address on the first controller
/dev/rdsk/c0t0d0s2	Raw interface to the third slice (which represents the whole disk) on the first disk at the first SCSI target address on the first controller
/dev/rdsk/c0t1d0s6	Raw interface to seventh (/usr) slice on the first disk at the second SCSI target address on the first controller

Figure 3.3 shows the naming convention for disks with direct controllers. If you have only one controller on your system, *X* is always 0. Use slice 2 to specify the entire disk.

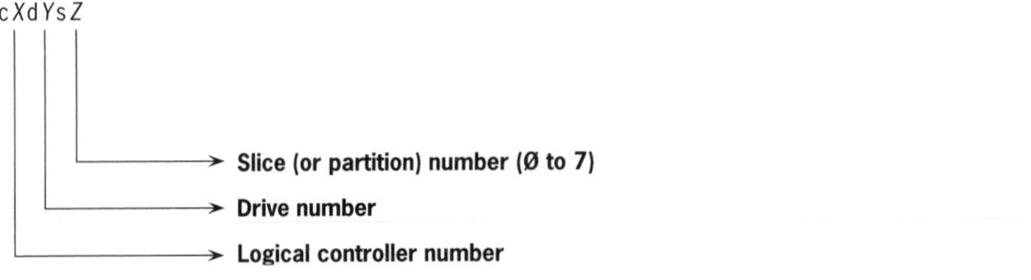

Figure 3.3 Naming convention for disks with direct controllers

Table 3.7 shows some examples of raw device names for disks with direct controllers.

Table 3.7 Examples of Device Names for Disks with Direct Controllers

Device Name	Description
/dev/rdsk/c0d0s0	Raw interface to the first controller on the first disk to the first slice (root).
/dev/rdsk/c0d0s2	Raw interface to the first controller on the first disk to the third slice (the entire disk).
/dev/rdsk/c0d1s6	Raw interface to the first controller on the second disk to the seventh (/usr) slice. By convention, the slice numbers are assigned to specific file systems, as shown in Table 3.5.

Disk Use Check (du)

To find the number of 512-byte disk blocks used per file or directory, type **du** and press Return. When directories contain subdirectories, the subdirectories and their contents are included in the block count.

```
oak% du
2913    ./3.0templates
639     ./Art
347     ./Howto
1998    ./Clipart
607     ./Newtemplates
38      ./Modemstuff
2004    ./Config/Art
6593    ./Config
13280   .
oak%
```

The output is displayed in 512-byte blocks. To convert to megabytes, divide by 2048. In this example 13280/2048 = 6.48 Mb.

Disk Information Check (prtvtoc)

New with SVR4.

Use the prtvtoc (print volume table of contents) command to display information about disk partitioning. The prtvtoc command only works when the slice you specify has space allocated to it. Otherwise, it displays the error message "No such device or address". If you use the standard slice naming conventions, specifying slice 2 displays the contents of the entire disk.

1. Become superuser.

2. Type **prtvtoc /dev/rdsk/c<*n*>*t*<*n*>*d*<*n*>*s*<*n*>** and press Return. Information for the disk you specify is displayed.

```
oak% su
Password:
oak# prtvtoc /dev/rdsk/c0t1d0s2
* /dev/rdsk/c0t1d0s2 partition map
*
* Dimensions:
*     512 bytes/sector
*      35 sectors/track
*       6 tracks/cylinder
*     210 sectors/cylinder
*    1019 cylinders
*     974 accessible cylinders
*
* Flags:
*   1: unmountable
*  10: read-only
*

*                        First
* Partition  Tag  Flags    Sector
      0       0    00         0
      1       0    00     24150
      2       0    00         0
      6       0    00     74550
Sector    Last
Count    Sector  Mount Directory
24150     24149
50400     74549
204540    204539    /
129990    204539
oak#
```

Bad-Disk Repair

The following sections describe the steps for repairing a bad disk or reinstalling a new one.

Try Archiving the Files

If you can access the drive, do a ufsdump of all the file systems on the disk. See Chapter 4 for information on how to use the ufsdump command.

Try Copying Data from the Disk

If you cannot run ufsdump on the disk, find another disk of the same type, connect it to the system, and use the dd command to copy the data from the bad disk. See the dd(1M) manual page for information on how to use this command.

Try Repairing Any Bad Blocks

If the disk has bad blocks, you may be able to repair them using the format command. See the format(1M) manual page for more information.

Try Reformatting the Disk

If the disk is bad, reformatting it may fix the problem. Use the format command to reformat a disk. See the format(1M) manual page for more information. Remember that formatting the disk destroys all data.

Replacing the Bad Disk

If reformatting and repairing bad blocks do not work, replace the disk. See the disk installation manual for more information.

Adding Defect List, Format, Partition, and Label Disk (format)

Follow these steps to put a defect list on a new disk, format, partition, and label it.

CAUTION! *You must format the disk after you add the defect list. Any data on the disk will be destroyed by formatting. If the disk is not new, be sure the data is backed up before you proceed. See Chapter 4 for complete information on how to back up and restore file systems.*

1. Become superuser.
2. Type **format** and press Return. A list of available disks is displayed.

```
AVAILABLE DISK SELECTIONS:
 0. c0t0d0 at scsibus0 slave 24
 sd0: <SUN0207 cyl 1254 alt 2 hd 9 sec 36>
```

3. Type the number of the new disk from the list that is displayed. The format menu and the format> prompt are displayed.
4. Type **defect** and press Return.
5. Type **primary** and press Return. The original defect list is added to the disk.

```
defect> primary
Extracting primary defect list . . . Extraction complete.
Current Defect List updated, \
total of 30 defects.
```

6. Type **quit** and press Return. The format> prompt is displayed.
7. Type **format** and press Return. The disk begins formatting. Formatting takes about 10 minutes for a 107Mb disk, longer for bigger disks.
8. When the format> prompt is redisplayed, type **partition** and press Return.
9. Re-create the partitions to match the partitions on the defective disk.
10. Type **label** and press Return. The disk is labeled.
11. Type **quit** and press Return. The format menu and format> prompt are redisplayed.
12. Type **quit** and press Return. The shell prompt is redisplayed.

```
oak% su
Password:
# format
Searching for disks...done


AVAILABLE DISK SELECTIONS:
        Ø. sdØ at espØ slave 24
           sdØ: <SUNØ2Ø7 cyl 1254 alt 2 hd 9 sec 36>
        1. sd2 at espØ slave 16
           sd2: <SUNØ2Ø7 cyl 1254 alt 2 hd 9 sec 36>
Specify disk (enter its number): 1
selecting cØtØdØ
[disk formatted]
FORMAT MENU:
        disk       - select a disk
        type       - select (define) a disk type
        partition  - select (define) a partition table
        current    - describe the current disk
        format     - format and analyze the disk
        repair     - repair a defective sector
        label      - write label to the disk
        analyze    - surface analysis
        defect     - defect list management
        backup     - search for backup labels
        verify     - read and display labels
        save       - save new disk/partition definitions
        inquiry    - show vendor, product and revision
        volname    - set 8-character volume name
        quit
```

```
format > defect
defect > primary
Extracting primary defect list . . . Extraction complete.
Current Defect List updated, total of 30 defects.
defect > quit
format > format
format> partition
PARTITION MENU:
        0      - change '0' partition
        1      - change '1' partition
        2      - change '2' partition
        3      - change '3' partition
        4      - change '4' partition
        5      - change '5' partition
        6      - change '6' partition
        7      - change '7' partition
        select - select a predefined table
        modify - modify a predefined partition table
        name   - name the current table
        print  - display the current table
        label  - write partition map and label to the disk
        quit
partition> <partition the disk>
partition> label
partition> quit
format > quit
#
```

Remaking the File Systems (newfs)

A disk must be formatted, partitioned, and labeled before you can create ufs file systems on it. If you are re-creating an existing ufs file system, unmount the file system before following these steps.

1. Become superuser.
2. Type **newfs /dev/rdsk/c<*n*>t<*n*>d<*n*>s<*n*>** and press Return. You are asked if you want to proceed.

CAUTION! *Be sure you have specified the correct device name for the partition before performing the next step. If you specify the wrong partition, you will erase its contents when the new file system is created.*

3. Type **y** to confirm. The newfs command uses optimized default values to create the file system.

This example creates a file system on /dev/rdsk/c0t3d0s7:

```
oak% su
Password:
# newfs /dev/rdsk/c0t3d0s7
newfs: construct a new file system /dev/rdsk/c0t3d0s7 (y/n)? y
/dev/rdsk/c0t3d0s7:     163944 sectors in 506 cylinders of 9 tracks, 36 sectors
        83.9MB in 32 cyl groups (16 c/g, 2.65MB/g, 1216 i/g)
super-block backups (for fsck -b #) at:
 32, 5264, 10496, 15728, 20960, 26192, 31424, 36656, 41888,
 47120, 52352, 57584, 62816, 68048, 73280, 78512, 82976, 88208,
 93440, 98672, 103904, 109136, 114368, 119600, 124832, 130064, 135296,
 140528, 145760, 150992, 156224, 161456,
#
```

Mounting the File System on a Temporary Mount Point (mount)

Type **mount /dev/dsk/c<*n*>t<*n*>d<*n*>s<*n*> /mnt** and press Return. The file system is mounted on the /mnt temporary mount point. To mount the disk, specify the block device directory (/dev/dsk), not the raw device directory.

Restoring Files to the File System (ufsrestore)

New with SVR4.

Restore the contents of the latest full backup, and then restore subsequent incremental backups from lowest to highest level (ufsrestore), by following these steps:

1. Type **cd /mnt** and press Return. You have changed to the mount point directory.
2. Write-protect the tapes for safety.
3. Insert the first volume of the level 0 tape into the tape drive.
4. Type **ufsrestore rvf /dev/rmt/<*unit*>** and press Return. If this is a multivolume restore, when prompted, remove the first tape and insert the last tape in the tape drive. Follow instructions about the order of the rest of the tapes. The level 0 tape is restored.
5. Remove the tape and load the next lowest level tape in the drive. Always restore tapes starting with 0 and continuing until you reach the highest level.
6. Type **ufsrestore rvf /dev/rmt/<*unit*>** and press Return. The next level tape is restored.
7. Repeat steps 5 and 6 for each additional tape.
8. Type **ls** and press Return.
9. A list of files in the directory is displayed. Check the listing to verify that all the files are restored.

10. Type **rm restoresymtable** and press Return. The restoresymtable created by ufsrestore is removed.

Unmounting the File System from Its Temporary Mount Point (umount)

1. Type **cd /** and press Return.
2. Type **umount /mnt** and press Return. The file system is unmounted from the temporary mount point.

Checking the File System for Inconsistencies (fsck)

Type **fsck /dev/rdsk/c<*n*>t<*n*>d<*n*>s<*n*>** and press Return. The file system is checked for consistency.

Performing a Level 0 Backup of the Restored File System (ufsdump)

New with SVR4.

You always should do an immediate backup of a newly created file system because ufsrestore repositions the files and changes the inode allocation.

1. Remove the last tape and insert a new write-enabled tape in the tape drive.
2. Type **ufsdump 0uf /dev/rmt/<*unit*> /dev/rdsk/c<*n*>t<*n*>d<*n*>s<*n*>** and press Return.

Mounting the File System at Its Permanent Mount Point (mount)

Type **mount /dev/dsk/c<*n*>t<*n*>d<*n*>s<*n*>** and press Return. The restored file system is mounted and available for use.

Understanding the Service Access Facility

The SunOS 5.*x* system software uses the Service Access Facility (SAF) to register and monitor port activity for modems, terminals, and printers. SAF is new with the SunOS 5.*x* system software. The SAF controls the resources that let users:

- Log in (either locally or remotely)
- Access printers across the network
- Access files across the network

The SAF is a complex hierarchy of background processes and administrative commands. Explaining the SAF in depth is beyond the scope of this book. The following sections provide a brief introduction to the elements of the SAF.

Port Monitors and Service Access

A port monitor is a program that continuously watches out for requests to log in or requests to access printers or files. Once a port monitor detects a request, it sets the parameters that are needed to establish communication between the operating system and the device that is requesting service. Then the port monitor transfers control to other processes that provide the services needed.

The SunOS 5.*x* system software provides two types of port monitors: listen and ttymon. The listen port monitor controls access to network services, fielding remote print and file system requests. The ttymon port monitor controls access to login services. You will need to set up a ttymon port monitor (using SAF) to process login requests from modems.

NOTE. *The ttymon port monitor replaces the SunOS 4.*x *getty port monitor. A single ttymon can replace multiple getties.*

SAF Control of Port Monitors and Services

You use three SAF commands to administer modems and alphanumeric terminals: sacadm, pmadm, and ttyadm.

The sacadm command adds and removes port monitors. This command is your main link with the Service Access Controller (SAC) and its administrative file (/etc/saf/_sactab).

The pmadm command adds or removes a service, and associates a service with a particular port monitor.

The ttyadm command formats information for inclusion in various SAF administrative files. A ttyadm command often is embedded within a sacadm or pmadm command to provide some of the data needed by those commands. Table 3.8 lists the programs associated with specific SAF functions. See the manual pages for more information about each command.

Printer Port Monitors Set-Up

This section provides steps for setting up port monitors for printing. Each SunOS 5.*x* print server and print client must have the port monitor configured to be able to handle network printing requests. If you use the Printer Manager (available with SunOS 5.1), you do not need to follow these steps. The Printer Manager automatically sets up the port monitors as part of the printer configuration process.

1. Become superuser.
2. Type **sacadm -a -p tcp -t listen -c "/usr/lib/saf/listen tcp" -v 'nlsadmin -V' -n 9999** and press Return. The network listen service that listens for incoming TCP/IP requests is started. The options are described in Table 3.9.

Table 3.8 SAF Functions and Associated Programs

Function	Program	Description
Overall administration	sacadm	Command for adding and removing port monitors
Service Access Controller	sac	SAF's master program
Port monitors	ttymon	Monitors serial port login requests
	listen	Monitors requests for network services
Port monitor Service Administrator	pmadm	Command for controlling port monitors' services
Services	logins; remote procedure calls; other	Services to which SAF provides access

Table 3.9 The sacadm Command Options

Option	Description
-a	Adds the -p port
-t	Identifies the type of service
-c	Tells which command to use to start the port monitor
-v	Indicates the version of the network listen process
-n	Specifies the number of times the Service Access Controller will restart the process, if it dies

3. Type **sacadm -l** and press Return. Look at the output to verify that the network listen status is enabled, as shown in this example:

```
# sacadm -l
PMTAG       PMTYPE    FLGS RCNT STATUS     COMMAND
tcp         listen     -    9999 ENABLED    /usr/lib/saf/listen tcp #
```

NOTE. *It may take several minutes before the network listen service is enabled.*

4. Type **lpsystem -A** and press Return. The system's universal address is displayed, as shown in this example:

```
# lpsystem -A
000202038194180e0000000000000000
```

The universal address has four parts, as shown in Figure 3.4. The last part, RFU, means Reserved for Future Use and could be used for other families of addresses (for example, Open Systems Interface) in the future.

Figure 3.4 Parts of the universal address

```
ØØØ2      Ø2Ø3      8194148Øe0ØØØ    ØØØØØØØØØØØØ
Internet  TCP Port       IP               RFU
```

The first four digits identify the Internet family. The fifth through eighth digits identify the TCP port. For the modified version, replace the fifth through eighth digits with 0ACE. (The first character is a zero.) For example, the modified version of the universal address shown in the example above is:

```
ØØØ2ØACE819418ØeØØØØØØØØØØØØØØØØ
```

NOTE. *You must type the characters* \x *at the beginning of the universal (or modified universal) address in the next steps exactly as shown. In addition, the address must be enclosed in single quotation marks so the backslash is not stripped off.*

1. To register listen service 0, type **pmadm -a -p tcp -s 0 -i root -m 'nlsadmin -c /usr/lib/saf/nlps_server -A '\x<*modified_address*>'' -v 'nlsadmin -V'** and press Return. The port monitor is configured to listen for requests from listen service 0.

2. To receive print requests from SunOS 5.0 print clients, type **pmadm -a -p tcp -s lp -i root -m 'nlsadmin -o /var/spool/lp/fifos/listenS5' -v 'nlsadmin -V'** and press Return. The port monitor is configured to listen for requests from listenS5, which registers print requests from SunOS 5.*x* print clients.

3. To receive print requests from SunOS 4.*x* print clients, type **pmadm -a -p tcp -s lpd -i root -m 'nlsadmin -o /var/spool/lp/fifos/listenBSD -A '\x<*address*>'' -v 'nlsadmin -V'** and press Return. The port monitor is configured to listen for requests from listenBSD, which registers print requests from SunOS 4.*x* print clients.

4. Type **cat /var/saf/tcp/log** and press Return. Examine the messages displayed to make sure that the services are enabled and initialized. In this example, all three network listen services are registered:

```
# lpsystem -A
ØØØ2Ø2Ø38194180eØØØØØØØØØØØØØØØØ
# pmadm -a -p tcp -s lp -i root -m `nlsadmin -o
/var/spool/lp/fifos/listenS5` -v `nlsadmin -V`
# pmadm -a -p tcp -s lpd -i root -m `nlsadmin -o
```

```
/var/spool/lp/fifos/listenBSD -A
'\x000202038194180e0000000000000000'` -v `nlsadmin -V`
# pmadm -a -p tcp -s 0 -i root -m `nlsadmin -c
/usr/lib/saf/nlps_server -A
'\x00020ACE8194180e0000000000000000'` -v `nlsadmin -V`
pine# cat /var/saf/tcp/log
10/28/91 10:22:51; 178; @(#)listen:listen.c     1.19.9.1
10/28/91 10:22:51; 178; Listener port monitor tag: tcp
10/28/91 10:22:51; 178; Starting state: ENABLED
10/28/91 10:22:51; 178; Service 0: fd 6 addr \x00020ACE8194180e0000000000000000
10/28/91 10:22:51; 178; Service lpd: fd 7 addr
\x000202038194180e0000000000000000
10/28/91 10:22:52; 178; Net opened, 2 addresses bound, 56 fds free
10/28/91 10:22:52; 178; Initialization Complete
#
```

Setting Up a Bidirectional Modem

To set up a bidirectional modem you need information for these variables:

- *<port-name>* Which port the modem is connected to (typically, ttya or ttyb).
- *<svctag>* The name of the port monitor service (for Sun systems, zsmon)
- *<port-device-name>* The name of the device for the port (typically /dev/cua/a or /dev/cua/b).
- *<short-port-device-name>* The name for the port without the complete path.
- *<modem-label>* The entry in the /etc/ttydefs file that is used to set the proper baud rate and line discipline.
- *<modem-type>* The type of the modem from the /etc/uucp/Dialers file. For example, the type for a Hayes modem is hayes.

Follow these steps to configure a modem:

1. Halt the system.
2. Make sure hardware carrier detect is disabled. On Sun systems you can use the eeprom command or type **setenv ttyb-ignore-cd=false** and press Return.
3. Reboot the system.
4. Connect the modem and make sure any modem switches are set to allow bidirectional use.

5. To remove the existing service for the port name so that the modem can be connected, type **pmadm -r -p <*svctag*> -s <*port-name*>**, and press Return. If you get the message "Invalid request, <*svctag*> does not exist," the <*svctag*> port monitor is not configured. To configure the <*svctag*> port monitor, type **sacadm -a -p <*svctag*> -t ttymon -c /usr/lib/saf/ttymon -v \`ttyadm -V\`** and press Return.

6. To set up the port monitor for use with the modem, type **pmadm -a -p zsmon -s ttyb -i root -fu -v 1 -m "\`ttyadm -b -d /dev/term/b -1 contty3H -m ldterm,ttcompat -s /usr/bin/login -S n\`"** and press Return. The -b option sets the bidirectional flag. The -m options specify STREAMS modules to be pushed.

7. To make sure the /etc/remote file has an entry for /dev/cua/<*n*> and that it is set to the correct baud rate, type **grep cua<*n*> /etc/remote** and press Return. In this example the information for cuab is correct:

```
# grep cuab /etc/remote
cuab:dv=/dev/cua/b:br#2400*
#
```

   If the entry is not in the /etc/remote file, edit the file and add the entry.

8. Edit the /etc/uucp/Devices file and add this entry:

```
ACU term/<short-port-device-name>,M - <modem-label> <modem-type>
```

Follow these steps to configure a bidirectional Hayes-compatible modem for dialing in and dialing out on serial port B. The default switch settings for a Hayes Smartmodem 2400 work properly.

1. Halt the system.

2. Hardware carrier detect must be disabled. To reset the PROM setting to disable hardware carrier detect on Sun systems, type **setenv ttyb-ignore-cd=false** and press Return.

3. Reboot the system.

4. Connect the modem and make sure any modem switches are set to allow bidirectional use. Note that the Hayes Smartmodem 2400 requires no changes to the default switch settings to work properly. Connect the modem cable to serial port B.

5. To remove the existing service for ttyb so that the modem can be connected, type **pmadm -r -p zsmon -s ttyb** and press Return. If you get the message "Invalid request, zsmon does not exist", the zsmon port monitor

is not configured. To configure the zsmon port monitor, type **sacadm -a -p zsmon -t ttymon -c /usrlib/saf/ttymon -v** '**ttyadm -V**' and press Return.

6. To set up the port monitor for use with the modem, type **pmadm -a -p zsmon -s b -i root -fu -v 1 -m** "'**ttyadm -b -d /dev/cua/b -l contty3H -m ldterm,ttcompat -s /usr/bin/login -S y**'" and press Return. The -b option sets the bidirectional flag. The -m options specify STREAMS modules to be pushed.

7. To make sure the /etc/remote file has an entry for /dev/cua/b and that it is set to the correct baud rate, type **grep cuab /etc/remote**. If the following information is displayed, the entry is correct:

```
# grep cuab /etc/remote
cuab:dv=/dev/cua/b:br#2400*
#
```

If the entry is not in the /etc/remote file, edit the /etc/uucp/devices file and type **ACU term/b,M - contty3H hayes**.

Using a Modem

To connect through the modem, type **tip -<*baud rate*> <*phone number*>** and press Return. With the Hayes Smartmodem 2400, this command dials and connects to the system. When the software on the connecting system is configured properly, the remote system dials the modem phone number and the modem answers automatically.

This example uses the information phone number, which is not a dial-in modem number:

```
oak% tip -2400 5551212
dialing ... connected
<Login messages>
```

CHAPTER

4

Administering File Systems

FILE SYSTEM IS A STRUCTURE OF DIRECTORIES USED TO LOCATE and store files. The term file system is used in several different ways:

- To describe the entire file tree from the root directory downward
- To describe a particular type of file system: disk-based, network-based, or pseudo
- To describe the data structure of a disk slice or other media storage device
- To describe a portion of a file tree structure that is attached to a mount point on the main file tree so that that portion is accessible

Usually, you can tell from context which meaning is intended.

The SunOS 5.*x* system software uses the virtual file system (VFS) architecture, which provides a standard interface for different file system types. The kernel handles basic operations—such as reading, writing, and listing files—without requiring the user or program to know about the underlying file system type.

The file system administrative commands provide a common interface that allows you to maintain file systems of different types. These commands have two components: a generic component and a component specific to each type of file system. The generic commands apply to most types of file systems; the specific commands apply to only one type of file system.

Administering the SunOS 5.*x* file system is one of your most important system administration tasks. The file system story is a complex one, and understanding it can help you more effectively administer file systems. This chapter describes:

- The types of file systems
- The default SunOS 5.*x* file system
- The virtual file system table (/etc/vfstab)
- The file system administrative commands
- Making local and remote files available to users
- Backing up and restoring file systems

Types of File Systems

The SunOS 5.*x* system software supports three types of file systems:

- Disk-based
- Network-based
- Pseudo

Disk-Based File Systems

Disk-based file systems are stored on physical media such as hard disks, CD-ROMs, and diskettes. Disk-based file systems can be written in different formats. The available formats are:

- **ufs** UNIX file system (based on the BSD Fat Fast File system that was provided in the 4.3 Tahoe release). The default disk-based file system in SunOS 5.*x* system software is ufs.
- **hsfs** High Sierra and ISO 9660 file system. High Sierra is the first CD-ROM file system; ISO 9660 is the official standard. The hsfs file system is used on CD-ROM, and is a read-only file system. The SunOS 5.*x* hsfs supports Rock Ridge extensions, which provide all ufs file system semantics and file types except for writability and hard links.
- **pcfs** PC file system, which allows read/write access to data and programs on DOS-formatted floppy disks written for DOS-based personal computers.

The System V (S5) file system traditionally provided with System V releases is not included in the SunOS 5.*x* system software because of significant limitations, such as a maximum of 64,000 files in a file system, a restriction of 14 characters for file names, and lack of a quota facility.

Each type of disk-based file system is customarily associated with a particular media device:

- ufs with hard disk and any other media (tape, CD-ROM, diskette)
- hsfs with CD-ROM
- pcfs with diskette

These associations are not, however, restrictive. For example, CD-ROMs and diskettes can have ufs file systems installed on them.

Network-Based File Systems

Network-based file systems are file systems that are accessed over the network. Typically, network-based file systems are file systems that reside on one system and are accessed by other systems across the network. The available network-based file systems are:

- NFS—network or distributed file system
- rfs—remote file sharing

The default SunOS 5.*x* distributed file system is NFS. You administer distributed file systems by sharing them (exporting them from a server) and mounting them on individual systems. See "Making File Systems Available" later in the chapter for more information.

Pseudo File Systems

Pseudo file systems are virtual or memory-based file systems that provide access to special kernel information and facilities. Pseudo file systems do not use file system disk space. Some pseudo file systems, such as the temporary file system, may, however, use the swap space on a physical disk.

The Temporary File System (tmpfs)

New with SVR4.

The Temporary File System, or tmpfs file system, uses local memory for disk reads and writes. Access to files in a tmpfs file system is typically much faster than access to files in a ufs file system. Files in the temporary file system are not permanent. They are deleted when the file system is unmounted and when the system is shut down or rebooted.

The default file system type for the /tmp directory in the SunOS 5.*x* system software is tmpfs. You can copy or move files into or out of the /tmp directory, just as you would in a ufs /tmp file system.

Using tmpfs file systems can improve system performance by saving the cost of reading and writing temporary files to a local disk or across the network. For example, temporary files are created when you compile a program. The operating system generates a lot of disk or network input and output activity while manipulating these files. Using tmpfs file systems to hold these temporary files may significantly speed up their creation, manipulation, and deletion.

The tmpfs file system uses swap space as a temporary storage area. If a system with a tmpfs file system does not have adequate swap space, two problems can occur:

- The tmpfs file system can run out of space, just as a regular file system can fill up.
- Because tmpfs allocates swap space to save file data (if necessary), some programs may not be able to execute because there is not enough swap space.

See Chapter 9 for information about increasing swap space.

The Loopback File System (lofs)

The lofs file system lets you create a new virtual file system. You can access files using an alternative path name. For example, you can create a loopback mount of /onto/tmp/newroot. The entire file system hierarchy looks like it is duplicated under /tmp/newroot, including any file systems that were mounted from NFS servers. All files are accessible either with a path name starting from /, or with a path name starting from /tmp/newroot until a different file system is mounted in /tmp/newroot or any of its subdirectories.

NEW

New with SVR4.

The Process File System (procfs)

The procfs file system resides in memory. It contains a list of active processes, by number, in the /proc directory. Information in the /proc directory is used by commands such as ps. Debuggers and other development tools can also access the address space of the processes using file system calls. This example shows a partial listing of the contents of the /proc directory:

```
oak% ls -l /proc
total 144944
-rw-------   1 root     root          0 Dec 19 15:45 00000
-rw-------   1 root     root     196608 Dec 19 15:45 00001
-rw-------   1 root     root          0 Dec 19 15:45 00002
-rw-------   1 root     root    1028096 Dec 19 15:46 00073
-rw-------   1 root     root    1445888 Dec 19 15:46 00091
-rw-------   1 root     root    1142784 Dec 19 15:46 00093
-rw-------   1 root     root    1142784 Dec 19 15:46 00095
(Some processes removed from this example)
-rw-------   1 ignatz   staff   1576960 Dec 19 15:50 00226
-rw-------   1 ignatz   staff    192512 Dec 19 15:51 00236
-rw-------   1 ignatz   staff   1269760 Dec 19 15:52 00240
-rw-------   1 ignatz   staff   6090752 Dec 19 15:52 00241
-rw-------   1 ignatz   staff    188416 Dec 19 15:52 00247
-rw-------   1 ignatz   staff   2744320 Dec 19 15:52 00256
```

CAUTION! *Do not delete the files in the /proc directory. Deleting processes from the /proc directory is not the recommended way to kill them. See Chapter 1 for information on how to kill a process. Remember, /proc files do not use disk space, so there is little reason to delete files from this directory. The /proc directory does not require any system administration.*

Additional Pseudo File Systems

These additional types of pseudo file systems are listed for your information. They do not require administration.

- **fifofs** (first-in first-out)   Named pipe files that give processes common access to data
- **fdfs** (file descriptors)   Provides explicit names for opening files using file descriptors
- **namefs**   Used mostly by STREAMS for dynamic mounts of file descriptors on top of files
- **specfs** (special)   Provides access to special character and block devices

- **swapfs** File system used by the kernel when you create additional swap space with the mkfile and swap commands

The Default SunOS 5.*x* File System

The SunOS 5.*x* file system is hierarchical, starting with the root directory (/) and continuing downward through a number of directories. The SunOS 5.*x* system software installs a default set of directories and uses a set of conventions to group similar types of files together. Table 4.1 describes the default SunOS 5.*x* file system, and shows the type of each file system.

Table 4.1 The Default SunOS 5.*x* File System

File System	File System Type	Description
/	ufs	The top of the hierarchical file tree. The root directory contains the directories and files critical for system operation, such as the kernel (/kernel/unix), the device drivers, and the programs used to start (boot) the system. It also contains the mount point directories where local and remote file systems can be attached to the file tree.
/etc	ufs	Contains system-specific files used in system administration.
/usr	ufs	Contains system files and directories that can be shared with other users. Files that run on only certain types of systems are in the /usr directory (for example, SPARC executables). Files (such as manual pages) that can be used on all types of systems are in /usr/share.
/home	NFS, ufs	The mount point for the users' home directories, which store users' work files. By default, /home is an automounted file system. On stand-alone systems, /home may be a ufs file system on a local disk slice.
/var	ufs	Contains system files and directories that are likely to change or grow over the life of the local system. These include system logs, vi and ex backup files, uucp files, and mail and calendar files.
/opt	NFS, ufs	Mount point for optional, third-party software. On some systems, /opt may be a ufs file system on a local disk slice.
/tmp	tmpfs	Temporary files, cleared each time the system is booted or unmounted.
/proc	procfs	Contains a list of active system processes, by number.

The root (/) and /usr file systems are both needed to run a system. Some of the most basic commands from the /usr file system (such as mount) are included in the root file system so that they are available when the system boots up or is in single-user mode.

The Virtual File System Table (/etc/vfstab)

New with SVR4.

Each system has a virtual file system table, /etc/vfstab, that lists all the disk slices and file systems available to the system. The file system table also specifies the mount point and options for each file system. In the SunOS 4.*x* system software, the file system table is called /etc/fstab. The /etc/vfstab file replaces /etc/fstab and functions in a similar manner. The default file system configuration table (the /etc/vfstab file) depends on the selections made for each system when system software was installed. You should edit the /etc/vfstab file for each system to automatically mount local ufs file systems, essential NFS file systems, and any other appropriate file systems.

This section describes the contents of the /etc/vfstab file and provides information on how to edit and use the file. The file system table is an ASCII file. Comment lines begin with #. This example shows an /etc/vfstab file for a system with two disks and two NFS file systems mounted.

```
# more /etc/vfstab
#device          device              mount          FS      fsck    auto-   mount
#to mount        to fsck             point          type    pass    mount?  options
/dev/dsk/c0t0d0s0 /dev/rdsk/c0t0d0s0 /              ufs     1       no      -
/proc            -                   /proc          proc    -       no      -
/dev/dsk/c0t0d0s1 -                  -              swap    -       no      -
swap             -                   /tmp           tmpfs   -       yes     -
/dev/dsk/c0t0d0s6 /dev/rdsk/c0t0d0s6 /usr           ufs     2       no      -
/dev/dsk/c0t3d0s7 /dev/rdsk/c0t3d0s7 /files7        ufs     2       no      -
cheers:/export/svr4/man.ja5   -   /usr/man          nfs     -       yes     hard
cheers:/export/svr4/openwinV3.ja4 -      /usr/openwin      nfs     -       yes
hard
#
```

Note that, for / and /usr, the automount field value is specified as no because these file systems are mounted as part of the boot sequence before the mountall command is run. If the automount field value is specified as yes, the mountall program redundantly (and unnecessarily) tries to mount these already-mounted file systems.

The file system table has seven fields, each separated by a Tab, as described in Table 4.2.

NOTE. *You must have an entry in each field in the /etc/vfstab file. If there is no value for the field, be sure to enter a hyphen (-).*

Table 4.2 Fields in the /etc/vfstab File

Field	Description
Device to mount	The device to mount can be • The block special device for local ufs file systems (for example, /dev/dsk/c0t0d0s0) • The resource name for remote file systems (for example, myserver:/export/home for an NFS file system) • The name of the slice on which to swap (for example, /dev/dsk/c0t3d0s1) • The /proc directory and proc file system type • CD-ROM as hsfs file system type • /dev/diskette as pcfs or ufs file system type. This field is also used to specify swap file systems.
Device to fsck	The raw (character) special device that corresponds to the file system identified by the *<special>* field (for example, /dev/rdsk/c0t0d0s0). This determines the raw interface that is used by fsck. Use a hyphen (-) when there is no applicable device, such as for a read-only file system or a network-based file system.
Mount point	The default mount point directory (for example, /usr for /dev/dsk/c0t0d0s6).
FS type	The type of file system identified by the *<special>* field.
fsck pass	The pass number used by fsck to decide whether to check a file system. When the field contains a hyphen (-), the file system is not checked. When the field contains a value of 1 or more, the file system is checked; non-ufs file systems with a zero fsck pass are checked. For ufs file systems only, when the field contains a zero (0), the file system is not checked. When fsck is run on multiple ufs file systems that have fsck pass values greater than 1 and the preen option (-o p) is used, fsck automatically checks the file systems on different disks in parallel to maximize efficiency. When the field contains a value of 1, the file system is checked sequentially. Otherwise, the value of the pass number does not have any effect.
Automount?	Indicate yes or no for whether the file system should be automatically mounted by mountall when the system is booted. Note that this field has nothing to do with the automounter software.
Mount options	A list of comma-separated options (with no spaces) that are used in mounting the file system. Use a hyphen (-) to show no options. See the mount_*<file-system-type>*(1M) manual page for a list of the available options.

* In SunOS 5.*x* system software, fsck pass does not explicitly specify the order in which file systems are checked as it did with SunOS 4.*x* system software.

Creation of an Entry in the File System Table

Follow these steps to create an entry in the file system table:

1. Become superuser.
2. Edit the /etc/vfstab file using an editor such as vi.
3. Add the entry, separating each field with white space (a space or a Tab). If a field has no entry, enter a hyphen (-).
4. Save the changes.
5. Check to be sure the mount point directory is present. If not, create it.
   a. Change to the directory where you want to create the mount point.
   b. Type **mkdir *<directory-name>*** and press Return.
6. Type **mount *<mount-point>*** and press Return. The entry is mounted.

This example mounts the disk slice /dev/dsk/c0t3d0s7 as a ufs file system attached to the mount point directory /files1 with the default mount options (read/write). It specifies the raw character device /dev/rdsk/c0t3d0s7 as the device to fsck. The fsck pass value of 2 means that the file system will be checked, but not sequentially.

```
#device            device             mount       FS     fsck    auto-    mount
#to mount          to fsck            point       type   pass    mount?   options
#
/dev/dsk/c0t3d0s7  /dev/rdsk/c0t3d0s7 /files1     ufs    2       yes      -
```

This example mounts the directory /export/man from the system oak as an nfs file system on mount point /usr/man. You do not specify a device to fsck or a fsck pass for NFS file systems. In this example, mount options are ro (read-only) and soft. For greater reliability, specify the hard mount option for read/write NFS file systems.

```
#device            device             mount       FS     fsck    auto-    mount
#to mount          to fsck            point       type   pass    mount?   options
oak:/export/man    -                  /usr/man    nfs    -       yes      ro,soft
```

This example mounts a CD-ROM drive on a mount point named /hsfiles. CD-ROM files typically are read-only, so you specify ro for the mount options. Specify no for automount because you are most likely to mount and unmount a CD-ROM from the command line. Because the hsfs is read-only, specify no device to fsck and no fsck pass number.

```
#device            device             mount       FS     fsck    auto-    mount
#to mount          to fsck            point       type   pass    mount?   options
/dev/dsk/c0t6d0s2  -                  /hsfiles    hsfs   -       no       ro
```

This example mounts the diskette drive on a mount point named /pcfiles. Specify no for automount because you are most likely to mount and unmount a diskette from the command line. Specify no device to fsck or fsck pass option, because the pcfs file system does not support fsck.

```
#device         device      mount         FS     fsck   auto-    mount
#to mount       to fsck     point         type   pass   mount?   options
/dev/diskette   -           /pcfiles      pcfs   -      no       rw
```

This example mounts the root file system on a loopback mount point named /etc/newroot. Specify yes for automount, no device to fsck, and no fsck pass number. Loopback file systems must always be mounted after the file systems used to make up the loopback file system. Be sure that the loopback entry is the last entry in the /etc/vfstab file so that it follows the entries that it depends on.

```
#device         device      mount         FS     fsck   auto-    mount
#to mount       to fsck     point         type   pass   mount?   options
/               -           /tmp/newroot  lofs   -      yes      -
```

File System Administrative Commands

This section lists the file system administrative commands and describes the syntax.

Most file system administrative commands have a generic and a file system-specific component. Use the generic commands, which use the file system-specific component. Table 4.3 lists the generic file system administrative commands, which are located in the /usr/sbin directory. Most of these commands also have a file system-specific counterpart.

CAUTION! *Do not use the file system-specific commands directly. If you specify an operation on a file system that does not support it, the generic command displays this error message:* <command>*: Operation not applicable for FSType* <type>.

Syntax of Generic Commands

Most of the generic commands use this syntax:

```
<command> [-F <type>] [-V] [<generic-options>] [-o <specific-options>]
[<special|mount-point>] [<operands>]
```

The options and arguments to the generic commands are shown in the Table 4.4.

Table 4.3 Generic File System Administrative Commands

Command	Description
clri(1M)	Clears inodes.
df(1M)	Reports the number of free disk blocks and files.
ff(1M)	Lists file names and statistics for a file system.
fsck(1M)	Checks the integrity of a file system and repairs any damage found.
fsdb(1M)	File system debugger.
fstyp(1M)	Determines the file system type.
labelit(1M)	Lists or provides labels for file systems when copied to tape (for use by the volcopy command only).
mkfs(1M)	Makes a new file system.
mount(1M)	Mounts file systems and remote resources.
mountall(1M)	Mounts all file systems specified in a file system table.
ncheck(1M)	Generates a list of path names with their i-numbers.
umount(1M)	Unmounts file systems and remote resources.
umountall(1M)	Unmounts all file systems specified in a file system table.
volcopy(1M)	Makes an image copy of a file system.

Manual Pages for Generic and Specific Commands

Both the generic and specific commands have manual pages. The specific manual page is a continuation of the generic manual page. To look at a specific manual page, append an underscore and the file system type abbreviation to the generic command name. For example, to see the specific manual page for mounting an hsfs file system, type **man mount_hsfs** and press Return. lofs, pcfs, and procfs do not have specific manual pages for the mount command.

How File System Commands Determine File System Type

The generic file system commands determine the file system type by following this sequence:

1. From -F, if supplied.

Table 4.4 Description of Generic File System Command Syntax

Option	Description
-F <*type*>	Specifies the type of file system. If you do not use this option, the command looks for an entry that matches special, raw device, or mount point in the /etc/vfstab file. Otherwise, the default is taken from the file /etc/default/fs for local file systems and from the file /etc/dfs/fstypes for remote file systems.
-V	Echoes the completed command line. The echoed line may include additional information derived from /etc/vfstab. Use this option to verify and validate the command line. It does not execute the command.
<*generic-options*>	Options common to different types of file systems.
-o <*specific-options*>	A list of options specific to the type of file system. The list must have the following format: -o followed by a space, followed by a series of <*keyword*> [=<*value*>] pairs separated by commas with no intervening spaces.
<*special*| *mount-point*>	Identifies the file system. Name either the <*mount point*> or the <*special*> device file for the slice holding the file system. For some commands, the <*special*> file must be the raw (character) device, and for other commands it must be the block device. See Chapter 3 for more information about disk device names. In some cases, this argument is used as a key to search the file /etc/vfstab for a matching entry from which to obtain other information. In most cases, this argument is required and must come immediately after <*specific-options*>. However, it is not required when you want a command to act on all the file systems (optionally limited by type) listed in the /etc/vfstab file.
Operands	Arguments specific to a type of file system. See the specific manual page of the command (for example, mkfs_ufs) for a detailed description.

2. By matching a special device with an entry in /etc/vfstab (if <*special*> is supplied). For example, fsck first looks for a match against the fsck device field; if no match is found, it then checks against the <*special*> device field.
3. By using the default specified in /etc/default/fs for local file systems and in /etc/dfs/fstypes for remote file systems.

Type of File System

If you want to determine the type of a file system, you can obtain the information from the same files that the generic commands use:

- The FS type field in the file system table (/etc/vfstab)

- The /etc/default/fs file for local file systems
- The /etc/dfs/fstypes file for remote file systems

To find a file system's type in the /etc/vfstab file, type **grep <*mount-point*> /etc/vfstab** and press Return. Information for the mount point is displayed.

```
drusilla% grep /tmp /etc/vfstab
swap            -               /tmp            tmpfs   -       yes     -
drusilla%
```

If vfstab does not have an entry for a file system, use one of the following procedures to determine the file system's type.

To identify a mounted file system's type, type **grep <*mount-point*> /etc/mnttab** and press Return. Information on the mount point is displayed.

```
drusilla% grep /home /etc/mnttab
drusilla:(pid129)  /home nfs  ro,ignore,map=/etc/auto_home,indirect,dev=21c0004
693606637
bigriver:/export/home/bigriver  /tmp_mnt/home/bigriver  nfs     rw,dev=21c0005
695409833
drusilla%
```

Or type **mount** and press Return. A list of the mounted file systems is displayed.

```
drusilla% mount
/ on /dev/dsk/c0t3d0s0 read/write on Tue Dec 24 12:29:22 1991
/usr on /dev/dsk/c0t1d0s6 read/write on Tue Dec 24 12:29:22 1991
/proc on /proc read/write on Tue Dec 24 12:29:22 1991
/usr/man on swsvr4-50:/export/svr4/man read/write/remote on Mon Dec 30 12:49:11
1991
/usr/openwin on swsvr4-50:/export/svr4/openwinV3 read/write/remote on Mon Dec
30 \  13:50:54 1991
/tmp on swap o on Wed Jan  8 13:38:45 1992
/mnt on swsvr4-50:/export/svr4 read/write/remote on Fri Jan 10 15:51:23 1992
/tmp_mnt/home on bigriver:/export/home read/write/remote on Tue Jan 14 \
09:23:53 1992
drusilla%
```

Or follow these steps:

1. Type **devnm <*mount-point*>** and press Return. The raw device name is displayed.
2. Become superuser.
3. Type **fstyp /dev/rdsk/c<*n*>t<*n*>d<*n*>s<*n*>** and press Return. The type of the file system is displayed.

```
drusilla% devnm /usr
/dev/dsk/c0t1d0s6 /usr
```

```
drusilla% su
Password:
# fstyp /dev/rdsk/c0t3d0s0
ufs
#
```

Making File Systems Available

Once you have created a file system, you need to make it available; you do this by mounting it. A mounted file system is attached to the system directory tree at the specified mount point and becomes available to the system. The root file system is always mounted. Any other file system can be connected or disconnected from the root file system.

You can mount a local file system in these ways:

- By creating an entry in the /etc/vfstab (virtual file system table) file. The /etc/vfstab file contains a list of file systems that are automatically mounted when the system is booted in multiuser state. See the section "The Virtual File System Table (/etc/vfstab)" earlier in this chapter for a description of the /etc/vfstab file.
- From a command line using the mount command.

File systems on disk slices must always be mounted on the server system and shared (exported) before other systems can access them. See "Sharing Files from a Server" later in this chapter for information about sharing file systems. When file systems are shared from a server, a client can mount them as NFS file systems in any of these three ways:

- By adding an entry to the /etc/vfstab file so that the file system is automatically mounted when the system is booted in multiuser state.
- By using the automount program to automatically mount or unmount the file system when a user changes into (mount) or out of (umount) the automounting directory.
- By using the mount command at a command line.

Understanding Mounting and Unmounting

File systems can be attached to the hierarchy of directories available on a system. This process is called *mounting*. To mount a file system you need:

- To be superuser.

- A mount point on the local system. The mount point is a directory to which the mounted file system is attached.
- The resource name of the file system to be mounted (for example, /usr).

As a general rule, local disk slices should always be included in the /etc/vfstab file. Any software from servers, such as OpenWindows or manual pages, and home directories from a server can either be included in the /etc/vfstab file or be automounted, depending on the policy at your site.

When you mount a file system, any files or directories that might be present in the mount point directory are unavailable as long as the file system is mounted. These files are not permanently affected by the mounting process and become available again when the file system is unmounted. However, mount directories usually are empty, because you usually do not want to obscure existing files.

The system tracks the mounted file systems in the /etc/mnttab (mount table) file. Whenever you mount or unmount a file system, the /etc/mnttab file is modified to show the list of currently mounted file systems. You can display the contents of the mount table using the cat or more command, but you cannot edit the mount table, as you would the /etc/vfstab file. Here is an example of a mount table file:

```
drusilla% more /etc/mnttab
/dev/dsk/c0t3d0s0       /       ufs     rw,suid 693186371
/dev/dsk/c0t1d0s6       /usr    ufs     rw,suid 693186371
/proc   /proc   proc    rw,suid 693186371
swap    /tmp    tmpfs   ,dev=0 693186373
swsvr4-50:/export/svr4/openwinV3 /usr/openwin    nfs     rw,dev=21c0000
693186443
swsvr4-50:/export/svr4/man      /usr/man        nfs     rw,dev=21c0001
693186447
drusilla:(pid127)    /nse  nfs
ro,ignore,map=/etc/auto.nse,indirect,dev=21c0002 693186449
drusilla:(pid127)    /net    nfs     ro,ignore,map=-
hosts,indirect,dev=21c0003   693186449
drusilla:(pid127)       /home   nfs
ro,ignore,map=/etc/auto_home,indirect,dev=21c0004       693186449
bigriver:/export/home/bigriver  /tmp_mnt/home/bigriver  nfs     rw,dev=21c0005
693186673
drusilla%
```

Using Mount and Unmount File System Commands

Table 4.5 lists the commands in the /usr/sbin directory that you use to mount and unmount file systems.

New with SVR4.

The mount commands will not mount a read/write file system that has inconsistencies. If you receive an error message from the mount or mountall command, you may need to check the file system.

Table 4.5 Commands for Mounting and Unmounting File Systems

Command	Description
mount(1M)	Mounts file systems and remote resources.
mountall(1M)	Mounts all file systems specified in a file system table.
umount(1M)	Unmounts file systems and remote resources.
umountall(1M)	Unmounts all file systems specified in a file system table.

The umount commands will not unmount a file system that is busy. A file system is considered busy if a user is in a directory in the file system, or if a program has a file open in that file system.

Finding the Mounted File Systems

To display a list of mounted file systems, type **mount** and press Return. All the file systems currently mounted are displayed.

```
oak% mount
/ on /dev/dsk/c0t0d0s0 read/write/setuid on Wed Oct 23 10:08:50 1991

/usr on /dev/dsk/c0t0d0s6 read/write/setuid on Wed Oct 23 10:08:50 1991

/proc on /proc read/write/setuid on Wed Oct 23 10:08:50 1991

/tmp on swap on Wed Oct 23 10:08:52 1991

/usr/openwin on cheers:/export/openwin hard/remote on Wed Oct 23
10:11:08 1991

/home on blowup:(pid136) read only/intr/map=auto.home/indirect on Wed Oct 23
10:11:10 1991

/vol on blowup:(pid136) read only/intr/map=auto.vol/indirect on Wed Oct 23
10:11:10 1991

/nse on blowup:(pid136) read only/intr/map=/etc/auto.nse /indirect on Wed Oct
23 10:11:10 1991
oak%
```

Mounting All File Systems in the /etc/vfstab File

Follow these steps to mount all file systems in the /etc/vfstab file:

1. Become superuser.
2. Type **mountall** and press Return.

All of the file systems in the local /etc/vfstab file are mounted.

```
oak% su
Password:
mountall
oak#
```

Mounting All File Systems of a Specific Type

Follow these steps to mount all file systems of a specific type that are in the /etc/vfstab file. The most common file system types are ufs for local disk slices and NFS for network file systems. See "Types of File Systems" early in the chapter for a complete list of file system types.

1. Become superuser.

2. Type **mountall -F** ***<filesystem-type>*** and press Return.

All of the file systems of the type you specify that are in the local /etc/vfstab file are mounted.

In this example, all nfs file systems are mounted:

```
oak% su
Password:
mountall -F nfs
oak#
```

Mounting a Single File System (mount)

Follow these steps to mount a single file system that has an entry in the /etc/vfstab file:

1. Become superuser.

2. Type **mount** ***<mount-point>*** and press Return.

The file system is mounted.

```
oak% su
Password:
# mount /opt
#
```

Unmounting All Remote File Systems (umountall -F nfs)

Follow these steps to unmount all remote file systems:

1. Become superuser.

2. Type **umountall -F nfs** and press Return.

All of the remote file systems in the local /etc/vfstab file are unmounted.

```
oak% su
Password:
umountall -F nfs
oak#
```

CAUTION! *If you unmount all file systems (umountall without any arguments), the system may be unusable and you may need to reboot it.*

Unmounting Individual File Systems (umount)

You cannot unmount a directory that is being used. If you want to unmount a directory that is being used, all users must change out of the directory.

1. Become superuser.
2. If necessary, have users change out of the directory you want to unmount.
3. Type **umount <*mount-point*>** and press Return.

The file system you specify is unmounted.

In this example, the mount command is used first to find the mount point for the file system to be unmounted:

```
oak% mount
/ on /dev/dsk/c0t0d0s0 read/write/setuid on Wed Oct 23 10:08:50 1991

/usr on /dev/dsk/c0t0d0s6 read/write/setuid on Wed Oct 23 10:08:50 1991

/proc on /proc read/write/setuid on Wed Oct 23 10:08:50 1991

/tmp on swap on Wed Oct 23 10:08:52 1991

/usr/openwin on cheers:/export/openwin hard/remote on Wed Oct 23
10:11:08 1991

/home on blowup:(pid136) read only/intr/map=auto.home/indirect on Wed Oct 23
10:11:10 1991

/vol on blowup:(pid136) read only/intr/map=auto.vol/indirect on Wed Oct 23
10:11:10 1991

/nse on blowup:(pid136) read only/intr/map=/etc/auto.nse /indirect on Wed Oct 23
10:11:10 1991
[41]oak% su
Password:
# cd /
# umount /home
#
```

The Automounter

You can mount file systems shared through NFS using a method called *automounting*. The automount program runs in the background and mounts and unmounts remote directories as they are needed. Whenever a user on a client system running the automounter accesses a remote file or directory available through the automounter, the automounter mounts the file system on the user's system. The remote file system remains mounted as long as the user remains in the directory and is using a file. If the remote file system is not accessed for a certain period of time, it is automatically unmounted. The automounter mounts and unmounts file systems, as required, without any intervention on the part of the user other than changing into or out of a directory.

You can mount some file hierarchies with automount, and others using the /etc/vfstab file and the mount command. A diskless machine *must* have entries for / (root), /usr, and /usr/kvm in the /etc/vfstab file. Because shared file systems should always remain available, do not use the automounter to mount /usr/share.

The automounter works with the file systems specified in maps. These maps can be maintained as NIS, NIS+, or local files.

The automounter maps can specify several remote locations for a particular file. This way, if one of the servers is down, the automounter can try to mount from another machine. You can specify which servers are preferred for each resource in the maps by assigning each server a weighting factor.

The automounter starts automatically when a system enters run level 3. You can also start it from a command line. (Describing how to set up and administer the automounter is beyond the scope of this book.) By default, the SunOS 5.*x* system software automounts /home.

Sharing Files from a Server

NFS is a distributed file system that can be used to tie together computers that are running different operating systems. For example, systems running DOS can share files with systems running UNIX.

NFS makes the actual physical location of the file system irrelevant to the user. You can use NFS to allow users to see all the relevant files, regardless of location. Instead of placing copies of commonly used files on every system, NFS allows you to place one copy on one system's disk and let all other systems access it across the network. Under NFS, remote file systems are virtually indistinguishable from local ones.

A system becomes an NFS server if it has file systems to share or export over the network. A server keeps a list of currently exported file systems and their access restrictions (such as read/write or read-only).

You may want to share resources, such as files, directories, or devices from one system on the network (typically, a server) with other systems. For example, you might want to share third-party applications or source files with users on other systems.

When you share a resource, you make it available for mounting by remote systems.

You can share a resource in these ways:

New with SVR4.

- Using the share or shareall command
- Adding an entry to the /etc/dfs/dfstab (distributed file system table) file

The default /etc/dfs/dfstab file shows you the syntax and an example of entries:

```
cinderella% more /etc/dfs/dfstab

#  place share(1M) commands here for automatic execution
#  on entering init state 3.
#
#  share [-F fstype] [ -o options] [-d "<text>"] <pathname> [resource]
#  .e.g,
#  share  -F nfs  -o rw=engineering  -d "home dirs"  /export/home2
share -F nfs /var/mail

cinderella%
```

Checking the Data Consistency of a File System (fsck)

The ufs file system relies on an internal set of tables to keep track of inodes and used and available blocks. When these internal tables are not properly synchronized with data on a disk, inconsistencies result and file systems need to be repaired.

File systems can be damaged or become inconsistent because of abrupt termination of the operating system in these ways:

- Power failure
- Accidental unplugging of the system
- Turning the system off without proper shutdown procedure
- A software error in the kernel

File system corruption, though serious, is not common. When a system is booted, a file system consistency check is done automatically. Most of the time, this file system check repairs problems it encounters.

File systems are checked with the fsck (file system check) program. The fsck command puts files and directories that are allocated but unreferenced in the lost+found directory in that file system. The inode number of each file is assigned as the name. If the lost+found directory does not exist, fsck creates it. If there is not enough space in the lost+found directory, fsck increases its size.

You may need to interactively check file systems

- When they cannot be mounted
- When they develop problems while in use

When an in-use file system develops inconsistencies, strange error messages may be displayed in the console window, or the system may crash. Before using fsck, you may want to refer to the fsck(1M) manual page for more information.

Finding Out If a File System Needs Checking

Follow these steps to determine whether or not a file system needs to be checked:

1. Become superuser.
2. Type **fsck -m /dev/rdsk/c<*n*>t<*n*>d<*n*>s<*n*>** and press Return.

The state flag in the superblock of the file system you specify is checked to see whether the file system is clean or requires checking.

If you omit the device argument, all the ufs file systems listed in /etc/vfstab with a fsck pass value greater than 0 are checked. In this example, the first file system needs checking; the second file system does not:

```
# fsck -m /dev/rdsk/c0t0d0s6
** /dev/rdsk/c0t0d0s6
ufs fsck: sanity check: /dev/rdsk/c0t0d0s6 needs checking
# fsck -m /dev/rdsk/c0t0d0s7
** /dev/rdsk/c0t0d0s7
ufs fsck: sanity check: /dev/rdsk/c0t0d0s7 okay
#
```

Checking File Systems Interactively

Follow these steps to check all file systems interactively:

1. Become superuser.
2. Unmount the file system.
3. Type **fsck** and press Return.

All file systems in the /etc/vfstab file with entries in the fsck pass field greater than zero are checked. You can also specify the mount point directory or

/dev/rdsk/c<*n*>t<*n*>d<*n*>s<*n*> as arguments to fsck. Any inconsistency messages are displayed.

In this example, /dev/rdsk/c0t0d0s6 is checked and the incorrect block count is corrected:

```
# fsck /dev/rdsk/c0t0d0s6
checkfilesys: /dev/rdsk/c0t0d0s6
** Phase 1 - Check Block and Sizes
INCORRECT BLOCK COUNT I=2529 (6 should be 2)
CORRECT? y

** Phase 2 - Check Pathnames
** Phase 3 - Check Connectivity
** Phase 4 - Check Reference Counts
** Phase 5 - Cylinder Groups
Dynamic 4.3 FFFS
929 files, 8928 used, 2851 free (75 frags, 347 blocks,
0.6% fragmentation)
/dev/rdsk/c0t0d0s6 FILE SYSTEM STATE SET TO OKAY

***** FILE SYSTEM WAS MODIFIED *****
```

Backing Up and Restoring File Systems

Backing up files means making copies of them, usually on removable media, as a safeguard in case the originals get lost or damaged. Backup tapes are convenient for restoring accidentally deleted files, but they are essential in case of serious hardware failures or other disasters.

Backing up files is one of the most crucial system administration functions. You must plan and carry out a procedure for regularly scheduled backups of your file systems for three major reasons:

- To ensure file system integrity against a possible system crash
- To protect user files against accidental deletion
- To act as an important safeguard before reinstalling or upgrading a system

When you back up file systems as scheduled, you have the assurance that you can restore anyone's files to a reasonably recent state. In addition, you may want to back up file systems to transport them from one system to another or to *archive* them—saving files on a transportable media—so that you can remove or alter the files that remain on the system.

When you plan a backup schedule, you need to consider

- Which command to use to back up the file systems
- What media to use
- What backup schedule to use
- Which file systems to back up
- Which files are critical to users on this system
- Where the files are located: Are they in a single file system?
- How often these files change
- How quickly you would need to restore these files in the event of damage or loss
- How often the relevant file systems can be unmounted so that they are available for backup

Outlining possible backup strategies is beyond the scope of this book. See the ufsdump(1M) manual page for a suggested dump schedule. The discussions that follow describe how to use the ufsdump command to make backups and how to retrieve files using the ufsrestore command.

Backing Up a File System Using QIC-150 Cartridge Tapes (ufsdump)

New with SVR4.

To do a full backup on a file system, all users must be logged out and you must bring the system to single-user mode. (See "Tape Device Naming Conventions" in Chapter 3 if you need information about tape device names.)

You can dump or restore files from a remote drive by adding *<remote-host:>* to the front of the tape device name. Here is the syntax:

```
<remote-host:>/dev/rmt/<unit>
```

For example, the device name for a remote tape drive /dev/rmt/0, on the system oak, would be oak:/dev/rmt/0.

Follow these steps to do a level 0 (full) backup of a file system:

1. Type **init s** and press Return. The system is brought to single-user mode, which ensures that no users can change the file system you are backing up.
2. Insert a tape cartridge in the QIC-150 tape drive.
3. Type **ufsdump 0cuf /dev/rmt/*<unit>* c*<n>*t*<n>*d*<n>*s*<n>*** and press Return. The 0 option specifies a level 0 (complete) dump. The c option specifies

cartridge tape. The u option updates the dump record. The f option followed by the device name specifies the device file. Type the raw disk slice for the file system you want to back up. For example, **c0t0d0s7** for /files1.

```
oak% su
Password:
# init s
# ufsdump 0cuf /dev/rmt/0 c0t0d0s7
  DUMP: Date of this level 0 dump: Wed Mar 11 10:16:53 1992
  DUMP: Date of last level 0 dump: the epoch
  DUMP: Dumping /dev/rdsk/c0t3d0s7 (/export/home) to
/dev/rmt/0
  DUMP: mapping (Pass I) [regular files]
  DUMP: mapping (Pass II) [directories]
  DUMP: estimated 956 blocks (478KB)
  DUMP: Writing 63 Kilobyte records
  DUMP: dumping (Pass III) [directories]
  DUMP: dumping (Pass IV) [regular files]
  DUMP: level 0 dump on Wed Mar 11 10:16:53 1992
  DUMP: 956 blocks (478KB) on 1 volume
  DUMP: DUMP IS DONE
#
```

4. If the dump requires more than one tape, the ufsdump command tells you when to change to a new tape.
5. Label the tape with the command, file system, and date.

Accomplishing Incremental Backups

You can specify different backup levels with the ufsdump command, making it possible to back up only those files that were changed since a previous backup at a lower level. Follow these steps to back up incremental changes since the last complete dump:

1. Bring the system to single-user mode.
2. Become superuser.
3. Put a tape into the tape drive.
4. Type **ufsdump *[1-9]*ucf /dev/rmt/<*unit*> /dev/rdsk/c<*n*>*t*<*n*>d<*n*>*s*<*n*>** and press Return. Type the level of the backup at the beginning of the ufsdump arguments. For example, for a level 9 backup, type **9ucf**.
5. Remove the tape from the tape drive and label it.

Restoring a Backed-Up File System (ufsrestore)

New with SVR4.

The ufsrestore command copies files from backups created using the ufsdump command into the current working directory. You can use ufsrestore to reload an entire file system hierarchy from a level 0 dump and incremental dumps that follow it, or to restore one or more single files from any dump tape. Files are restored with their original owner, last modification time, and mode (permissions).

Before you start to restore files or file systems, you need to know:

- Which tapes (or diskettes) you need
- The raw device name for the file systems you want to back up
- The type of tape drive you will use
- The device name (local or remote) for the tape drive

Determining Which Tapes to Use

Before you can begin restoring file systems or files, you must determine which backup tapes you need. When restoring an entire file system, you always need the most recent level 0 backup tape. You also need the most recent incremental backup tapes made at each of the higher levels. Refer to the backup plan that you are using to determine the levels and number of tapes you need. For example, if you make level 0 and level 9 backups, you need the most recent level 0 and level 9 backup tapes made.

Use this checklist to determine which tapes to use to restore individual files or file systems:

1. Ask the user the date when the file or file system was lost, or the approximate date of the files to be recovered.
2. Refer to your backup plan to find the date of the last backup that would have the file or file system on it. Note that you do not necessarily use the most recently backed up version of the file. To retrieve the most recent version of a file, work backward through the incremental backups from highest to lowest level and most recent to least recent.
3. If you have on-line archive files created using the ufsdump -a option, type **ufsrestore ta *<archive-name>* /path/*<filename(s)>*** and press Return. Be sure to use the complete path for the *<filename(s)>*. A list of the files and the media they are stored on is displayed.
4. Retrieve the media containing the backups. Be aware of the storage organization of backup media at your site so that you can locate media that are months or years old.

5. This step is optional. Insert media in the drive and type **ufsrestore tf** ***<device-name>* /*<path>*/*<filename(s)>*** and press Return. Be sure to use the complete path for the *<filename(s)>*. If a file is in the backup, its name and inode number are listed. Otherwise, a message says it is not on the volume.

6. If you have multiple dump files on the same tape, you can use the *-s n* option to position the tape at the dump you want to use. For example, type **ufsrestore xfs /dev/rmt0 5** and press Return to position the tape at the fifth dump and restore it.

Restoring a Full Backup

Follow these steps to restore a full backup of a file system, using QIC-150 cartridge tape:

CAUTION! *This procedure completely destroys any data already in the file system by creating a new file system on the slice.*

1. Become superuser.

2. Type **init s** and press Return. The system is brought to single-user mode, which ensures that no one is using the file system you are restoring.

3. Type **umount *<mount-point>*** and press Return. The mount point you specify (for example, /files1) is unmounted.

4. Type **newfs /dev/rdsk/c*<n>*t*<n>*d*<n>*s*<n>*** and press Return. The raw device file for the disk slice (for example, /dev/rdsk /c0t0d0s7 for the /home slice) is wiped clean and the file system is rebuilt.

5. Type **mount /dev/dsk/c*<n>*t*<n>*d*<n>*s*<n>*** and press Return. The file system, specified as the block file device (for example, /dev/dsk/c0t0d0s7 for /files1), is remounted at the mount point you specify.

6. Type **cd *<mount-point>*** and press Return. You are in the directory you want to restore.

7. Insert the tape cartridge in the QIC-150 tape drive.

8. Type **ufsrestore rvf /dev/rmt/0h** and press Return. The file system is restored.

   In this example, the /files1 slice c0t0d0s7 is restored.

```
oak% su
Password:
# init s
# umount /files1
```

```
# newfs /dev/rdsk/c0t0d0s7
# mount /dev/dsk/c0t0d0s7 /files1
# cd /files1
# ufsrestore rvf /dev/rmt/0h
#
```

Restoring Files Interactively

When restoring individual files and directories, it is a good idea to restore them to a temporary directory such as /var/tmp. After you verify them, you can move the files to their proper locations. You can restore individual files and directories to their original locations. If you do so, be sure you are not overwriting newer files with older versions from the backup tape.

Follow these steps to restore files interactively:

1. Become superuser.
2. Write-protect the tape for safety.
3. Put the backup tape in the tape drive.
4. Type **cd /var/tmp** and press Return. If you want to restore the files to a different directory, substitute the directory name for /var/tmp in this step.
5. Type **ufsrestore if /dev/rmt/<*unit*>** and press Return. Some informational messages and the restore > prompt are displayed.
6. Create a list of files to be restored.
   - To list the contents of a directory, type **ls** and press Return.
   - To change directories, type **cd <*directory-name*>** and press Return.
   - To add a directory or file name to the list of files to be restored, type **add <*filename*>** and press Return.
   - To remove a directory or file name from the list of files to be restored, type **delete <*filename*>** and press Return.
   - To keep the mode of the current directory unchanged, type **setmodes** and press Return. Then type **n** and press Return.
7. When the list is complete, type **extract** and press Return. Then, ufsrestore asks you which volume number to use.
8. Type the volume number and press Return. If you have only one volume, type **1** and press Return. The files and directories in the list are extracted and restored to the current working directory.
9. Type **quit** and press Return. The shell prompt is displayed.

10. Use the ls -l command to list the restored files and directories. A list of files and directories is displayed.
11. Check the list to be sure all the files and directories you specified in the list have been restored.
12. Use the mv command to move the files to the proper directories.

In this example, the files backup.examples and junk are restored from the pubs directory.

```
# cd /var/tmp
# ufsrestore if /dev/rmt/0
ufsrestore > ls
.:
 lost+found/   pubs/

ufsrestore > cd pubs
ufsrestore > ls
 ./pubs:
 .Xauthority            .login
.profile               backup.examples%
 .Xdefaults             .mtdeletelog
.wastebasket/          core
 .cshrc                 .openwin-init
Junk/                  dead.letter
 .desksetdefaults       .openwin-init.BAK
backup.examples        junk

ufsrestore > add backup.examples
ufsrestore > add junk
ufsrestore > setmodes
set owner/mode for '.'? [yn] n
ufsrestore > extract
You have not read any volumes yet.
Unless you know which volume your file(s) are on you
should start
with the last volume and work towards the first.
Specify next volume #: 1
set owner/mode for '.'? [yn] n
ufsrestore > quit
# ls -l
total 6
drwxrwxrwt   3 sys      sys           512 Mar 11 10:36 ./
drwxrwxr-x  18 root     sys           512 Mar 10 16:43 ../
```

```
drwxr-xr-x   2 pubs     staff        512 Mar 11 10:11 pubs/
# pwd
/var/tmp
# cd pubs
# ls
./                 ../                backup.examples   junk
#
```

Restoring a Single File from a Backup Tape (ufsrestore)

Follow these steps to restore a single file from a backup tape:

1. Become superuser.
2. Put the backup tape in the tape drive.
3. Type **cd /var/tmp** and press Return. If you want to restore the files to a different directory, substitute the directory name for /var/tmp in this step.
4. Type **ufsrestore xf /dev/rmt/<*unit*> <*filename*>** and press Return. The x option tells ufsrestore to copy specific files or directories in the <*filename*> argument. The message set owner/mode for '.'? [yn] is displayed.
5. Type **n** and press Return. Directory modes remain unchanged.
6. Type the volume number where files are located and press Return. If there is only one volume, type **1** and press Return. The file is restored to the current working directory.
7. Type **ls -l <*filename*>** and press Return. A listing for the file is displayed.
8. Use the mv command to move the file to the proper directory.

CHAPTER

Administering Network Services

Checking on Remote System Status

Logging In to a Remote System (rlogin)

Transferring Files between Systems (rcp, ftp)

Administering NIS+ Databases (admintool)

THIS CHAPTER CONTAINS INFORMATION ABOUT CHECKING ON REMOTE system status, logging into a remote system, transferring files between systems, and administering the Network Information Service Plus (NIS+) databases.

Checking on Remote System Status

This section describes commands you use to find out the status of remote systems: rup, ping, and rpcinfo -d.

Determining How Long a Remote System Has Been Up (rup)

To find out how long a system has been up and the load average, type **rup <*system-name*>** and press Return. The host name, uptime, and load average are displayed.

```
oak% rup ash
ash    up 59 days,  3:42, load average: 0.12, 0.12, 0.01
oak%
```

You can also display a list of all remote hosts in the subnet by typing **rup** and pressing Return. If you display a list, you can use the options shown in Table 5.1 to sort the output.

Table 5.1 Options to the rup Command

Option	Description
-h	Sort the display alphabetically by host name.
-l	Sort the display alphabetically by load average.
-t	Sort the display by uptime.

In this example, the output is sorted alphabetically by host name:

```
oak% rup -h
ash    up  1 day,   1:42,  load average: 0.00, 0.31, 0.34

elm    up 14 days,  0 min,  load average: 0.07, 0.01, 0.00

maple  up 32 days,  14:39,  load average: 0.21, 0.05, 0.00

oak    up  8 days,  15:44,  load average: 0.02, 0.00, 0.00
oak%
```

Determining If a Remote System Is Up (ping, rup, rpcinfo -p)

Follow these steps to determine if a remote system is up:

1. Type **ping <*system-name*>** and press Return. The message "<*system-name*> is alive" means the system is accessible over the network. The message "ping: unknown host <*system-name*>" means the system name is not known on the network. The message "ping: no answer from <*system-name*>" means the system is known on the network but is not up at this time.

2. Type **rup <*system-name*>** and press Return. Information about how long the system has been up and the load average is displayed.

3. Type **rpcinfo -p <*system-name*>** and press Return. Information about RPC services is displayed.

4. Type **rlogin <*system-name*>** and press Return. You are logged on to the remote system.

```
cinderella% ping drusilla
drusilla is alive
cinderella% rup drusilla
   drusilla     up  3 days,  15:10   load average: 0.07, 0.08, 0.09
cinderella% rpcinfo -p drusilla
program  vers proto port  service
100000    3   udp    111  portmapper
100000    2   udp    111  portmapper
100000    3   tcp    111  portmapper
100000    2   tcp    111  portmapper
100007    3   tcp   1029  ypbind
100007    3   udp   1025  ypbind
100021    1   tcp   1030  nlockmgr
100021    1   udp   1026  nlockmgr
100024    1   tcp   1028  status
100024    1   udp   1027  status
100021    3   tcp   1030  nlockmgr
100021    3   udp   1026  nlockmgr
100020    2   tcp   4045  llockmgr
100020    2   udp   4045  llockmgr
100021    2   tcp   1030  nlockmgr
100021    2   udp   1026  nlockmgr
100087   10   udp   1031  adm_agent
100011    1   udp   1034  rquotad
100002    1   udp   1037  rusersd
100002    2   udp   1037  rusersd
100012    1   udp   1041  sprayd
100008    1   udp   1043  walld
100001    2   udp   1046  rstatd
```

```
100001    3   udp   1046  rstatd
100001    4   udp   1046  rstatd
100068    2   udp   1049  cmsd
100068    3   udp   1049  cmsd
100083    1   tcp   4049
cinderella% rlogin drusilla
Password:
Last login: Mon Mar  2 10:31:55 from cinderella
drusilla%
```

You can also use ping with a system's IP address by typing **ping <*IP-address*>** and pressing Return. The message "<*IP-address*> is alive" means the system is accessible over the network. The message "ping: no answer from <*IP-address*>" means the system is not available to the network. The message "ping: unknown host <*IP-address*>" means the system name is not known on the network.

```
oak% ping 129.144.52.119
129.144.52.119 is alive
oak% ping 129.137.67.234
ping: unknown host 129.137.67.234
oak% ping 129.145.52.119
ping: no answer from 129.145.52.119
oak%
```

Logging in to a Remote System (rlogin)

Follow these steps to log in to a remote system:

1. Type **rlogin <*system-name*>** and press Return. You may be prompted for a password.
2. If you have a local account on that system, type your local password. Otherwise, type your NIS+ password. Unless you have a home directory that is accessible on the remote system (because it is local on that system, or because it is hard-mounted or automounted), you log in to the root (/) directory.

```
oak% rlogin ash
Password:
No directory!  Logging in with home=/
Last login: Tue Sep 17 13:54:28 from 129.144.52.119
Sun Microsystems, Inc. SunOS 5.0 June 1992.
ash%
```

Transferring Files between Systems (rcp, ftp)

If the automounter is set up for your site, you can transfer files between systems using commands such as cp and mv. This section describes how to use the rcp and ftp commands to transfer files between systems.

Using the rcp Command

To transfer a file from a remote system to your system using the remote copy command, type **rcp** ***<system-name>:<source-pathname> <destination>*** and press Return. If you have proper security to access the remote system, the file is copied to the destination you specify.

In this example, the file quest is copied from the /tmp directory on the system ash to the current working directory on the system oak:

```
oak% rcp ash:/tmp/quest .
oak%
```

To transfer a file from a local system to a remote system, type **rcp** ***<pathname> <system-name>:<destination-pathname>*** and press Return. If you have proper security to access the remote system, the file is copied from the local system to the remote destination you specify.

In this example, the file quest is copied from the current working directory on the system oak to the /tmp directory on the system ash:

```
oak% rcp quest ash:/tmp
oak%
```

If you want, you can rename the file as part of the destination path name. For example, to rename the file quest to questions and put it in the /tmp directory, type **/tmp/questions** as the destination path name.

Using the File Transfer Program (ftp)

Follow these steps to transfer files from your local system to a remote system using the file transfer program.

NOTE. *You may need to have an account on each system and an entry in the / .rhosts file to use the file transfer program. Some systems allow read-only ftp access to anybody who logs in as anonymous and types a login name at the password prompt.*

If you have an NIS or an NIS+ account, you can use your login name and network password to access a remote system using ftp.

1. Type **ftp** and press Return. The ftp> prompt is displayed.

2. Type **open <*remote-system-name*>** and press Return. System connection messages are displayed, and you are asked for a user name.
3. Type the user name for your account on the remote system and press Return. If a password is required, you are asked to enter it.
4. Type the password (if required) for your account on the remote system and press Return. A system login message and the ftp> prompt are displayed.
5. Type **bin** to set binary format or **asc** to set ASCII format and press Return. The file type is set.
6. Type **put <*local-filename*> <*destination-filename*>** and press Return. File transfer messages and the ftp> prompt are displayed.
7. Type **quit** and press Return. A goodbye message and the command prompt are displayed.

```
oak% ftp
ftp> open elm
Connected to elm
220 elm FTP server (UNIX(r) System V Release 4.0) ready.

Name (elm:ignatz): ignatz
331 Password required for ignatz.
Password:
230 User ignatz logged in.
ftp> asc
ftp> put quest /tmp/quest
200 PORT command successful.

150 ASCII data connection for /tmp/quest
(129.144.52.119,1333).

226 Transfer complete.
ftp> quit
221 Goodbye.
oak%
```

You can use the send command as an alternative to the put command. You can copy multiple files using the mput command. There is no msend command. See the ftp(1) manual page for more information.

NOTE. *You must have an account on each system to use the file transfer program.*

If you have an NIS or an NIS+ account, you can use your login name and network password to access a remote system using ftp. Follow these steps to transfer files from a remote system to your local system using the file transfer program:

1. Type **ftp** and press Return. The ftp> prompt is displayed.
2. Type **open *<remote-system-name>*** and press Return. System connection messages are displayed, and you are asked for a user name.
3. Type the user name for your account on the remote system and press Return. If a password is required, you are asked to enter it.
4. Type the password (if required) for your account on the remote system and press Return. A system login message and the ftp> prompt are displayed.
5. Type **bin** to set binary format or **asc** to set ASCII format and press Return. The file type is set.
6. Type **get *<remote-filename> <destination-filename>*** and press Return. File transfer messages and the ftp> prompt are displayed.
7. Type **quit** and press Return. A goodbye message and the command prompt are displayed.

```
oak% ftp
ftp> open elm
Connected to elm
220 elm FTP server (UNIX(r)System V Release 4.0) ready.

Name (elm:ignatz): ignatz
331 Password required for ignatz.
Password:
230 User ignatz logged in.

ftp> asc
ftp> get quest /tmp/quest
200 PORT command successful.
150 ASCII data connection for /tmp/quest
(129.144.52.119,1333).
226 Transfer complete.

ftp> quit
221 Goodbye.
oak%
```

NOTE. *You can copy multiple files using the mget command. See the ftp(1) manual page for more information.*

Administering NIS+ Databases (admintool)

New with SVR4.

NIS+ provides a central store of information for network resources such as hosts, users, and mailboxes. NIS+ replaces NIS (Network Information Service) and provides these enhancements: an organizational framework that is simpler to administer in large companies, improved security, and improved distribution time to propagate changes through the network. In addition, the Solaris 2.0 environment provides a new name service switch file, /etc/nsswitch.conf, which lets you use several different network information services at once. The /etc/nsswitch.conf file also lets you specify which service provides which type of information. In previous SunOS releases, selection of the name service was hard-coded into the services, which made it difficult to switch to a new name service. The /etc/nsswitch.conf file defines the order in which local files and network databases are searched for information. Describing how to set up NIS+ is beyond the scope of this book.

The Solaris 2.0 environment provides an OpenWindows Administration Tool (admintool). Through Administration Tool you access a Database Manager that you can use to browse the contents of NIS+ tables, NIS maps, and local /etc files. If you have proper permissions, you can also use Administration Tool to edit NIS+ tables and local /etc files. This section describes NIS+ tables, using Administration Tool to look at the contents of NIS+ tables, setting Administration Tool security, and editing NIS+ tables.

Using NIS+ Tables

NIS+ tables correspond to NIS maps. The Solaris 2.0 environment provides 16 types of tables (shown in Figure 5.1) that store the network information used by NIS+.

Each table stores a different type of information about users, workstations, or resources on the network. For instance, the Hosts table stores the hostname and network address of every workstation in the domain; the Bootparams table stores the location of the root, swap, and dump directories of the diskless clients in the domain.

Each domain may have its own set of these NIS+ tables, which store all the NIS+ information for that particular domain. Table 5.2 lists the 16 NIS+ tables and the information they store.

NOTE. *You cannot use the Database Manager to administer the Cred, Aliases, and Auto_Master databases. To work on the information in those tables, use the nistbladm command.*

Table 5.2 NIS+ Tables

Table	Information in the Table
Hosts	Network address and hostname of every workstation in the domain
Bootparams	Location of the root, swap, and dump partition of every diskless client in the domain
Password	Password information about every NIS+ principal in the domain, plus a pointer to the shadow file
Cred	Credentials for principals who have permission to access the information or objects in the domain
Group	Password, group id, and members of every group in the domain
Netgroup	The netgroups to which workstations and users in the domain may belong
Aliases	Information about the aliases of workstations in the domain
Timezone	The time zone of every workstation in the domain
Networks	The networks in the domain and their canonical names
Netmasks	The networks in the domain and their associated netmasks
Ethers	The Ethernet address of every workstation in the domain
Services	The names of IP services used in the domain and their port numbers
Protocols	The list of IP protocols used in the domain
RPC	The RPC program numbers for RPC services available in the domain
Auto_Home	The location of all users' home directories in the domain
Auto_Master	Automounter map information

You can access information in NIS+ tables either by entry row or by column, as shown in Figure 5.2.

For example, if you wanted to find the network address of a workstation named drusilla, you could ask a search program to look through the hostname column until it found "drusilla," as shown in Figure 5.3. The program then searches the drusilla entry row to find its network address, as shown in Figure 5.4.

You can use either NIS+ commands or the Administration Tool's Database Manager to perform these types of searches for you. Using Administration Tool is the preferred way to edit NIS+ tables. If you need a programmatic interface to the NIS+ tables, use the commands listed in Table 5.3.

Figure 5.1
The 16 NIS+ tables

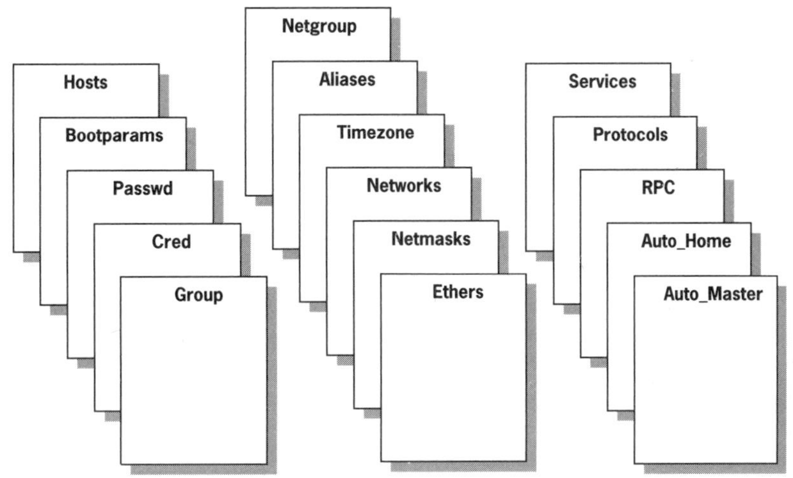

Figure 5.2
Entry rows and columns in a table

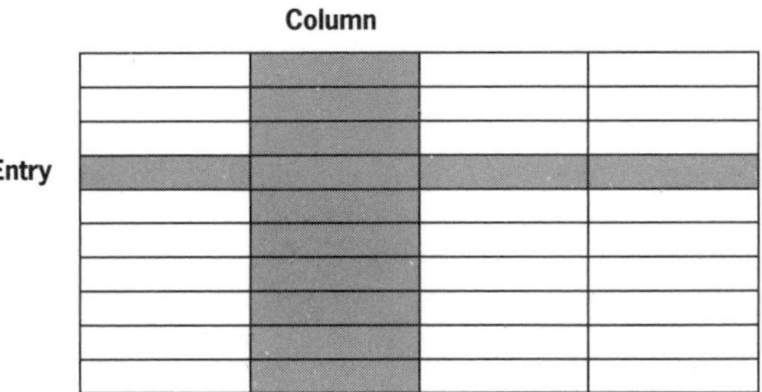

Figure 5.3
Searching the Hostname Column

Hostname column

	oak		
	grass		
	violin		
	drusilla		

Figure 5.4
Finding a network address

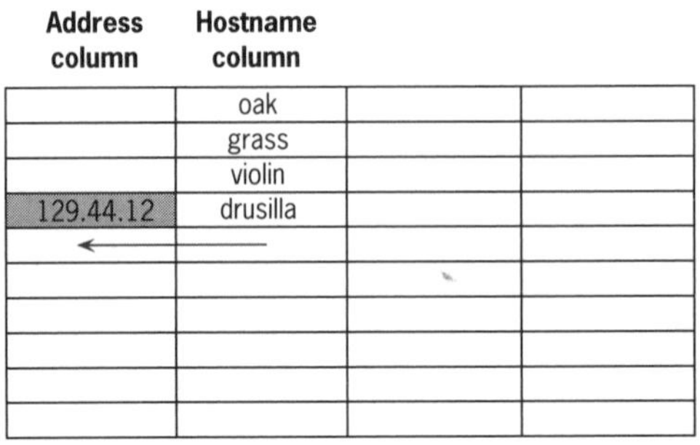

Table 5.3 **NIS+ Administrative Commands**

Command	Description
nistbladm	Displays, adds, modifies, and deletes information in an NIS+ table
nisgrep	Searches for information in an NIS+ table
nismatch	Searches for information in an NIS+ table
niscat	Displays the entire contents of an NIS+ table

See the manual pages for information about how to use these commands. The following sections describe how to use the Administration Tool's Database Manager to find information in NIS+ databases, how to set up Administration Tool security, and how to use the Database Manager to edit NIS+ tables.

Finding Information Using the Database Manager

Any user can browse through NIS+ databases without needing special permission. Follow the steps in this section to use the Database Manager to find information in NIS+ databases.

1. Start OpenWindows (if necessary) by typing **openwin** and pressing Return.

CAUTION! *Use your own login account to run Administration Tool. You should not run it as root.*

2. Start the Administration Tool by typing **admintool&** at a command prompt and pressing Return. The Administration Tool window is displayed, as shown in Figure 5.5.

Figure 5.5
Administration Tool window

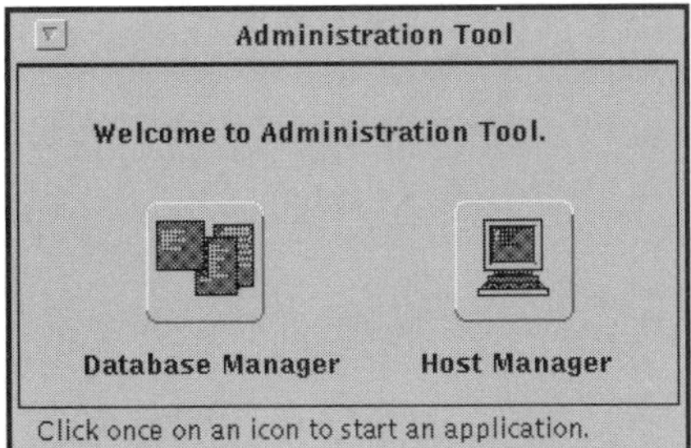

3. Move the pointer onto the Database Manager icon and click the SELECT mouse button once. The Load Database window is displayed, as shown in Figure 5.6.

Figure 5.6
Load Database window

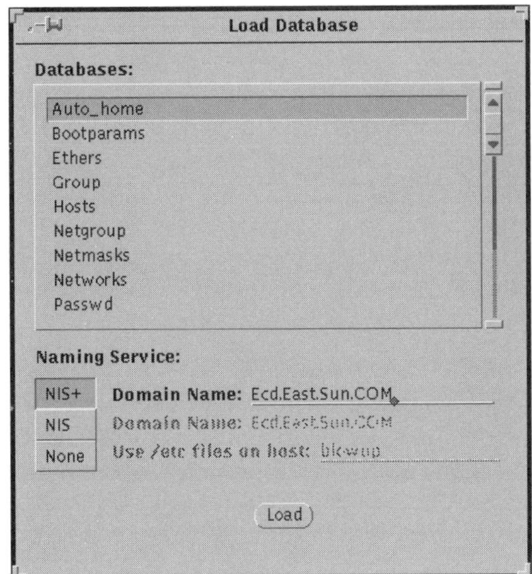

4. Select a database by moving the pointer onto the name of a database and clicking SELECT. The database is highlighted. In the example shown in Figure 5.7, the Passwd database is highlighted.

Figure 5.7
Highlighted database

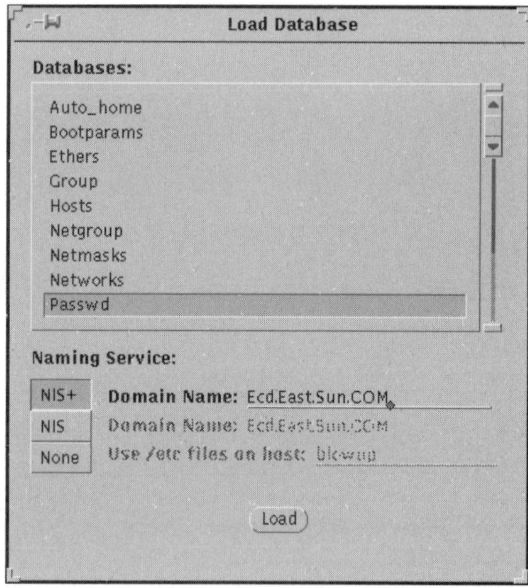

5. If you want to find information in NIS+ databases, click SELECT on the NIS+ setting. To find information in NIS maps, click on NIS. To find information in local /etc files, click on None.

6. If you want to view information for a different domain, type the domain name in the Domain Name text field. The current domain name is displayed by default.

7. Click SELECT on the Load button. The window for the database you selected is displayed. The scrolling list shows the beginning of the list of all of the entries in the database. In Figure 5.8, the Passwd database is displayed. Complete lines of text may not be displayed. Use the resize corners to change the width or height of the window to display more information.

Using the View Menu

Each database window has a View menu with the items shown in Figure 5.9. You can use the items on the View menu to match specific entries; to sort the entries by user name, by user ID, or by comment; and to find specific entries. This section describes how to use each of these items.

To show entries that match, choose Show Entries that Match from the View menu. The Show Entries that Match window is displayed, as shown in Figure 5.10.

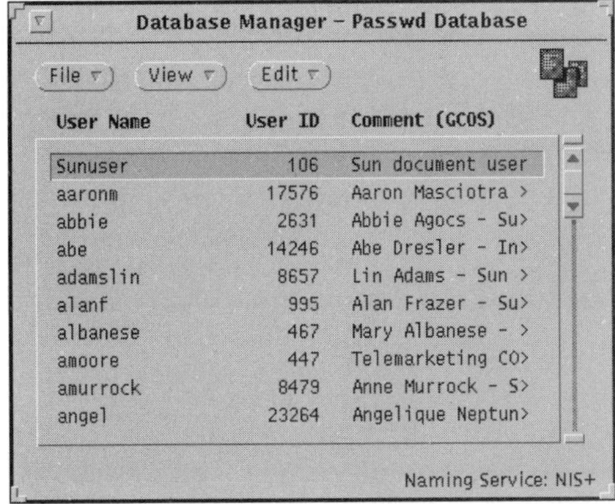

Figure 5.8
The Passwd Database window

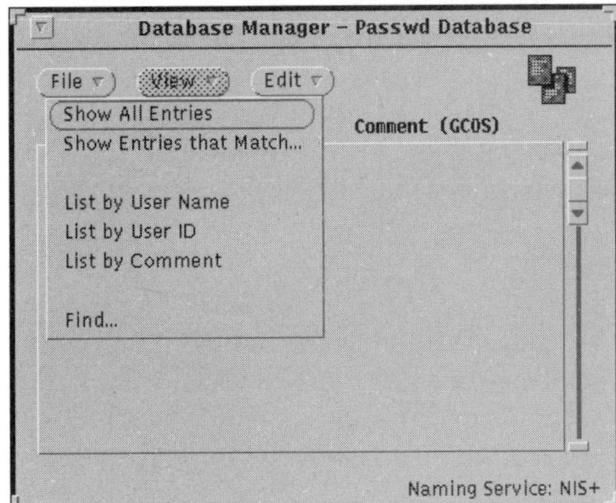

Figure 5.9
The View menu

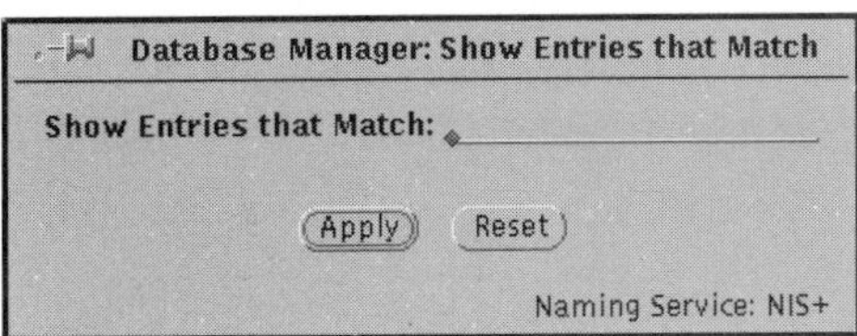

Figure 5.10
The Show Entries that Match window

Type the search string that you want to match in the text field and click SELECT on the Apply button. The table is reloaded, showing only entries that match the search string in the scrolling list.

To change the sorting order of the information displayed in the list, choose one of the List by entries from the View menu. The information in the scrolling list is sorted using the criterion that you specify.

To find a specific entry, choose Find from the View menu of the database window. The Find window is displayed, as shown in Figure 5.11.

Figure 5.11
The Find window

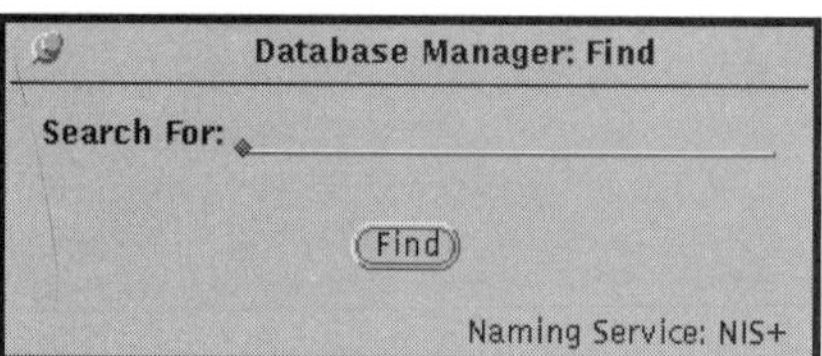

You can use file expansion syntax (* is a wildcard; strings in square brackets match any character in the string) in the Find text field. Type the name of the entry you want to match in the text field and click SELECT on the Find button. The information scrolls and the entry is displayed in the database window.

Setting Up Administration Tool Security

NIS+ uses a security authorization model that is similar to the UNIX file system model. It specifies that each item in the namespace as well as each record, each column, and each row has associated with it a set of access rights that are granted to three broad classes of principals:

- The owner of the item
- A group owner of the item
- All other principals

The specific access rights are different from the traditional read, write, and execute rights of file systems because of the nature of information services. Refer to your system manual for more information about NIS+ security.

When permitted by the NIS+ security authorization model, members of the sysadmin UNIX group (GID=14) are authenticated to use Administration Tool to add, modify, and delete administration information in NIS+ tables. However, Administration Tool cannot be used to add, modify, or delete information in NIS maps. This is because NIS does not provide a programmatic interface that the Administration Tool can use to access its maps.

Anyone with root permissions on a local system can use Administration Tool to modify, create, or delete information in the local /etc files for a system. If you want others to be able to edit local /etc files without granting root access, create a sysadmin UNIX group with a GID of 14 in the local /etc/group file and add privileged users to this group.

Follow these steps to set up a system administration group for editing NIS+ tables:

1. Log on as root to the root master server.
2. Start the Administration Tool (if necessary) by typing **admintool&** and pressing Return. The Administration Tool window is displayed.
3. Click SELECT on the Database Manager. The Load Database window is displayed.
4. Make sure the NIS+ naming service is selected. If it is not selected, click SELECT on NIS+.
5. The current domain name is displayed. If you want to look at a different domain name, type the name of the domain in the Domain Name text field.
6. Click SELECT on Group as shown in Figure 5.12.

Figure 5.12
The Load Database window

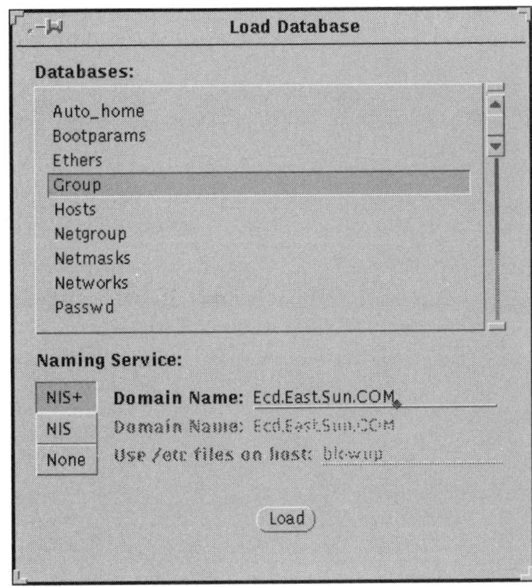

7. Click SELECT on the Load button. The Group Database window for the NIS+ naming service is displayed, as shown in Figure 5.13.

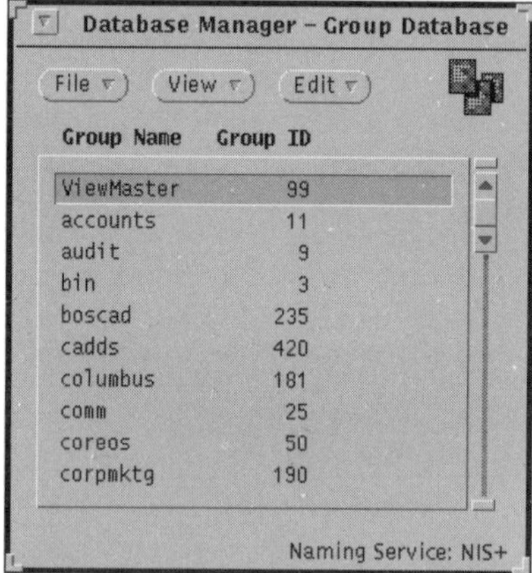

Figure 5.13
The Group Database window

8. Choose Add Entry from the Edit menu, as shown in Figure 5.14. The Add Entry window is displayed, as shown in Figure 5.15.

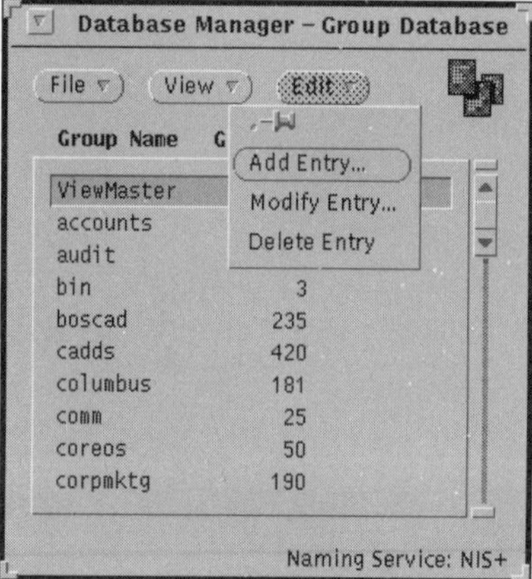

Figure 5.14
Edit menu

9. Type **sysadmin** in the Group Name text field.

10. Type **14** in the Group ID text field.

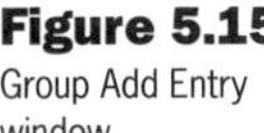

Figure 5.15 Group Add Entry window

11. Type the name of principal user in the Members List text field. You can add multiple users by typing a space between each name.
12. Click SELECT on the Add button. Group 14 is added to the NIS+ Group database along with the name of the user(s) you specify.
13. Check the local /etc/group file of the NIS+ root master server to make sure it does not contain an entry for GID 14. If it does, you may want to combine the two entries in the NIS+ Group database and remove the local entry, or move the group to a different group ID number. The default Name Service Switch configuration file, /etc/nsswitch.conf used with NIS+, specifies "files" before NIS+ tables for the group table, so a GID 14 entry on a local system will prevent access to members of the NIS+ GID 14 group unless the names of the group members are identical.
14. Repeat this process for all the domains that will use Administration Tool.

After completing these steps, NIS+ principals who are members of the sysadmin group (GID 14) in the domain's Group table can use the Database Manager to add, modify, or delete information in the NIS+ tables, subject to the access rights of each NIS+ table if they are using their own login identities and are not running Administration Tool as root. Principals can do this whether running the Database Manager from a workstation in the local domain or from a workstation in another domain.

Editing Information for an NIS+ Database (admintool)

To edit a database, you must be a member of the sysadmin group (GID 14). See "Using Administration Tool Security" just preceding this section for information on how to use Administration Tool to create a sysadmin authorization group. This section lists the steps for editing information in an NIS+ database. "Using Administration Tool Security" gives detailed examples.

1. Start OpenWindows (if necessary) by typing **openwin** and pressing Return.
2. Start the Administration Tool by typing **admintool&** at a command prompt and pressing Return. The Administration Tool window is displayed.
3. Move the pointer onto Database Manager and click the SELECT mouse button. The Load Database window is displayed.
4. Select a database by moving the pointer and clicking SELECT. The database is highlighted.
5. Click SELECT on NIS+.
6. If you want to view information for a different domain, type the domain name in the NIS+ Domain Name text field. The current domain name is displayed by default.
7. Click SELECT on the Load button. The database window is displayed.
8. To edit a database entry, use one of the items from the Edit menu (Add Entry, Modify Entry, Delete Entry) to display a pop-up window. A window is displayed showing the current information for the entry. The fields in the window are different for each database.
9. Type the information into the text fields. If you make a mistake or change your mind, click SELECT on the Reset button and retype the information.
10. Click SELECT on the Apply button. The information is loaded into the NIS+ databases.

CHAPTER

6

Administering Printing

Introducing the LP Print Service

Understanding the Structure of the LP Print Service

Setting Up Printing Services

Using Printing Commands

PRINTING IN THE SOLARIS 2.X ENVIRONMENT IS COMPLETELY DIFFERENT from printing with SunOS 4.*x*. Descriptions of printers are no longer stored in the /etc/printcap files. Instead, they are described by entries in the terminfo database. If you install the binary compatibility package (BCP), you can continue to use the lpr and lpc printing commands. These commands do not, however, use the lpr printing system. Instead, they call the appropriate LP print service commands to perform the requested actions.

The new printing service consists of the LP print service software, any print filters (programs that process data before printing) you may provide, and the hardware (the printer, workstation, and network connections).

This chapter briefly describes the LP print service; lists the files, daemons, and logs used by the LP print service; provides steps for setting up print servers and clients; and describes the basic commands used for printing.

Introducing the LP Print Service

The LP print service performs the following functions:

- Administers files and schedules local print requests
- Schedules network requests
- Filters files (if necessary) so that they print properly
- Starts programs that interface with the printers
- Tracks the status of jobs
- Tracks forms mounted on the printer
- Tracks printwheels that currently are mounted
- Delivers alerts to mount new forms or different printwheels
- Delivers alerts about printing problems

Administering Files and Scheduling Print Requests

The LP print service has a scheduler daemon, called lpsched. The scheduler daemon updates the LP system files with information about printer set-up and configuration, as shown in Figure 6.1.

The lpsched daemon also schedules all local print requests, as shown in Figure 6.2, regardless of whether the requests are issued by users from an application or from the command line. In addition, the scheduler tracks the status of printers and filters. When a printer finishes printing a request, the scheduler schedules the next request, if there is one in the queue.

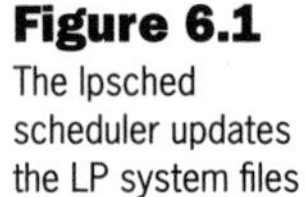

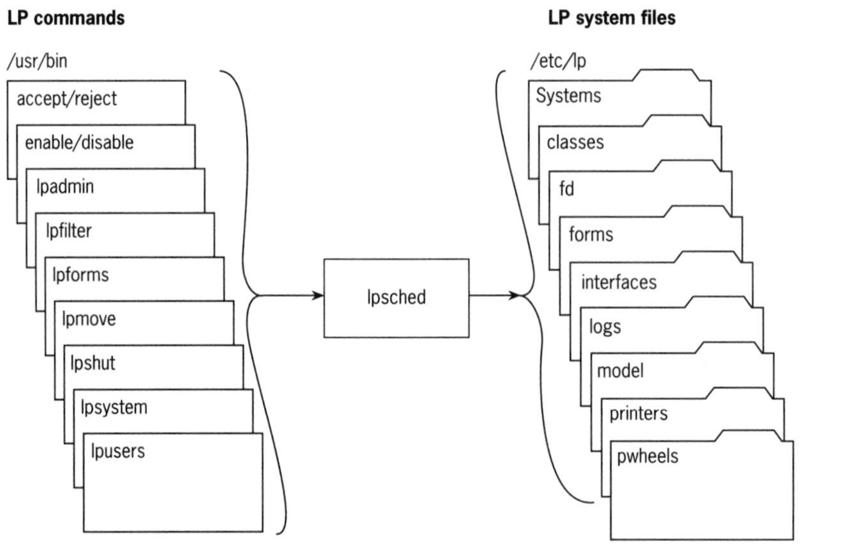

Figure 6.1 The lpsched scheduler updates the LP system files

Each print client and print server must have only one LP scheduler running. The scheduler is started when a system is booted (or enters run level 2) by the control script /etc/rc2.d/S80lp. Without rebooting the system, you can stop the scheduler with the /usr/sbin/lpshut command and restart the scheduler with the /usr/lib/lp/lpsched command. The scheduler for each system manages its own print requests. It waits for requests issued by the lp commands and then handles the requests in an appropriate manner.

Scheduling Network Print Requests

Each print client and print server must have at least one (and maybe several) lpNet daemon. The lpNet daemon schedules network print requests. The lpNet daemon is also started when a system is booted. If you stop and restart the scheduler (using the lpshut and lpsched commands), the lpNet daemon is also stopped and restarted.

Although the Service Access Facility (sacadm(1M), pmadm(1M)) is not part of the LP print system, the lpNet daemon needs a configured port monitor and registered listen services to handle incoming network requests on each print server running SunOS 5.0 system software. See Chapter 3 for more information about the Service Access Facility.

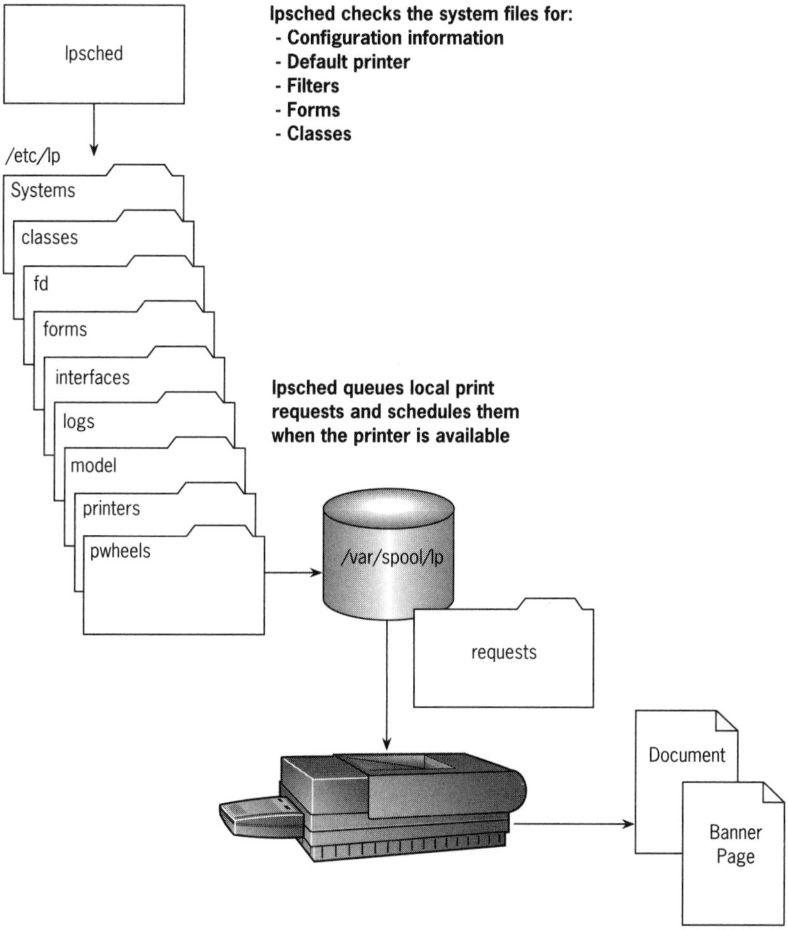

Figure 6.2
The lpsched scheduler schedules local print requests

lpsched

lpsched checks the system files for:
- Configuration information
- Default printer
- Filters
- Forms
- Classes

/etc/lp
Systems
classes
fd
forms
interfaces
logs
model
printers
pwheels

lpsched queues local print requests and schedules them when the printer is available

/var/spool/lp
requests
Document
Banner Page

Filtering Print Files

Print filters are programs that convert the content of a file from one format to another so that it can be printed. In network printing, print filters process the file on the print client before it gets transmitted to the server. The LP print service uses filters to:

- Convert a file from one data format to another so that it can be printed properly on a specific type of printer

- Handle the special modes of printing that users may request using the -y option to the lp command—for example, two-sided printing, landscape printing, draft- or letter-quality printing
- Detect printer faults and notify the LP print service of them so that the print service can deliver alerts

Not every print filter can perform all of these tasks. However, because each task is printer-specific, it can be implemented separately.

A print filter can be as simple or as complex as needed. SunOS 5.*x* system software provides print filters in the /usr/lib/lp/postscript directory to cover most PostScript printing situations where the destination printer requires the data to be in PostScript format. You have to create and add filters to the system for non-PostScript printers.

Starting the Printer Interface Program

The LP print service uses a standard printer interface program to interact with other parts of the operating system to:

- Initialize the printer port, if necessary. The standard printer interface program uses the stty command to initialize the printer port.
- Initialize the printer. The standard printer interface program uses the terminfo database and the TERM shell variable to find the appropriate control sequences.
- Print a banner page, if necessary.
- Print the correct number of copies specified by the print request.

The LP print service uses the standard interface program (found in the /usr/lib/lp/model directory) unless you specify a different one. You can create custom interface programs, but you must be careful that the custom program does not terminate the connection to the printer or interfere with proper printer initialization.

Tracking the Status of Print Jobs

The lpsched daemons on both the print server and the print client each keep a log of every print request that is processed and note any errors that occurred during the printing process. This log is kept in the /var/lp/logs/lpsched file. Every night, the lp cron job renames /var/lp/logs/lpsched to a new file lpsched.*n* and starts a new log file. If errors occur or jobs disappear from the print queue, you can use the log files to determine what lpsched has done with a printing job.

Tracking Forms

The LP print service helps you track which forms are mounted on each printer and notifies you when it cannot find the description of how to print on a form. You are responsible for creating form descriptions and mounting and unmounting the paper form in each printer, either as part of setting up a printer or in response to alerts from the LP print service.

Users can specify the form on which they want a job to print. You (root) can mount a specific form and then tell the LP print service that the form is available and on which printer it is mounted. Alternatively, users can submit print requests specifying a particular form and whether or not the form is mounted. When the LP print service receives the request, it sends an alert message to the system administrator (root) requesting that the form be mounted.

Tracking Printwheels

The procedure for tracking printwheels is similar to the procedure for tracking forms. Some printers (usually letter-quality printers) have removable print heads, such as daisy wheels or print balls, that provide a particular font or character set. A user can request a named character set. If that character set is not available, the LP print service notifies the system administrator (root) of the request. The job is stored in the print queue until the printwheel is changed.

Receiving Printing Problem Alerts

The LP print service performs sophisticated error checking. If a printing problem occurs, alerts are sent to the originator of a print request or to the system administrator, depending on the nature of the problem and what is required to fix it. Users are notified when a print request cannot be completed. If users request, they are notified by e-mail when a job is successfully completed. Administrators are alerted to problems with printers, and to requests for filters, forms, or character sets.

For problems that require an administrator's attention, the LP print service default is to write an alert message to the system administrator's console window (that is, to the terminal on which root is logged in).

As the system administrator, you can change the policy to receive alert messages via electronic mail or a program of your choice. Or, you can choose to receive no alerts when printing problems occur.

Understanding the Structure of the LP Print Service

The following sections explain the structure and directory hierarchy for the LP print service. The many files of the LP print service are distributed among seven directories, as shown in Table 6.1.

Table 6.1 Directories for the LP Print Service

Directory	Description
/usr/bin	The lp, lpstat, enable, and disable commands
/etc/lp	A hierarchy of LP configuration files
/usr/share/lib	The terminfo database directory
/usr/sbin	The lp commands
/usr/lib/lp	The LP daemons, directories for binary files and PostScript filters, and the model directory (which contains the standard printer interface program)
/var/lp/logs	The logs for LP activities
lpNet	Messages from lpNet
lpsched.*n*	Messages from lpsched
requests.*n*	Information about completed print requests
/var/spool/lp	The spooling directory where files are queued for printing

User Commands

The /usr/bin directory contains the lp and lpstat commands, with which users submit and monitor print requests. The directory also contains the enable and disable commands, with which printers are enabled and disabled.

Users can customize their print requests using options to the lp command specifying forms, character sets, filters, titles, banners, and so forth. Table 6.2 summarizes the frequently used options for the lp command. These options can be used individually or combined in any order on the command line. When combining options, use a space between options and repeat the dash (—). For example, the following command specifies a destination printer, requests e-mail notification, and prints six copies of a file:

```
% lp -d <printer-name> -m -n6 <filename>
```

Table 6.2 Summary of Frequently Used lp Command Options

Option	Description
-d	Destination. Specifies a destination printer by name.
-m	Mail. Sends e-mail to the user who submitted the print request when the file has printed successfully.
-n	Number. Specifies the number of copies to be printed.
-t	Title. Specifies a title for a print request (printed only on the banner page).
-o nobanner	Option. Suppresses printing of the banner page for an individual request.
-h	Header. Puts a header on each page of the print request.
-c	Copy. Copies the file before printing.
-w	Write. Writes a message to root's terminal when the file has printed successfully.

See the lp(1) manual page for a complete list of options.

LP Configuration Files

The scheduler stores configuration information in LP configuration files located in the /etc/lp directory. These configuration files serve the function of the /etc/printcap file in SunOS 4.1. You can check the contents of these files, but you should not edit them directly. The LP administrative commands provide input for the configuration files in the /etc/lp directory. The lpsched daemon administers and updates the configuration files. You should use the administrative commands any time you need to update any configuration file. Table 6.3 describes the contents of the /etc/lp directory.

The printers directory has a subdirectory for each printer (local or remote) known to the system. This example shows the subdirectories for the printers pinecone and sparc1:

```
%ls -l /etc/lp/printers
drwxrwxr-x 2 lp lp 512 Jan 23 23:53 pinecone
drwxrwxr-x 2 lp lp 512 Jan 11 17:50 sparc1
```

Within each of the printer-specific directories, the following files can describe the printer:

- alert.sh = Shell to execute in response to alerts
- alert.vars = Alert variables

- configuration = Configuration file
- users.deny = List of users to deny printer access
- comment = Printer description

Table 6.3 Contents of the /etc/lp Directory

File	Type	Description
Systems	ASCII file	Names of systems defined using the lpsystem command. Describes every remote system with which the local system can exchange print requests.
classes	Directory	Contains files identifying classes provided by the lpadmin -c command.
fd	Directory	Contains descriptions of existing filters.
forms	Directory	Location to put files for each form. Initially, this directory is empty.
interfaces	Directory	Contains printer interface program files.
logs	Link to /var/lp/logs	Contains log files of printing activities.
model	Link to /usr/lib/lp/model	Contains the standard printer interface program.
printers	Directory	Contains directories for each (remote or local) printer set-up. Each directory contains configuration information and alert files for an individual printer.
pwheels	Directory	Contains printwheel or cartridge files.

A typical configuration file for the printer pinecone, /etc/lp/printers/pinecone/configuration, would look like this:

```
Banner: on: Always
Content types: PS
Device: /dev/term/b
Interface: /usr/lib/lp/model/standard
Printer type: PS
Modules: default
```

Printer Definitions

The LP print service uses the terminfo database to initialize a local printer; to establish a selected page size, character pitch, line pitch, and character set;

and to communicate the sequence of codes to a printer. The terminfo database directory is located in /usr/share/lib.

Each printer is identified in the terminfo database with a short name. If necessary, you can add entries to the terminfo database, but it is a tedious and time-consuming process. Describing how to add entries to the terminfo database is beyond the scope of this book.

Daemons and LP Internal Files

The /usr/lib/lp directory contains daemons and files used by the LP print service, as described in Table 6.4.

Table 6.4 Contents of the /usr/lib/lp Directory

File	Type	Description
bin	Directory	Contains files for generating printing alerts, slow filters, and queue management programs.
lpNet	Daemon	Controls lp requests for network printing.
lpdata	ELF executable file	
lpsched	Daemon	Manages scheduling of LP print requests.
model	Directory	Contains the standard printer interface program.
postscript	Directory	Contains all PostScript filter programs provided by the SunOS 5.0 LP print service. These filters come with descriptor files in the /etc/lp/fd directory that tell the LP print service the characteristics of the filters and where to locate them.

LP Administrative Commands

The commands used to set up and administer the LP print service are in the /usr/sbin directory, as shown in Table 6.5.

Log Files

The LP print service maintains two sets of log files: a list of current requests that are in the print queue (/var/spool/lp) and an ongoing history of print requests (/var/lp/logs/requests).

Table 6.5 The lp Commands in the /usr/sbin Directory

Command	Purpose
accept/reject	Accepts print requests into the printer's queue or rejects print requests
lpadmin	Defines printer names, printer types, file content types, print classes, printer devices, and printer comments; removes printers or print classes; specifies fault recovery, interface programs (either custom or standard), printing options, banner/no banner; mounts forms; mounts printwheels or cartridges; defines allow and deny user lists
lpfilter	Adds, changes, deletes, and lists filters
lpforms	Adds, changes, deletes, and lists forms
lpmove	Moves queued print requests from one printer to another
lpshut	Halts the LP print service (the command lpsched, which starts the LP print service, is in the /usr/lib/lp directory)
lpsystem	Registers print servers and print clients with the LP print service
lpusers	Sets queue priorities for users

Print Queue Logs

The scheduler for each system keeps a log of print requests in the directories /var/spool/lp/requests/<*system*> and /var/spool/lp/tmp/<*system*>. Each print request has two files (one in each directory) that contain information about the request. The information in the /var/spool/lp/requests/<*system*> directory can be accessed only by root or lp. The information in the /var/spool/lp/tmp/<*system*> directory can be accessed only by root, lp, or the user who submitted the request.

The following example shows the contents of the /var/spool/lp/tmp/pine directory. See Table 6.6 later in the chapter for an explanation of the lp requests log codes.

```
pine% ls /var/spool/lp/tmp/pine
20-0 21-0
pine% cat 21-0
C 1
D slw2
F /etc/default/login
P 20
t simple
U winsor
s 0x1000
```

These files remain in their directories only as long as the print request is in the queue. Once the request is finished, the information in the files is combined and appended to the file /var/lp/logs/requests, which is described in the next section.

Use the information in the /var/spool/lp logs if you need to track the status of a print request that is currently in the queue.

History Logs

The LP print service records a history of printing services in three log files: lpNet, lpsched, and requests. These log files are located in the /var/lp/logs directory. You can use the information in these logs to diagnose and troubleshoot printing problems. Here is an example of the contents of the /var/lp/logs directory:

```
# cd /var/lp/logs
# ls
lpNet        lpsched.1    requests    requests.2
lpsched      lpsched.2    requests.1
#
```

The files with the .1 and .2 suffixes are copies of the previous day's logs. Each day, the lp cron job cleans out the lpsched and requests log files; it keeps copies for two days.

The two most important log files for troubleshooting are the lpNet log, which contains information about network printing; and the lpsched log, which contains information about local printing requests.

The requests log contains information about print requests that have completed and are no longer in the print queue. Once a request is finished printing, the information in the /var/spool/lp log files is combined and appended to the /var/lp/logs/requests file.

The requests log has a simple structure, and you can extract data using common UNIX shell commands. Requests are listed in the order they are printed and are separated by lines showing their request IDs. Each line below the separator line is marked with a single letter that identifies the kind of information contained in that line. Each letter is separated from the data by a single space.

Here is an example of the contents of a requests log:

```
# pwd
/var/lp/logs
# tail requests.2
= slw2-20, uid 200, gid 200, size 5123, Mon Nov 18
01:24:01 EST 1991
z slw2
```

```
C 1
D slw2
F /etc/motd
P 20
+ simple
U irving
s 0x0100
#
```

Table 6.6 shows the codes in the LP requests log.

Spooling Directories

Files queued for printing are stored in /var/spool/lp directory until they are printed. Table 6.7 shows the contents of the /var/spool/lp directory.

Table 6.6 Codes in the LP Requests Log

Character	Content of Line
=	The separator line. It contains the following items, separated by commas: the request ID, the user ID and group IDs of the user, the total number of bytes in the original (unfiltered) files, and the time when the request was queued. The user ID, group IDs, and file size are preceded by the words *uid*, *gid*, and *size*, respectively.
C	The number of copies printed.
D	The printer or class destination, or the word *any*.
F	The name of the file printed. The line is repeated for each file printed; files were printed in the order shown.
f	The name of the form used.
H	One of three types of special handling: resume, hold, and immediate. The only useful value found in this line will be immediate.
N	The type of alert used when the print request was successfully completed. The type is the letter *M* if the user was notified by e-mail or *W* if the user was notified by a message to the terminal.
O	The -o options.
P	The priority of the print request.
p	The list of pages printed.
r	This single-letter line is included if the user asked for raw processing of the files (the -r option of the lp command).

Table 6.6 Codes in the LP Requests Log (Continued)

Character	Content of Line
S	The character set or printwheel (or cartridge) used.
s	The outcome of the request, shown as a combination of individual bits expressed in hexadecimal form. Although several bits are used internally by the print service, the most important bits are listed below: 0x0004 Slow filtering finished successfully. 0x0010 Printing finished successfully. 0x0040 The request was canceled. 0x0100 The request failed filtering or printing.
T	The title placed on the banner page.
t	The type of content found in the file(s).
U	The name of the user who submitted the print request.
x	The slow filter used for the print request.
Y	The list of special modes to give to the print filters used to print the request.
z	The printer used for the request. This printer differs from the destination (the D line) if the request was queued for any printer or a class of printers, or if the request was moved to another destination.

Table 6.7 Contents of the /var/spool/lp Directory

File	Type	Description
SCHEDLOCK	File	Lock file for the scheduler. Check for this file if the scheduler dies and won't restart.
admins	Directory	Linked to /etc/lp.
bin	Directory	Linked to /usr/lib/lp/bin.
fifos	Directory	Contains pipes that convey networked print requests to and from the lpNet daemon.
logs	Link	Linked to ../lp/logs where completed print requests are logged.
model	Link	Linked to /usr/lib/lp/model.

Table 6.7 Contents of the /var/spool/lp Directory (Continued)

File	Type	Description
requests	Directory	Contains a directory for each configured printer where print requests are logged until printed. Users cannot access this log.
system	Directory	Contains a print status file for the system.
temp	Link	Linked to /var/spool/lp/tmp/<*printer-name*>, which contains the spooled requests.
tmp	Directory	Contains a directory for each configured printer where print requests are logged until printed. Changes to existing print requests are also recorded in this log.

Setting Up Printing Services

You need to decide which systems will have local printers directly cabled to them and which systems will connect to printers over the network. The system that has the printer connected to it and makes the printer available to other systems is called a *print server*. The system that has its printing needs met by a print server is called a *print client*.

Setting up printing services is composed of three basic tasks:

- Setting up local printers
- Setting up print servers
- Setting up print clients

You can have the following client-server combinations, as illustrated in Figure 6.3:

- SunOS 5.0 print clients with a SunOS 5.0 print server
- SunOS 5.0 and SunOS 4.1 print clients with a SunOS 5.0 print server
- SunOS 5.0 and SunOS 4.1 print clients with a SunOS 4.1 print server

This chapter describes how to set up a SunOS 5.0 print client to print from a server running SunOS 4.1 system software. When SunOS 5.0 systems are added to an existing SunOS 4.*x* network, this case is probably the most typical.

Appendix B describes how to set up print clients and print servers using the Solaris 2.1 Printer Manager, which you access from the Administration Tool. The Printer Manager automatically configures the port monitor as part of the printer set-up procedure.

Figure 6.3
Print client-server configurations

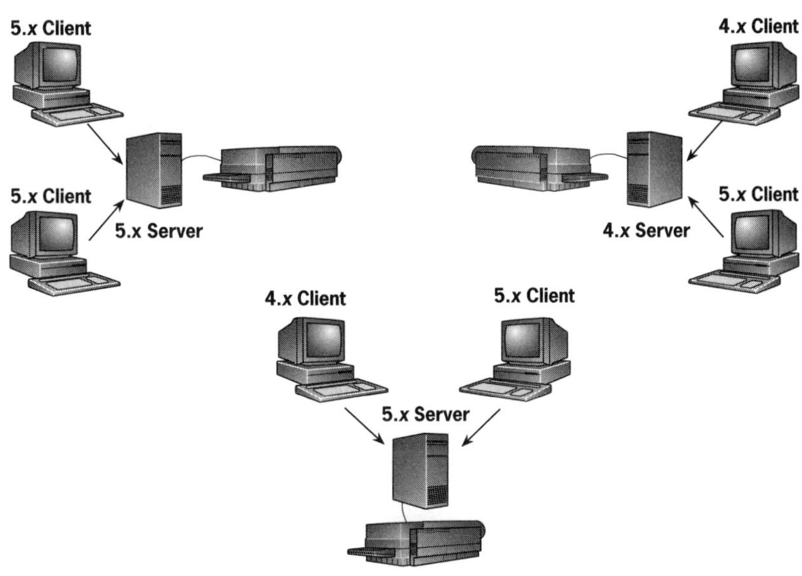

Setting Up a PostScript Print Client

This section describes how to set up a SunOS 5.0 print client to print on a SunOS 4.*x* print server that has a PostScript printer installed. You must complete the following tasks so the print client can use the printer connected to the print server:

- Identify the printer and server system to which the printer is connected.
- Define the characteristics of the printer.
- Set up the print filters.

You must have a network that enables access between systems to set up print clients. If your network is running the Network Information Service (NIS) or NIS+, follow the appropriate procedures for enabling access between systems. If your network is not running NIS or NIS+, you must include the Internet address and system name for each print client in the /etc/hosts file on the print server. You must also include the Internet address and system name of the print server in the /etc/hosts file of each print client system.

Before you start, you need superuser privileges on the print client system. You also need the name of the printer and the name of the print server system. You do not need to specify a printer type or file content type for a printer client. If no printer type is specified, the default is *unknown*. If no file content type is specified, the default is *any*, which allows both PostScript and ASCII files to be printed on a PostScript printer.

To set up a PostScript print client:

1. Become superuser on the print client system.
2. Type **lpsystem -t bsd <*server-system-name*>** and press Return. The print server system is identified as a bsd (SunOS 4.*x*) system.
3. Type **lpadmin -p <*printer-name*> -s <*server-system-name*>** and press Return. The printer and the server system name are registered with the client LP print service.
4. Type **cd /etc/lp/fd** and press Return.
5. Type **lpfilter -f download -F download.fd** and press Return.
6. Type **lpfilter -f dpost -F dpost.fd** and press Return.
7. Type **lpfilter -f postio -F postio.fd** and press Return.
8. Type **lpfilter -f postior -F postior.fd** and press Return.
9. Type **lpfilter -f postprint -F postprint.fd** and press Return.
10. Type **lpfilter -f postreverse -F postreverse.fd** and press Return. The PostScript filters are installed.
11. Type **accept <*printer-name*>** and press Return. The printer is now ready to begin accepting (queuing) print requests.
12. Type **enable <*printer-name*>** and press Return. The printer is now ready to process print requests in the print queue.
13. (Optional but recommended) Type **lpadmin -d <*printer-name*>** and press Return. The printer you specify is established as the default printer for the system. You should define a default printer even if there is only one printer configured for a system.
14. Type **lpstat -t** and press Return. Check the messages displayed to verify that the printer is accepted and enabled.
15. Type **lp <*filename*>** and press Return. If you have not specified a default printer, type **lp -d <*printer-name*> <*filename*>** and press Return. The file you choose is sent to the printer.

If you want to set up SunOS 5.0 print clients and print servers in addition to setting up the LP print system, you must also configure the port monitors using the Service Access Facility. See Chapter 3 for information on how to set up the port monitors. If you use the Solaris 2.1 Printer Manager, the port monitors are configured for you automatically. See Appendix A for information about the Printer Manager. To set up a SunOS 5.0 print client, in place of step 2 in the procedure described above, type **lpsystem** ***<server-system-name>*** and press Return. The print server system is identified as a SunOS 5.*x* system.

Using Printing Commands

The following sections describe how to use lp to submit requests from a command line. When a request is made, the LP print service places it in the queue for the printer, displays the request ID number, and then redisplays the shell prompt. The lp command has many options that can modify the printing process, as summarized in Table 6.2 earlier in the chapter. For a complete list of options, see the lp(1) manual page.

Printing to the Default Printer

When the LP print service is set up with a default printer, users can submit print requests without typing the name of the printer. Type **lp** ***<filename>*** and press Return. The file specified is placed in the print queue of the default printer, and the request ID is displayed.

The following example will print the /etc/passwd file:

```
pine% lp /etc/passwd
request id is pinecone-8 (1 file)
pine%
```

Printing to a Printer by Name

Whether or not a default printer has been designated for your system, you can submit print requests to any printer that is configured for your system. To submit a print request to an individual printer, type **lp -d** ***<printer-name> <filename>*** and press Return. The file specified is placed in the print queue of the destination printer, and the request ID is displayed.

The following example will print the /etc/passwd file on the printer acorn:

```
pine% lp -d acorn /etc/passwd
request id is acorn-9 (1 file)
pine%
```

If you submit a request to a printer that is not configured on your system, an information message is displayed, as shown in this example:

```
pine% lp -d thorn /etc/passwd
UX:lp: ERROR: Destination "thorn" is unknown to the
              LP print service.
pine%
```

Requesting Notification When a File Is Done Printing

When you submit a large file for printing, you may want the LP print service to notify you when printing is complete. You can request that the LP print service notify you either via an e-mail message or via a message to your console window.

To request e-mail notification, use the -m option when you submit the print request. Type **lp -m <*filename*>** and press Return.

To request that a message be written to your console window, use the -w option when you submit the print request. Type **lp -w <*filename*>** and press Return.

Printing Multiple Copies

You can print more than one copy of a file. When you request more than one copy, the file is printed the number of times you specify using the -n option to the lp command. The print request is considered as one print job, and only one header page is printed. To request multiple copies, type **lp -n<*number*> <*filename*>** and press Return.

The following example will print four copies of the /etc/passwd file:

```
pine% lp -n4 /etc/passwd
request id is pinecone-9 (1 file)
pine%
```

Determining Printer Status

Use the lpstat command to find out about the status of the LP print service. You can check on the status of your own jobs in the print queue, determine which printers are available for you to use, or determine request IDs of your jobs if you want to cancel them.

The Status of Your Print Requests

To find out the status of your own spooled print requests, type **lpstat** and press Return. A list of the files that you have submitted for printing is displayed.

In this example, on the system pine, one file is queued for printing to the printer pinecone:

```
pine% lpstat
pinecone-10            fred            1261   Mar 12 17:34 on pine
pine%
```

The lpstat command displays one line for each print job, showing the request ID and followed by the user who spooled the request, the output size in bytes, and the date and time of the request.

Availability of Printers

To find out which printers are configured on your system, type **lpstat -s** and press Return. The status of the scheduler is displayed followed by the default destination and a list of the systems and printers that are available to you.

In this example, on the system elm, the scheduler is running, the default printer is pinecone, and two network printers are available:

```
elm% lpstat -s
scheduler is running
system default destination: pinecone
system for pinecone: pine
system for acorn: oak
elm%
```

Display of All Status Information

The -t option for lpstat gives you a short listing of the status of the LP print service. To display a short listing of all status information, type **lpstat -t** and press Return. All available status information is displayed.

In this example, there are no jobs in the print queue. When files are spooled for printing, the status of those print requests is also displayed.

```
elm% lpstat -t
scheduler is running
system default destination: tom
system for slw2: bertha
system for slw1: bertha
device for tom: /dev/term/b
slw2 accepting requests since Mon May 11 11:01:54 EDT 1992
slw1 accepting requests since Wed May 27 16:26:38 EDT 1992
tom accepting requests since Wed Jun  3 14:25:41 EDT 1992
printer slw2 is idle. enabled since Mon May 11 11:01:55 EDT 1992. available.
printer slw1 is idle. enabled since Wed May 27 16:26:38 EDT 1992. available.
printer tom is idle. enabled since Wed Jun  3 14:25:41 EDT 1992. available.
character set usascii
character set english
```

```
character set finnish
character set japanese
character set norwegian
character set swedish
character set germanic
character set french
character set canadian_french
character set italian
character set spanish
character set line
character set security
character set ebcdic
character set apl
character set mosaic
elm%
```

The -l option for lpstat, when used with one of the other options, gives you a long listing of the status of the LP print service. To display a long listing of all status information, type **lpstat -tl** and press Return. All available status information is displayed.

In this example for the same system, additional information is displayed. When files are spooled for printing, the status of those print requests is also displayed.

```
{:44} lpstat -tl
scheduler is running
system default destination: tom
system for slw2: bertha
system for slw1: bertha
device for tom: /dev/term/b
slw2 accepting requests since Mon May 11 11:01:54 EDT 1992
slw1 accepting requests since Wed May 27 16:26:38 EDT 1992
tom accepting requests since Wed Jun  3 14:25:41 EDT 1992
printer slw2 is idle. enabled since Mon May 11 11:01:55 EDT 1992. available.
        Content types: any
        Printer types: unknown
        Description:
        Users allowed:
                (all)
        Forms allowed:
                (none)
        Banner not required
        Character sets:
                (none)
        Default pitch:
        Default page size:

printer slw1 is idle. enabled since Wed May 27 16:26:38 EDT 1992. available.
        Content types: simple
        Printer types: unknown
```

```
        Description: Located in ia lab
        Users allowed:
                (all)
        Forms allowed:
                (none)
        Banner not required
        Character sets:
                (none)
        Default pitch:
        Default page size:

printer tom is idle. enabled since Wed Jun  3 14:25:41 EDT 1992. available.
        Form mounted:
        Content types: PS
        Printer types: la100
        Description: hi
        Connection: direct
        Interface: /usr/lib/lp/model/standard
        After fault: continue
        Users allowed:
                (all)
        Forms allowed:
                (none)
        Banner required
        Character sets:
                usascii
                english
                finnish
               japanese
              norwegian
                swedish
               germanic
                 french
         canadian_french
                italian
                spanish
                   line
               security
                 ebcdic
                    apl
                 mosaic
        Default pitch: 10 CPI 6 LPI
        Default page size: 132 wide 66 long
(More information not shown in this example)
```

Display of Status for Printers

You can request printer status information for individual printers using the -p option to lpstat. This option shows whether the printer is active or idle, when it was enabled or disabled, and whether it is available to accept print requests.

To request status for all printers on a system, type **lpstat -p** and press Return. In this example, two printers are idle, enabled, and available. If one of those printers had jobs in the print queue, those jobs would also be displayed.

```
elm% lpstat -p
printer pinecone is idle. enabled since Wed Jan  1 18:20:22 PST 1992. available.
printer acorn is idle. enabled since Mon Mar  2 15:53:44 PST 1992. available.
elm%
```

To request status for an individual printer by name, type **lpstat -p** ***<printer-name>*** and press Return.

Display of Printer Characteristics

If you want to see all of the characteristics for a printer, use the -p option together with the -l (long) option to lpstat. This command can be especially useful for finding the printer type and content type.

To show characteristics for all printers on a system, type **lpstat -p -l** and press Return. A table shows all the configuration information that is used by the LP print service for each printer.

In this example, all of the fields are blank except for the content type and the printer type of the printer pinecone:

```
elm% lpstat -p pinecone -l
printer pinecone is idle. enabled since Wed Jan  1 18:20:22 PST 1992. available.
        Content types: PS
        Printer types: PS
        Description:
        Users allowed:
                (all)
        Forms allowed:
                (none)
        Banner not required
        Character sets:
                (none)
        Default pitch:
        Default page size:
elm%
```

Summary Table of lpstat Options

You can request different types of printing status information using the lpstat command. Table 6.8 summarizes the frequently used options for the lpstat command. Use these options individually or combine them in any order on the command line. When you combine options, use a space between options and repeat the hyphen (-). For example, to show a long list of status for an individual printer, type **lpstat -p** ***<printer-name>*** **-l** and press Return. See the lpstat(1) manual page for a complete list of options.

Table 6.8 **Summary of Frequently Used Options to the lpstat Command**

Option	Description
-a	Accept. Show whether print destinations are accepting requests.
-c	Class. Show classes and their members.
-d	Destination. Show default destination.
-f	Forms. Show forms.
-o	Output. Show status of output.
-p [*list*][-D][-l]	Printer/Description/Long list. Show status of printers.
-r	Request. Request scheduler status.
-R	Show position of job in the queue.
-S	Sets. Show character sets.
-s	Status. Show status summary.
-u [*username*]	User. Show requests by user.
-v	Show devices.

Canceling a Print Request

Use the cancel command to cancel a print request while it is in the queue or while it is printing. To cancel a request, you need to know its request ID. The request ID always includes the name of the printer, a hyphen, and the number of the print request. When you submit the print request, the request ID is displayed. If you do not remember your request ID, type **lpstat** and press Return. Only the user who submitted the request, or someone logged in as root or lp, can cancel a print request.

Cancellation of Print Request by ID Number

To cancel a print request, type **cancel <*request-ID*>** and press Return. A message is displayed telling you that the request is canceled. The next job in the queue begins printing.

In this example, two print requests are canceled:

```
elm% cancel pinecone-3 pinecone-4
request "pinecone-3" cancelled
request "pinecone-4" cancelled
elm%
```

Canceling a File That Currently Is Printing by Printer Name

You can also cancel just the job that currently is printing (if you submitted it) by typing the printer name in place of the request ID. Type **cancel *<printer-name>*** and press Return. A message is displayed telling you that the request is canceled. The next job in the queue begins printing.

In this example, the currently printing request has been canceled:

```
elm% cancel pinecone
request "pinecone-3" cancelled
elm%
```

As system administrator, you can log in as root or lp and cancel the currently printing request using the printer name as the argument for the cancel command.

CHAPTER

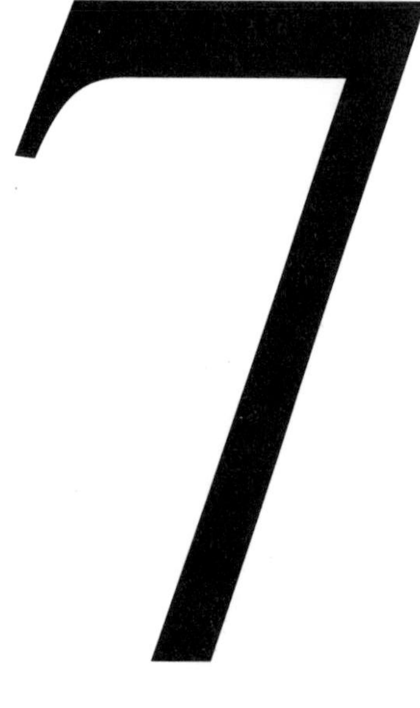

Administering User Accounts and Groups

Adding and Administering User Accounts

Setting Up and Administering Groups

THIS CHAPTER DESCRIBES HOW TO SET UP AND ADMINISTER USER ACCOUNTS and groups using the Administration Tool. You can use Administration Tool to edit both NIS+ databases and the files in the local /etc directory. You can also use Administration Tool to view information in NIS maps, but you cannot use the tool to edit them.

NOTE. *Solaris 2.x provides the following SVR4 useradd commands: useradd, userdel, usermod, groupadd, groupmod, and groupdel. Because these commands are only minimally network-aware, they are not described in this chapter. If you want to use these commands to administer user accounts on standalone systems, refer to the appropriate manual pages.*

Adding and Administering User Accounts

The following sections describe how to use the Administration Tool to add and delete user accounts. With Solaris 2.0, you must edit the Passwd database or the local /etc/passwd file to add users. Administration Tool does not automatically create the user's home directory, so you must do so, as described in the sections below. With Solaris 2.1, the User Manager edits the Passwd database and creates the home directory. The User Manager is described in Appendix B.

Adding User Accounts

Before you add users to the network, the users' systems must be installed and configured. When appropriate, NIS+ or NIS software should be installed and running on the network. (Only 4.*x* systems can be NIS servers. You can have either 4.*x* or 5.*x* systems installed as NIS clients.)

Adding users so that they can log in and start working has two steps: setting up the user account and providing the user with a working environment.

When you set up a user account, you:

- Edit the Passwd database
- Define the user's group(s)
- Create a home directory
- Define the user's environment
- Create a password

The next sections provide background information and describe how to do these tasks.

Editing the Passwd Database

Before you can use Administration Tool to edit the Passwd database or to edit the local /etc/passwd file, you must be a member of the sysadmin group (GID 14). If the system is running NIS+, you must also have the appropriate create and delete permissions for the NIS+ databases.

If you have the appropriate permissions, you can use the Administration Tool from any system on the network to make changes to a central NIS+ database or to the /etc/passwd file on a local system.

You need the following information for each user you plan to add:

- Login name
- User ID (UID)
- Primary Group ID (GID)
- Identifying information (name, office, extension, home phone)
- Home directory
- Login shell

Follow these steps to add users to the network NIS+ database or to a local /etc/passwd file:

1. Start OpenWindows (if necessary) by typing **openwin** and press Return.
2. Start Administration Tool (if necessary) by typing **admintool&** and press Return. The Administration Tool window is displayed.
3. Click SELECT on the Database Manager icon (if necessary). The Database Manager window is displayed.
4. Highlight the Passwd database, then click SELECT on either the NIS+ naming service or None (local /etc files), and click SELECT on the Load button. The Passwd Database window is displayed, as shown in Figure 7.1.
5. If you have a large network, you may want to search for the login name and UID to make sure that they are not already in use. Choose Find from the View menu, type the login name or the UID in the text field, and click SELECT on the Find button. If an entry matches, the list scrolls and the match is highlighted. If there is no match, the message "No match" is displayed in the footer of the Passwd Database window.
6. Choose Add Entry from the Edit menu. The Add Entry window is displayed, as shown in Figure 7.2.
7. Type the user name and the user ID in the appropriate text fields.

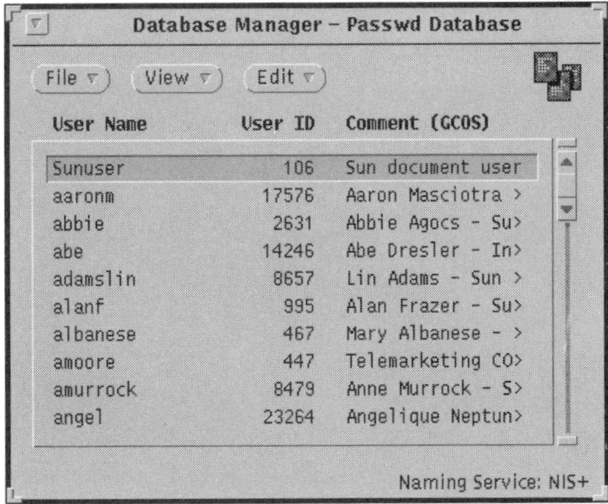

Figure 7.1
The Passwd Database window

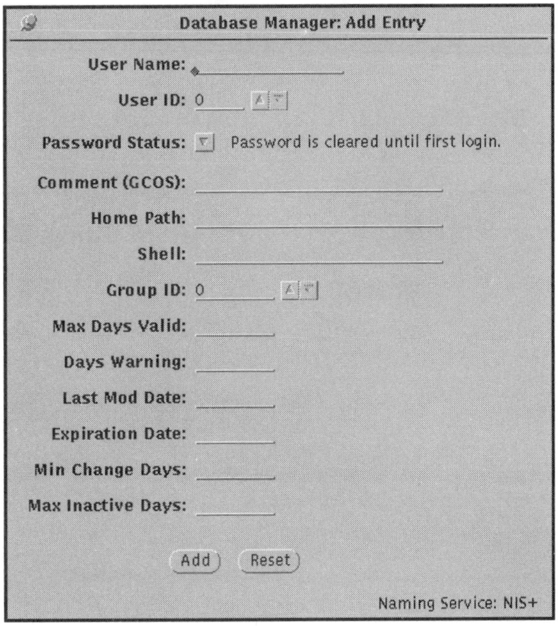

Database Manager: Add Entry
User Name:
User ID: 0
Password Status: Password is cleared until first login.
Comment (GCOS):
Home Path:
Shell:
Group ID: 0
Max Days Valid:
Days Warning:
Last Mod Date:
Expiration Date:
Min Change Days:
Max Inactive Days:
Add Reset
Naming Service: NIS+

Figure 7.2
The Add Entry window

8. The default password status is to be cleared until the first time the user logs in. If you want a different password status, choose other options from the Password Status menu, shown in Figure 7.3. The items in the menu are described in Table 7.1.

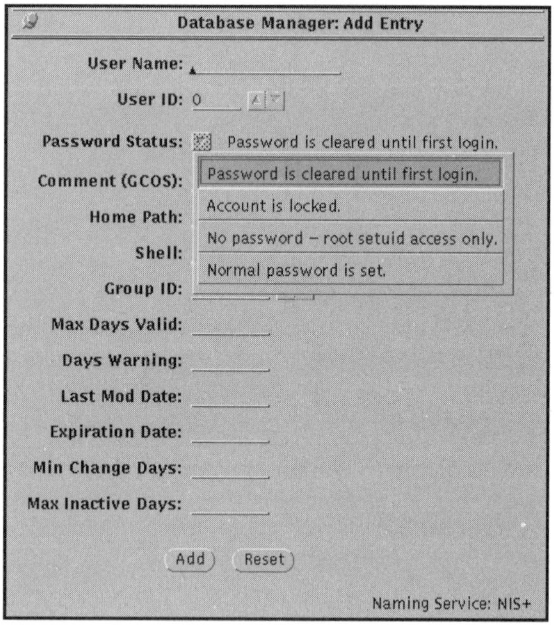

Figure 7.3
The Password Status menu

Table 7.1 **Password Status Choices from the Password Status Menu**

Password Status	Description
Password is cleared until first login.	Account requires a password; login prompts for password the first time the user logs in to the account.
Account is locked.	Account is disabled with an invalid password and can be unlocked by assigning a new password. This type of account allows a user to own files but not log in.
No password—root setuid access only.	Account cannot be logged into directly. This allows programs such as lp or uucp to run under an account, without allowing a user to log in.
Normal password is set.	Choose this item when an existing account already has a password.

NOTE. *You cannot create an account that does not require a password, and you cannot define a password for the account from Database Manager. Use either the nispasswd, yppasswd, or passwd command to create a password for an account.*

9. Type the rest of the user account information into the text fields. Table 7.2 describes the contents of each field. The Database Manager also provides on-line help. To get more information about an entry, move the pointer onto the entry label or into the text field and press the Help key on the keyboard of the field contents.

Table 7.2 Contents of Fields in the Passwd Database Add Entry Window

Field	Description
User Name	Enter a unique public name with two to eight characters (including numbers) that is used to log in.
User ID	Enter a unique number between 100 and 60000 that identifies the user internally to the system.
Password Status	See Table 7.1.
Comment (GCOS)	Enter optional information, such as user's full name, phone number, and organization. (Originally the GCOS field.)
Home Path	Enter the path to the user's home directory. By convention, the path should be /home/*<login-name>*. Note that in Solaris 2.*x* the system name is no longer included as part of the user's home directory path.
Shell	Enter the complete path of the shell that starts up at login: /bin/sh for the Bourne shell, /bin/csh for the C shell, or /bin/ksh for the Korn shell. The default is the Bourne shell.
Group ID	Enter a unique number between 0 and 60000 that identifies the primary group to which the user belongs.
Max Days Valid	Enter the maximum number of days the password will be valid. If you leave the field blank, the password does not expire.
Days Warning	Enter the number of days to begin warning the user before the password expires.
Last Mod Date	The date when the password was last changed is displayed in this field as the number of days since January 1, 1970 (for example, 8085 stands for January 28, 1992). You should not change this field.
Expiration Date	Enter the absolute date that the user account expires, as the number of days since January 1, 1970 (for example, 8085 stands for January 28, 1992). If you leave this field blank, the password does not expire.
Min Change Days	Enter the minimum number of days allowed between password changes.
Max Inactive Days	Enter the number of days an account can go unused (no login) before it is locked.

10. When you have entered all of the information correctly, click SELECT on Add. The information is entered into the Passwd database or the /etc/passwd file, depending on which of these you chose to edit. If the message "...cannot execute method, access denied..." is displayed, edit the NIS+ group table or the /etc/group file and create or add your login name to the sysadmin group with GID 14.

To complete the user set-up after editing the Passwd database, you must also create a home directory and set up the user's environment, as described in a later section.

Adding a User Account to the NIS+ Passwd Database (Example)

Figure 7.4 shows an example of adding a user account with this information:

- Login name: ignatz
- UID: 6987
- Default GID: 112
- Identifying information: Iggy Ignatz
- Home directory: /home/ignatz
- Login shell: /bin/csh

Figure 7.4
Example of adding a user

Database Manager: Add Entry

User Name: ignatz
User ID: 6387
Password Status: Password is cleared until first login.
Comment (GCOS): Iggy Ignatz
Home Path: /home/ignatz
Shell: /bin/csh
Group ID: 112
Max Days Valid: 0
Days Warning: 0
Last Mod Date:
Expiration Date:
Min Change Days: 0
Max Inactive Days: 0

Add Reset

Naming Service: NIS+

Defining the User's Group(s)

If you add the user to any groups, you must edit the Groups database and add the user's login name to the list that defines the members of the group. This section describes how to add a user to a group. To do this, you need the user's login name and user ID (UID) and the name and ID for groups to which you will add the user.

You can add users to groups defined in the network NIS+ Group database or to a local /etc/group file.

1. From the Database Manager window, highlight the Group database, press SELECT on NIS+ or None (local /etc files), and click SELECT on Load. The Group Database window is displayed, as shown in Figure 7.5.

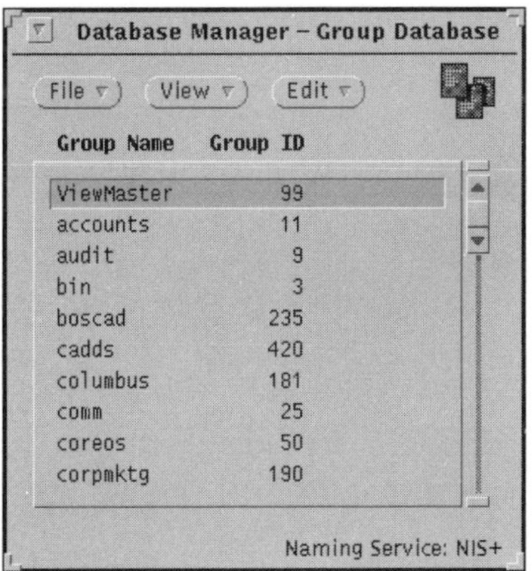

Figure 7.5 The Group Database window

2. Click SELECT on the entry you want to modify. The entry is highlighted.
3. Choose Modify Entry from the Edit menu. The Modify Entry window is displayed, showing the current information in the Group database (or file) for the selected entry, as shown in Figure 7.6.
4. Add the user's login name to the Members List text field. If you make a mistake or change your mind, click SELECT on the Reset button, and retype the information.
5. Click SELECT on Modify. The Group database (or local /etc/group file) is modified.
6. Repeat the steps for each secondary group to which you want to add the user, if you want the user to belong to any secondary groups.

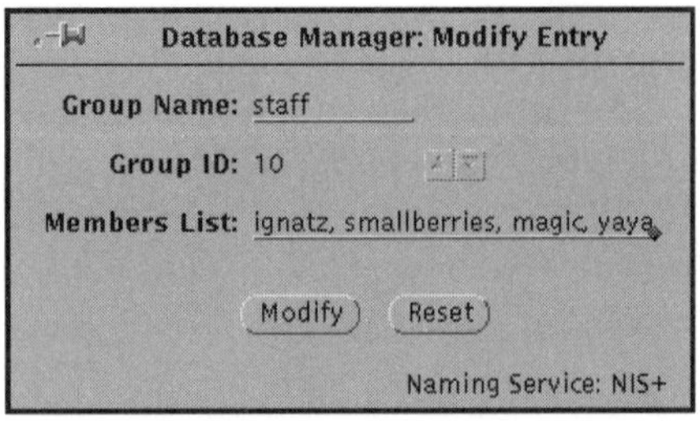

Figure 7.6 The Modify Entry window

NOTE. *If you are not using a naming service, repeat this procedure to update the /etc/group file on other systems with users who belong to the same group. To edit the /etc/group file for other systems, you must go back to the Load Database window and type the system name in the Use /etc files on host text field.*

Creating a Home Directory

The home directory is that portion of a file system that is allocated to an individual user for storing private files. The amount of space you allocate for a home directory may vary, depending on the kinds of files the users create and the type of work they do. You should probably allocate at least 15Mb of disk space for each user's home directory.

A user's home directory can be either on the local system or on a remote file server. In either case, by convention the home directory is created as /export/home/<*login-name*>. Note that this convention is new with Solaris 2.*x*. The server name is no longer included as part of the user's home directory path. On a large server that supports a number of users' home directories, there may be a number of directories under /export—such as home1, home2, home3, and so on—with directories for different users under them. Regardless of where their home directory is located, users access their home directory through a mount point named /home/<*login-name*>.

This section describes the default procedure for Solaris 2.*x*, which assumes that the user's system is on a network and that the Automounter is used to make the home directory accessible. Whether the home directory originates on a server or on the local system, you need to make it accessible to other systems by using the share command to export the file system so that the user can access the home directory from other systems on the network.

In addition, you need to define how the home directory is mounted by either:

- Adding an entry to the NIS+ Auto_home database, NIS auto.home map, or local /etc/auto_home files so that the home directory is automatically mounted. This is the preferred method.

- Adding an entry in /etc/vfstab file on the user's system to NFS-mount the home directory.

To support automatic mounting of home directories, the SunOS 5.*x* system software includes this entry in the /etc/auto_master file:

```
/home        /etc/auto_home
```

This entry tells the Automounter to mount the directories specified in the auto_home database onto the /home mount point on the local system. The entries in auto_home use this format:

```
<login-name>     <system-name>:/export/home/<login-name>
```

When a user logs in with *<login-name>*, the Automounter mounts the specified directory (/export/home/*<login-name>*) from the specified system (*<system-name>*) onto the /home mount point on the system to which the user is logged in.

This method works even when the home directory is stored on the same system to which the user has logged in. But more importantly, the user can log in to any other system and have his or her home directory mounted on /home on that system.

NOTE. *When the Automounter is used to mount home directories, you are not permitted to create any directories under the /home mount point on the user's system. The system recognizes the special status of /home when the Automounter is active.*

To create a home directory, you must already have created the user's account by editing the Passwd database. You need this information:

- User's login name and UID.
- The name of the system on which to create the home directory. If the home directory is accessed over the network, the home directory system should be on the same network segment as the user's local system. Use the df command to check the servers to make sure there is enough space for a new home directory.
- The name of the directory where you will create the user's account. By convention, the home directory is named /export/home. However, on a large file server you may have multiple directories—/export/home1, /export/home2, and so on. Under each directory, different subdirectories are created for different users (for example, /export/home/*<login-namea>*, /export/home/*<login-nameb>* ... /export/home1/*<login-namey>* ... /export/home2/*<login-namez>*, and so forth).

All of these steps apply regardless of whether the home directory is created on the local system or on a remote file server:

1. Become superuser on the system where you want to create the home directory.
2. Type **cd /export/*<home-dir>*** and press Return. The *<home-dir>* is the name of the directory where you want to create the user's home directory. For example, to change to the directory /export/home1, type:

   ```
   # cd /export/home1
   ```

3. Type **mkdir *<login-name>*** and press Return. The *<login-name>* is the login name of the user. You have created a directory that matches the login name of the user. For example, to create a directory for a user with a login name of ignatz, type:

   ```
   # mkdir ignatz
   ```

4. Type **chown *<login-name>* *<login-name>*** and press Return. The user now owns the home directory. For example, for user ignatz, type:

   ```
   # chown ignatz ignatz
   ```

5. Type **chgrp *<primary-GID>* *<login-name>*** and press Return. The user is assigned to the primary group you specified in the Passwd database for the user account, for example, the staff group.

   ```
   # chgrp staff ignatz
   ```

6. Type **chmod 755 /export/*<home-dir>*/*<login-name>*** and press Return. The user's home directory permissions are set to rwx for owner, r-x for group, and r-x for other.

   ```
   # chmod 755 /export/home1/ignatz
   #
   ```

NOTE. *The following steps describe how to share a home directory from a 5.*x *server. The procedure for sharing home directories from a 4.*x *server uses the export command.*

1. Type **share** and press Return to find out if the home directory has already been shared. If the home directory is listed, you will see information that looks like this:

   ```
   oak% su
   Password:
   # share
   ```

```
-               /export/home       rw     ""
#
```

If the home directory is not listed, perform the following steps to set it up so that it can be shared by other systems. You perform these steps once for each /export/<*home-dir*> directory. By convention, these are named /export/home, /export/home1, /export/home2, and so on.

2. Edit the file /etc/dfs/dfstab and add this line:

   ```
   share -F nfs /export/<home-dir>
   ```

3. Type **shareall -F nfs** and press Return. All the share commands in the /etc/dfs/dfstab file are executed so that you do not need to reboot the system. If you reboot the system, the share command is automatically run.

4. Type **ps -ef | grep mountd** and press Return. If the daemon mountd is running, the procedure is complete. This example shows that a mountd is not running. If the mountd is not running, follow the next step.

   ```
   # ps -ef | grep mountd
       root     221     218  16  18:07:25 pts/1  0:00 grep
   mountd
   ```

5. Type **/etc/init.d/nfs.server start** and press Return. The daemons required for sharing file directories are started.

NOTE. *If your network is not running NIS or NIS+, you need to add the home directory server's Internet Protocol (IP) address and system name to the /etc/hosts file on the user's system. You can use Database Manager to edit the local /etc/hosts file.*

If you use disk quotas, set up a disk quota for the user.

Once you have created the user's home directory, you must make it available. You make the home directory available either by adding it to the Auto_home database (the preferred method) for use by the automounter, or by adding an entry to the /etc/vfstab file on the user's system for NFS mounting.

Automounting the Home Directory Before you follow the procedures in this section, you should have created the user's home directory and have the Automounter set up and running. Use the Administration Tool Database Manager to edit the NIS+ Auto_home database. You must be a member of the sysadmin group (GID 14) and have the appropriate create and delete permissions for the Auto_home database.

You can use the Administration Tool from any system in the network to make changes to a central NIS+ Auto_home database or to the /etc/auto_home file on the local or other specified system, as long as you have the appropriate permissions.

To edit the Auto_home database you need the user's login name and the name of the home directory to be mounted.

All of these steps apply whether the home directory is created on the local system or on a remote file server:

1. Start Administration Tool (if necessary) and click SELECT on the Database Manager icon. The Load Database window is displayed, as shown in Figure 7.7. The Auto_home database and NIS+ are already selected.

Figure 7.7
The Load Database window

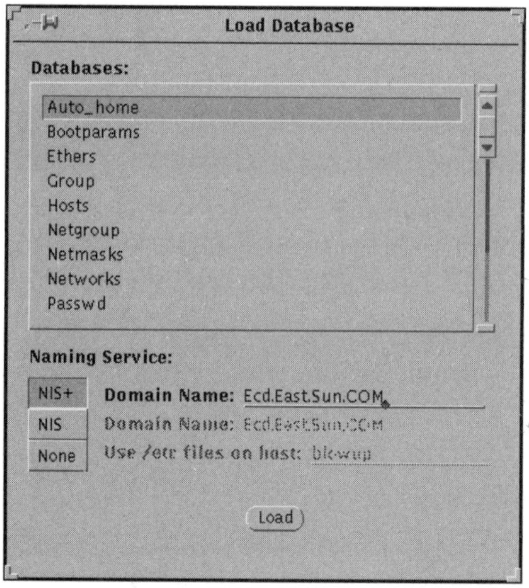

2. The default domain name is displayed. If the system is in a different domain, type the domain name in the text field. If you are editing the Auto_home file on a local system, click SELECT on None and type the name of the system in the Host Name text field.

3. Click SELECT on the Load button. The Auto_home Database window is displayed, as shown in Figure 7.8.

4. Choose Add Entry from the Edit menu. The Add Entry window is displayed, as shown in Figure 7.9.

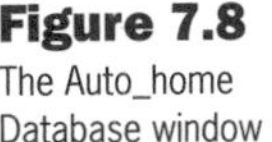

Figure 7.8
The Auto_home Database window

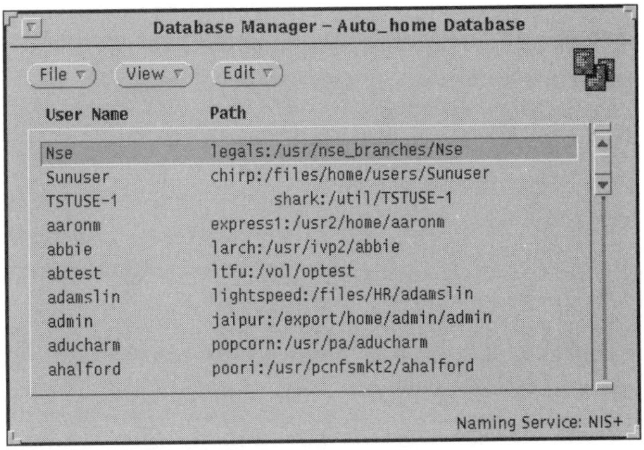

Figure 7.9
The Add Entry window

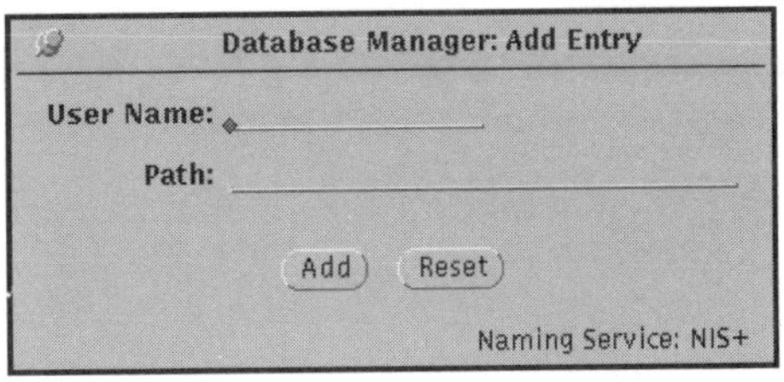

5. Type ***<login-name>*** in the User Name text field.

6. Type ***<system-name>*:/export/*<homen>*/*<login-name>*** in the Path text field. The *<system-name>* is the name of the server where the home directory was created.

7. Click SELECT on Add. The information is added to the Auto_home database or local /etc/auto_home file. The first time the user logs in, the home directory is automatically mounted under /home/*<login-name>*.

NFS-Mounting the Home Directory If the directory (disk space) for a user's home directory is located on another system and the Automounter is not being used to make that space available, follow these steps to NFS-mount the home directory:

1. Become superuser on the user's system.

2. Edit the /etc/vfstab file and create an entry for the user's home directory. For example, to create an entry for user ignatz with a home directory on server oak, you would add this line to the file:

```
oak:/export/home1/ignatz - /home/ignatz nfs - yes rw,intr
```

3. To create the mount point on the user's system, type **mkdir /home/ <*login-name*>** and press Return.

NOTE. *The home directory does not have the same name on the user's system as it does on the server. For example, /export/home/ignatz on the server is mounted as /home/ignatz on the user's system.*

4. Type **chown <*login-name*> /home/<*login-name*>** and press Return. The user now owns the home directory.

5. Type **chgrp <*primary-GID*> /home/<*login-name*>** and press Return. The user's primary group has permission to access the user's home directory.

6. Type **mountall** and press Return. All entries in the current vfstab file (whose automnt fields are set to Yes) are mounted.

7. To verify that all entries are mounted, type **mount** and press Return. The file systems that are mounted are displayed.

Defining the User's environment

To completely set up the user account, you must also:

- Define default initialization files
- Set up a mail account
- Set up a printer

Defining Initialization Files When a user logs in, the login program sets a number of variables, such as HOME, LOGNAME, and TZ. Then a file called the system profile (initialization file) is run to set system-wide defaults such as PATH, message of the day, and umask. Finally, the user profile initialization file (or files) that sets variables specific to the user is run. For example, the user profile may modify the PATH to include applications run by only that user.

Each shell has its own initialization file (or files), as shown in Table 7.3.

The SunOS 5.*x* system software provides default user initialization files for each shell in the /etc/skel directory, as shown in Table 7.4.

Table 7.3 Shell User Initialization Files

Shell	Initialization File	Purpose
C	$HOME/.login	Defines user's environment at login
	$HOME/.cshrc	Defines user's environment for all C shells invoked after login shell
Bourne	$HOME/.profile	Defines user's environment at login
Korn	$HOME/.profile	Defines user's environment at login
	$HOME/*<ksh-env>*	Defines user's environment at login in the file specified by the *<ksh-env>* environment variable

Table 7.4 Default Home Directory Initialization Files

Shell	File Name
C	/etc/skel/local.login
C	/etc/skel/local.cshrc
Bourne or Korn	/etc/skel/local.profile

Here is the default /etc/skel/local.login file:

```
# @(#)login 1.7 89/09/05 SMI
stty -istrip
setenv TERM 'tset -Q -'
```

Here is the default /etc/skel/local.cshrc file:

```
# @(#)cshrc 1.11 89/11/29 SMI
umask 022
set path=(/bin /usr/bin /usr/ucb /etc .)
if ( $?prompt ) then
        set history=32
endif
```

Here is the default /etc/skel/local.profile file:

```
stty istrip
PATH=.:/usr/bin:/usr/ucb:/etc
export PATH
```

As you can see, these files define a minimal environment. To minimize the need to edit the customization files for each user, you can customize the files in /etc/skel to set as many system-wide default variables as you can. You will need to edit individual users' customization files to set the user's path.

To set up initialization files, you must already have created the user's home directory and know which shell (C, Bourne, or Korn) is set in the user's account entry in the Passwd database. Follow these steps to set up the user's initialization files:

1. Become superuser on the system with the user's home directory.
2. Type **cd /*<home-dir>*/*<login-name>*** and press Return. You are in the user's home directory. For example to change to user ignatz's directory which is in /export/home1, type: # **cd /export/home1/ignatz**.
3. Type **cp /etc/skel/local.*** **.** and press Return. You have copied all of the default user initialization files to the user's home directory.
4. Type **chmod 744 local.*** and press Return. Permissions are set for the initialization files.
5. Type **chown *<login-name>*** * and press Return. The user now owns the initialization files.

```
# chown ignatz *
#
```

6. Type **chgrp *<primary-GID>* local.*** and press Return. The files are assigned to the primary group (for example, sysadmin) you specified in the Passwd database for the user account.

```
# chgrp 10 local.*
#
```

7. Rename the shell initialization files. If the user's shell is the C shell, type **mv local.login .login; mv local.cshrc .cshrc** and press Return. If the user's shell is the Korn or Bourne shell, type **mv local.profile .profile** and press Return.
8. Type **rm local.*** and press Return. You have removed the unused shell initialization files.
9. Mount the user's home directory.
10. On the user's system, log in as the user.
11. Assign the user an interim password. See "Creating a Password" later in the chapter for information on how to create passwords.

12. Check to make sure the user's environment is set up correctly.

13. Edit the user's initialization file (or files) and make changes as needed.

    To edit the user's initialization file (or files):

1. Set the user's default path to include the home directory and directories or mount points for the user's windowing environment and applications.

2. To change the path setting, add or modify the line for PATH as follows. For the C shell, type **set path =(. /*<dirname1>* /*<dirname2>* /*<dirname3>* ...)**. For example, enter a line like this in the user's $HOME/.cshrc file:

```
set path=(. /usr/openwin/bin /usr/bin /$home/bin /lib /usr/lib $home/bin)
```

   For the Bourne or Korn shell, type **PATH=.:/*<dirname1>*:/*<dirname2>*:/*<dirname3>* ...;export PATH**. For example, enter a line such as the following in the user's $HOME/.profile file:

```
PATH=.:/usr/openwin/bin:/usr/bin:/$HOME/bin:/lib:/usr/lib; export PATH
```

3. To check that the environment variables are set correctly, type **env** and press Return. Note that the variables are shown using Bourne or Korn shell syntax, even if the user's shell is the C shell. Type **man =s5 environ** and press Return for more information.

```
$ env
HOME=/home/ignatz
HZ=100
LOGNAME=ignatz
MAIL=/var/mail/ignatz
MANSECTS=\1:1m:1c:1f:1s:1b:2:\3:3c:3i:3n:3m:3k:3g:3e:3x11:3xt:3w:3b:9:4:5:7:8
PATH=:/usr/openwin/bin:/sbin:/usr/sbin:/usr/bin:/etc:/$HOME/bin:/lib:/usr/lib
SHELL=/bin/sh
TERM=sun
TZ=EST5EDT
$
```

4. Add or change the settings of environment variables. For the C shell, type **setenv *<VARIABLE>* *<value>*** (or **set *<variable>*=*<value>*** for the path and term variables). For example, this line sets the history to the last 100 commands:

```
setenv HISTORY 100
```

   For the Bourne or Korn shell, type ***<VARIABLE>*=*<value>*;export *<VARIABLE>***. For example, this line sets the user's default mail directory:

```
MAIL=/var/mail/ignatz;export MAIL
```

5. Check the umask setting. If you need to change it, type **umask <*nnn*>** and press Return. You can either include or omit leading zeros. For example, to set file permissions to 644, type **umask 022.** Table 7.5 shows the file permissions that are created for each of the octal values of umask.

Table 7.5 Permissions for umask Values

Octal Value	File Permissions
0	rwx
1	rw-
2	r-x
3	r--
4	-wx
5	-w-
6	--x
7	---(none)

The LANG variable and LC environment variables determine the locale-specific conversions and conventions the shell uses. These conversions and conventions include time zones, collation orders, and formats of dates, time, currency, and numbers. If necessary, set these variables in the user's initialization file. LANG sets all possible conversions and conventions for a given locale. If you have special needs, you can set various aspects of localization separately using the LC variables LC_COLLATE, LC_CTYPE, LC_MESSAGES, and LC_NUMERIC. Table 7.6 shows the values for several locales.

If the system needs to support multibyte characters (for example, Japanese), add this command to the system initialization file (/etc/profile or /etc/.login): stty cs8 defeucw. When the initialization files are complete, log out of the user's account.

Setting Up a User's Mail Account Each user has a mailbox either on a local system or on a mail server and a mail alias in the /etc/mail/aliases file that points to the location of the mailbox. To set up a mail client with a mailbox on a mail server:

1. Become superuser on the mail client's system.

Table 7.6 Values for LANG and LC Variables

Value	Locale
de:	German
fr:	French
iso_8895_1	English and European
it	Italian
japanese	Japanese
korean	Korean
sv	Swedish
tchinese	Taiwanese

2. Create a /var/mail mount point on the mail client's system.
3. Edit the /etc/vfstab file and add an entry for the /var/mail directory on the mail server, mounting it on the local /var/mail directory. The client's mailbox will automatically be mounted any time the system is rebooted.
4. Type **mount -a** to mount the mailbox. The client's mailbox is mounted.
5. Use the Administration Tool to edit the /etc/hosts file and add an entry for the mail server.

NOTE. *The sendmail program automatically creates mailboxes in the /var/mail directory the first time a message is delivered. You do not need to create individual mailboxes for your mail clients.*

If you are using NIS+, follow these steps to set up mail aliases for the user:

1. Compile a list of each of your mail clients, the locations of their mailboxes, and the names of the mail server systems.
2. Become superuser on any system.
3. For each alias, type **aliasadm -a *<alias>* *<expanded-alias>*[*<options>* *<comments>*]** and press Return. The alias is added to the NIS+ aliases table. For example, adding an alias for user iggy.ignatz would look like this:

```
# aliasadm -a iggy iggy.ignatz@oak "Iggy Ignatz"
```

4. Type **aliasadm -m <*alias*>** and press Return. The entry you created is displayed.
5. Check the entry to be sure it is correct.

Setting Up a User's Printer After adding users to a system, make sure they have access to a printer. See Chapter 6 for information on how to set up printing services.

Creating a Password

Passwords are an important part of system security. Each user account should be assigned a password of six to ten characters using a combination of letters and numbers. See the passwd(1), yppasswd(1), or nispasswd(1) manual pages for information about changing passwords and password attributes.

New with SVR4.

In the SunOS 4.*x* system, encrypted passwords were stored in the /etc/passwd file along with the rest of the information about the user. In SunOS 5.*x*, the encrypted password and associated password aging information are stored in the Shadow field of the NIS+ Passwd database (or in the local /etc/shadow file). Permissions on the Shadow field are restricted. Permissions for the /etc/shadow file are -r--------. Only root can read the /etc/shadow file, and only the passwd, yppasswd, and nispasswd commands can write to the file.

Here is an example of an /etc/shadow file:

```
root:XzVuaelvazZsw:8223::::::
daemon:NP:6445::::::
bin:NP:6445::::::
sys:NP:6445::::::
adm:NP:6445::::::
lp:NP:6445::::::
smtp:NP:6445::::::
uucp:NP:6445::::::
nuucp:NP:6445::::::
listen:*LK*:::::::
nobody:NP:6445::::::
noaccess:NP:6445::::::
janice:gzqgrmlKcfy7A:8223::::::
```

To create or modify passwords, use one of these commands:

- /usr/bin/passwd (for no naming service)
- /usr/bin/nispasswd (for the NIS+ naming service)
- /usr/bin/yppasswd (for the NIS naming service)

Users can create or change their own password at any time. You must be root to create the initial password for any other user. In addition, to create an NIS+ password, you must have the appropriate NIS+ privileges and you must have established the necessary network-wide credentials. (See the nispasswd(1) manual page.)

Follow these steps to create an NIS+ password:

1. Become superuser on the NIS+ server.
2. Type **nispasswd *<login-name>*** and press Return. The message "New NIS+ password:" is displayed.
3. Type the new password and press Return. The prompt "Retype new NIS+ password:" is displayed.
4. Retype the password and press Return. The password is assigned and added to the NIS+ database.

   In this example, a new password is assigned for the user ignatz:

```
oak% su
Password:
# nispasswd ignatz
New NIS+ password:
Retype new NIS+ password:
#
```

Follow these steps to change an NIS+ password:

1. Become superuser on the NIS+ server.
2. Type **nispasswd *<login-name>*** and press Return. The prompt "Old password:" is displayed.
3. Type the old password and press Return. The prompt "New password:" is displayed.
4. Type the new password and press Return. The prompt "Re-enter new password:" is displayed.
5. Retype the password and press Return. The password is assigned and added to the /etc/shadow file.

   In this example, the password for user ignatz is changed:

```
oak% su
Password:
# nispasswd ignatz
```

```
Old password:
New password:
Re-enter new password:
#
```

NOTE. *You can also use nispasswd to define, change, and view password attributes, such as password aging. See the nispasswd(1) manual page for more information.*

Follow these steps to create an NIS password:

1. Become superuser on any system in the NIS domain.
2. Type **yppasswd <*login-name*>** and press Return. The message "Changing NIS password for <*login-name*>" and the prompt "New password:" are displayed.
3. Type the new password and press Return. The prompt "Retype new password:" is displayed.
4. Retype the password and press Return. The password is assigned and added to the NIS master file.

In this example, the NIS password is changed for user yaya:

```
oak% su
Password:
# yppasswd yaya
Changing NIS password for yaya
New password:
Retype new password:
NIS entry changed on eucalyptus
#
```

Changing an NIS password is similar to changing an NIS+ password. When prompted to do so, type the old password, and then the new password two times.

Follow these steps to create a local password:

1. Become superuser on the local system.
2. Type **passwd <*login-name*>** and press Return. The prompt "New password:" is displayed.
3. Type the new password and press Return. The prompt "Re-enter new password:" is displayed.

4. Retype the password and press Return. The password is assigned and added to the /etc/shadow file.

```
oak% su
# passwd smallberries
New password:
Re-enter new password:
#
```

NOTE. *You can also use passwd to define, change, and view password attributes, such as password aging. See the passwd(1) manual page for more information.*

Changing a local password is similar to changing an NIS+ password. When prompted to do so, type the old password, and then the new password two times.

Administering User Accounts

Administering user accounts includes modifying, removing, and disabling the accounts.

Modifying User Accounts

When information about the user changes, use the Database Manager to edit the information in the Passwd database. Unless you define a user (login) name or UID that conflicts with existing ones, you probably will not need to modify a user account's login name or UID.

In a network environment, you may need to use the Database Manager to change the Auto_home database for the user's home directory when users move from one system to another, and from one server to another.

If you need to modify user passwords, use the passwd (no naming service), yppasswd (NIS), and nispasswd (NIS+) commands.

Removing User Accounts

Here is a checklist for removing a user account:

1. Delete the user's entry from the NIS+ Passwd database, NIS map, or /etc/passwd files.
2. Remove the user's name from entries in the NIS+ Group database, NIS map, or /etc/group files.
3. Remove the user from any printer access or deny lists.
4. Decide whether you want to delete or archive all of the user's files.

5. Delete the user's mail file.
6. Remove the user from the Auto_home database.

Disabling User Accounts

Occasionally, you may need to temporarily or permanently disable a login account. You should have good reason for taking such action. For example, the user may be on leave of absence or you may have strong evidence that the account is being misused or security is being violated.

The easiest way to disable a login account is to use the Database Manager to lock the password for an account in the Passwd database.

On a local system, you can control access to a user's account by requiring password aging, by setting an expiration date for the login account, or by requiring that a user access the account at regular intervals. Another way that you can disable a login is to temporarily change the password.

Setting Up and Administering Groups

The Group database (map, or local /etc/group file) stores information about user groups, traditionally called UNIX groups. A user group is a collection of users who can share files and other system resources. For example, a set of users who are working on the same project could be formed into a user group.

Each group has a GID (group identification number, analogous to the UID), which identifies it internally to the system. A group should have a name and a list of user names. User groups can be defined in two ways:

- Implicitly, by the GID for the user's primary group, which is defined in the user account. Whenever a new GID appears in the Group field of the Passwd database, a new group is defined.
- Explicitly, by name, GID, and user list, as entered into the Group database.

It's better to explicitly define all groups so every group has a name.

All users belong to at least one group—their primary group—which is indicated by the Group field of their user account. Although it is not required by the operating system, you should add the user to the member list of the group you've designated as his or her primary group. Optionally, users can belong to up to 16 secondary groups. To belong to a secondary group, the user must be added to the group's member list.

The groups command shows the groups to which a user belongs. For any user, only one group can be considered the primary group at a time.

However, users can temporarily change the primary group (with the newgrp command) to any other group they belong to.

Some applications, such as the file system, look at the user's primary group only. For example, ownership of files created, and recorded accounting data, reflects only the primary group. Other applications may take into account a user's membership across groups. For example, a user has to be a member of the sysadmin group to use the Administration Tool to make changes to a database, but it doesn't matter if sysadmin is the current primary group.

User groups probably are best known as the groups referred to by the read-write-execute permissions for the user, group, and world on files and directories. These permissions are a cornerstone of security. You cannot access others' files (if they do not allow world access) unless your primary or a secondary group has permission to access the files. For example, a group called techwrite could be created for technical writers, and a central directory of document files could be set up with write permission for the techwrite group. That way, only writers would be able to change the files.

User groups can be local to a workstation or used across a network. Across the network, user groups allow a set of users on the network to access a set of files on a workstation or file server without making those files available to everyone.

NOTE. *NIS+ supports another, unrelated kind of group called NIS+ group, which assigns access rights to NIS+ objects. These groups have nothing to do with using NIS+ to maintain a database of user groups.*

Setting Up Fields in the Group Database

The Group database (map, or local /etc/group file) has these fields:

- Group Name
- Group ID
- User (Member) List

There is an additional field that rarely is used: the Group Password. The Group Password field is a relic of earlier versions of UNIX. It is usually left empty or filled with an asterisk. If a group has a password, the newgrp command prompts users to enter it. However, there is no utility to set the password.

Setting Up a Group Name Field

This field contains the name assigned to the group. For example, members of the chemistry department in a university may be called chem. Group names can have a maximum of nine characters.

Setting Up a Group ID Field

This field contains the group's numerical ID. It must be unique from all other group IDs on a system and should be unique across the entire organization. Each GID number must be a whole number between 0 and 60002, but customarily you use numbers from 100 to 60000. (Numbers 60001 and 60002 are assigned to nobody and noaccess, respectively, and numbers under 100 are reserved for system default group accounts.) When you use the Administration Tool to add user accounts, you must specify the user's primary group; otherwise, the default primary group is root with a GID of 0. You do not want users to have a group of root.

Setting Up a User (Member) List Field

This field contains a list of the users in the group. User names are separated by commas. These names must be the official login names defined in the Passwd database. As already noted, each user can belong to a maximum of 17 groups.

Identifying Default UNIX User Groups

By default, all SunOS 5.*x* workstations and servers have these groups:

```
root::0:root
other::1:
bin::2:root,bin,daemon
sys::3:root,bin,sys,adm
adm::4:root,adm,daemon
uucp::5:root,uucp
mail::6:root
tty::7:root,tty,adm
lp::8:root,lp,adm
nuucp::9:root,nuucp
staff::10:
daemon::12:root,daemon
nobody::60001:
noaccess::60002:
```

You can add a sysadmin group with a GID of 14 to the NIS+ Group database, NIS Group map, or local /etc/group files. This group specifies the users who have access to all functions of the Administration Tool.

Creating New Groups

System administrators frequently create new group accounts. You must create a group and assign it a GID number before you can assign users to it.

Use the Administration Tool to create and maintain both network and local groups. You must be a member of the sysadmin group (GID 14) before you can use Administration Tool to create or edit group accounts. If the network is running NIS+, you must also have create and delete permissions for the NIS+ databases.

You need this information to create a new group:

- Login names of users who will belong to the group
- User IDs (UIDs) of users who will belong to the group
- Group name
- Group ID (GID)

Follow these steps to add groups to the network-wide NIS+ database or a local /etc/group file:

1. Start the Administration Tool (if necessary) by typing **admintool&** and pressing Return.
2. Click SELECT on the Database Manager icon. The Database Manager window is displayed.
3. Click SELECT on the Group database, then click SELECT on either the NIS+ naming service or None (local /etc files).
4. Click SELECT on Load. The Group Database window is displayed, as shown in Figure 7.10.

Figure 7.10
The Group Database window

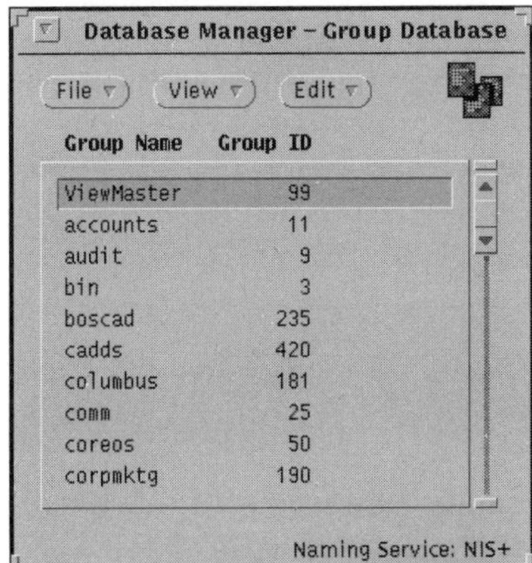

5. Choose Add Entry from the Edit menu. The Group Database: Add Entry window is displayed, as shown in Figure 7.11.

Figure 7.11
The Group Database: Add Entry window

Database Manager: Add Entry

Group Name:

Group ID: 0

Members List:

Add Reset

Naming Service: NIS+

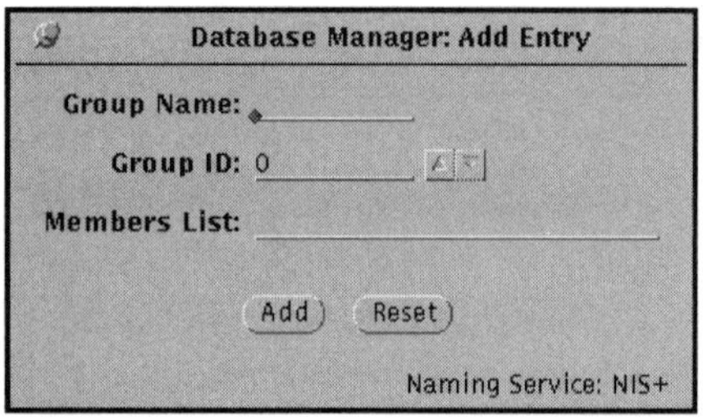

6. Type the group name, the group ID, and the list of members in the appropriate text fields, separated by a comma.
7. Click SELECT on Add. The group is added to the Group database (or local /etc/group file). Repeat the last two steps to add more groups.

Modifying or Deleting Groups

Membership in group accounts can change frequently as new employees are hired and other employees change job responsibilities. Consequently, you have to modify existing group accounts to add or remove users. If you choose to have a user belong to secondary groups, you have to modify those groups to add the user to the user lists. When adding groups, you may make a mistake. The ability to delete groups helps you correct such mistakes.

When projects finish, groups set up for them may no longer be needed, and these groups can be deleted. You should be careful to avoid conflicts if you reuse the GIDs from deleted groups.

Modifying a Group

Follow these steps to modify a group entry:

1. Click SELECT on Group, choose either NIS+ or None, and click SELECT on Load. The Group Database window is displayed.
2. Click SELECT on the name of the database you want to modify.
3. Choose Modify Entry from the Edit menu. The Modify Entry window is displayed, showing the current entries for the group.
4. Add or delete user names from the text field, then click SELECT on Modify. The entry in the Group database is modified.

Deleting a Group

If a group account is no longer needed, you can delete the group name. Follow these steps to delete a group:

1. Click SELECT on Group, choose either NIS+ or None, and click SELECT on Load. The Group Database window is displayed.
2. Click SELECT on the name of the database you want to delete.
3. Choose Delete Entry from the Edit Menu. The message "Do you really want to delete this entry?" is displayed.
4. If you do not want to delete the entry, click SELECT on Cancel. If you want to delete the entry, click SELECT on Delete. The group is deleted from the Group database.

CHAPTER

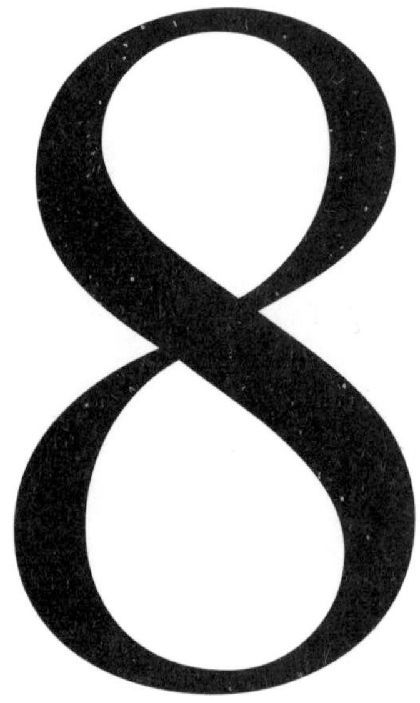

Understanding Shells

Commands Common to All Shells

The Bourne Shell

The C Shell

The Korn Shell

THE SOLARIS 2.X ENVIRONMENT PROVIDES THREE SHELLS FOR USE AS COMmand interpreters: the Bourne shell (the default), the C shell, and the Korn shell. One shell is defined as the default shell for each user, but users can start a new shell from any command line. This chapter describes elements that are common to all three shells and then provides a section for each shell that describes some of the prevalent shell features.

Table 8.1 lists the basic shell features and shows which shells provide each feature.

Table 8.1 Basic Features of Bourne, C, and Korn Shells

Feature	Bourne	C	Korn
Aliases	No	Yes	Yes
Command line editing	No	Yes	Yes
Enhanced cd	No	Yes	Yes
History list	No	Yes	Yes
Ignore CTRL-D (ignoreeof)	No	Yes	Yes
Initialization file separate from .profile	No	Yes	Yes
Job control	Yes	Yes	Yes
Logout file	No	Yes	No
Protect files from overwriting (noclobber)	No	Yes	Yes
Syntax compatible with Bourne shell	Yes	No	Yes

Commands Common to All Shells

The following sections describe commands that can be used with any shell.

Setting a Default Shell

The user's login shell is set in the last field of the user's entry in the Passwd database or /etc/passwd file. Use Database Manager to edit the Passwd database. Before you can use Administration Tool to edit the Passwd database or to edit the local /etc/passwd file, you must be a member of the sysadmin group, GID 14. If the system is running NIS+, you must also have the appropriate create and delete permissions for the NIS+ databases.

1. If necessary, open the Database Manager from Administration Tool.

2. Click SELECT on the Passwd database, then click SELECT on NIS+ or None to choose whether you will edit the NIS+ Passwd database or the local /etc/passwd file.
3. Click SELECT on Load. The Passwd database window is displayed.
4. Click SELECT on the name of the user account you want to edit, then choose Modify Entry from the Edit menu.
5. Change the entry in the Shell text field: enter /bin/sh for the Bourne shell, /bin/csh for the C shell, or /bin/ksh for the Korn shell.
6. Click SELECT on Modify to apply the changes. The next time the user logs out and logs in again, the new shell is used.

Changing Shells from a Command Line (csh, ksh, sh)

If you want to use another shell without modifying the Passwd database, you can change shells at a command line prompt by simply typing the name of the shell you want to use.

To change to the C shell, type **csh** and press Return. The default C shell prompt is the system name followed by a percent sign (%).

```
$ csh
oak%
```

To change to the Korn shell, type **ksh** and press Return. The default Korn shell prompt is a dollar sign ($).

```
oak% ksh
$
```

To change to the Bourne shell, type **sh** and press Return. The Bourne shell prompt also is a dollar sign ($).

```
$ sh
$
```

Quitting from a Shell (exit)

If you start a new shell from the command line, you can quit it and return to the old shell. To quit from a shell, type **exit** and press Return. If you have started (layered) another shell, you are returned to the original shell prompt.

```
$ exit
oak%
```

Clearing a Shell Window (clear)

You can clear the contents of a shell window and redisplay the prompt to the top of the window. To clear the contents of a shell window, type **clear** and press Return.

```
oak% which openwin
no openwin in . /home/ignatz /usr/deskset/bin /usr/bin
/home/ignatz/bin /bin /home/bin /etc /usr/etc /usr/ucb
oak% clear
```

The window is cleared and the prompt is redisplayed at the top.

The Bourne Shell

The default shell for the Solaris 2.*x* environment is the Bourne shell, developed by Steve Bourne when he was at AT&T Bell Laboratories. The Bourne shell is a small shell for general-purpose use. It also provides a full-scale programming language that is used to develop shell scripts to capture frequently performed commands and procedures. Describing how to write shell scripts is beyond the scope of this book.

Reviewing the Bourne Shell Initialization File

The Bourne shell uses one initialization file, .profile, in the user's home directory to set the user's environment. When the user logs in or starts a Bourne shell from the command line, the .profile file is read. Use this file to set the user's path and any environment variables.

Defining Bourne Shell Environment Variables

The syntax for defining an environment variable is the same for both the Bourne and Korn shells; type **<*VARIABLE*>=<*value*>;export <*VARIABLE*>** and press Return.

```
$ PS1=oak$;export PS1
$
```

The C Shell

The C shell, written by Bill Joy when he was at UC Berkeley, is popular with many users of Berkeley UNIX. The C shell is completely different from the Bourne and Korn shells and has its own syntax. The most important advantages of the C shell are command history, command editing, and aliases. Command history stores a record of the most recent commands that you have used. You can display these commands and reuse them as originally issued. You can also change a command by editing it. Aliases let you type short names for frequently used commands. You can also combine sequences of frequently used commands and provide an alias for the sequence.

Reviewing C Shell Initialization Files

The C shell uses two initialization files in the user's home directory to set the user's environment: .login and .cshrc (C shell run control).

When the user logs in, the .login file is read, and then the .cshrc file. When you start the C shell from a command line, only the .cshrc file is read. Because the .login file is not always read, you should set environment variables and the user's path in the .cshrc file.

Defining C Shell Environment Variables

To define an environment variable for the C shell, type **setenv <*VARIABLE*> <*value*>** and press Return.

```
oak% setenv DISPLAY rogue:0
oak%
```

Creating Aliases for the C Shell

Define any aliases for the user in the .cshrc file. The syntax for creating an alias is alias <*alias-name*> <*command sequence*>. For example, you can shortcut the alias command so that you type only the letter *a* by adding this line to the .cshrc file:

```
alias a alias
```

Here are some examples of aliases from a .cshrc file. Note that if the command contains spaces, you enclose the entire command in quotes. In these examples, both double and single quotes are used:

```
alias a alias
a h history
a c clear
a lf ls -F
a ll "ls -l | more"
a la ls -a
a s "source .cshrc"
a f 'find ~ -name core -print'
a copytotape "tar cvf /dev/rmt/0 *"
```

Setting History for the C Shell

To set history for the C shell, on a command line type **set history=<*n*>** and press Return. History is set to the number of lines you specify.

```
oak% set history=10
oak%
```

You can set the history temporarily for a shell window or set it "permanently" by entering the command as a line in your .cshrc file.

Using History for the C Shell

To display the history for the C shell, on a command line type **history** and press Return. The last <*n*> commands that you had set for the history are displayed.

```
oak% history
     26  pwd
     27  kermit
     28  cd Howto
     29  tar xvf /dev/rmt/0
     30  ls -l howto*
     31  cd
     32  cd Config/Art
     33  ls -l
     34  tar cvf /dev/rmt/0
     35  history
oak%
```

To repeat the previous command in a C shell, type **!!** and press Return. The previous command is executed again.

```
oak% history
     26  pwd
     27  kermit
     28  cd Howto
     29  tar xvf /dev/rmt/0
     30  ls -l howto*
     31  cd
     32  cd Config/Art
     33  ls -l
     34  tar xvf /dev/rmt/0
     35  history
oak% !!
```

```
history
    27  kermit
    28  cd Howto
    29  tar xvf /dev/rmt/0
    30  ls -l howto*
    31  cd
    32  cd Config/Art
    33  ls -l
    34  tar xvf /dev/rmt/0
    35  history
    36  history
oak%
```

To repeat the last word of the previous command in a C shell, type **!$** and press Return. The last word from the previous command is used as part of the command-line argument.

For example, you might list the complete path name of a file, and then use the path name as the argument to edit the file using vi, or to print it:

```
oak% ls -l /home/ignatz/quest
oak% lp !$ lp
/home/ignatz/quest
oak%
```

You can use the !$ command anywhere within the command line. In this example, the file /home/ignatz/quest is copied to the /tmp directory:

```
oak% ls -l /home/ignatz/quest
oak% cp !$ /tmp
cp /home/ignatz/quest /tmp
oak%
```

To repeat a numbered command in a C shell, type **!<*n*>** and press Return. The number in the shell prompt is <*n*>. The command is executed again.

```
oak% history
29  tar xvf /dev/rmt/0
30  ls -l howto*
31  cd
32  cd Config/Art
33  ls -l
34  tar xvf /dev/rmt/0
35  ls -l
36  cd
37  lp howto*
```

```
38  history
oak% !32
cd Config/Art
oak%
```

Setting the Backspace Key for the C Shell (stty erase)

If you want to change the erase key from Delete to Backspace, type **stty erase**, then press Control and Shift together, and then type **H** and press Return. The Backspace key is set as the erase key.

```
oak% stty erase ^H
oak%
```

Incorporating a New Command for the C Shell (rehash)

The C shell builds an internal table of commands named with the path variable. When you add a new command to a directory, the command is not part of the internal table, and the shell cannot execute it. To incorporate a new command into the search path internal table, type **rehash** and press Return. Any new commands are incorporated into your command search path.

```
oak% newcommand
newcommand: Command not found
oak% rehash
oak% newcommand
oak%
```

Editing C Shell History Commands

You can edit commands retrieved from the history list using the s/*<oldstring>*/*<newstring>*/ form to substitute in the command as retrieved. In this example, an incorrectly typed command from the history list is corrected:

```
oak% history
    31  cd
    32  ls
    33  cd /home/frame3.1
    34  ls
    35  cd ..
    36  tar cvf /dev/rmt/0 frame3.1
    37  lp questionnaire
    38  lpstat -t
    39  echo $PaTH
```

```
    40  history
oak% !39:s/a/A/
echo $PATH
.:/home/winsor:/usr/openwin/bin:/usr/deskset/bin:/home/
winsor/bin:/bin:/home/bin:/etc:/usr/etc:/usr/bin:/home/
frame3.1/bin
oak%
```

The Korn Shell

The Korn shell, developed by David Korn of AT&T Bell Laboratories, is a superset of the Bourne shell. That is, the Korn shell uses the same syntax as the Bourne shell, but it has more built-in functions that can be defined directly from the shell. The Korn shell provides a more sophisticated form of command editing than does the C shell. The Korn shell also provides a command history and aliases.

The Korn shell provides a complete command and programming language. The following sections provide a brief introduction to some of the most basic features of the Korn shell.

Reviewing Korn Shell Initialization Files

The Korn shell uses two initialization files in the user's home directory to set the user's environment: .profile and .<*ksh-env*>, which is a file with any name you choose that controls the user's environment. You might want to name the file .kshrc, because its function is similar to the C shell .cshrc file.

When the user logs in, the .profile file is read and then the .<*ksh-env*> file. The .<*ksh-env*> file lets you configure the Korn shell session to your needs. Many of the commands that you would include in the .<*ksh-env*> file can be executed only by the Korn shell and cannot be included in the .profile file.

You must set the ENV environment variable to point to the .<*ksh-env*> file. The syntax for setting environment variables in the Korn shell is the same as for the Bourne shell: <*VARIABLE*>=<*value*>;export <*VARIABLE*>. As in the Bourne shell, you must export the variable to make it available to the shell. This example sets the environment variable for a .kshrc file:

```
$ ENV=$HOME/.kshrc;export ENV
$
```

You set this environment variable in the .profile file; otherwise, the .kshrc file will not be found when the user logs in. The ENV variable has no default setting. Unless you set it, the feature is not used. The .<*ksh-env*> file is read each time a user starts the Korn shell from a command line.

Using Korn Shell Options

The Korn shell has a number of options that specify the user's environment and control execution of commands. To display the current option settings, type **set -o** and press Return. In this example, the default options for the Korn shell for Solaris 2.*x* system software are displayed:

```
$ set -o
Current option settings
allexport       off
bgnice          on
emacs           off
errexit         off
gmacs           off
ignoreeof       off
interactive     on
keyword         off
markdirs        off
monitor         on
noexec          off
noclobber       off
noglob          off
nolog           off
nounset         off
privileged      off
restricted      off
trackall        off
verbose         off
vi              off
viraw           off
xtrace          off
$
```

The default options are described in Table 8.2.

Table 8.2 Korn Shell Options

Option	Default	Description
allexport	off	Automatically exports variables when defined.
bgnice	on	Executes all background jobs at a lower priority.
emacs	off	Sets emacs/gmacs as the in-line editor.

Table 8.2 Korn Shell Options (Continued)

Option	Default	Description
errexit	off	If a command returns a value of False, the shell executes the ERR trap (if set), and immediately exits.
gmacs	off	Sets gmacs as the in-line editor.
ignoreeof	off	When the interactive option is also set, the shell does not exit at End-of-file. Type **exit** to quit the shell.
interactive	on	The shell automatically turns the interactive option on so that shell prompts are displayed.
keyword	off	The shell puts each word with the syntax of a variable assignment in the variable assignment list.
markdirs	off	Displays a / following the names of all directories resulting from path name expansion.
monitor	on	Enables job control.
noclobber	off	Does not overwrite an existing file when the redirect operator > is used.
noexec	off	Reads commands but does not execute them. You can use this option for debugging shell scripts for syntax errors.
noglob	off	Disables file name expansion.
nolog	off	Does not store function definitions in the history file.
nounset	off	Displays an error message when the shell tries to expand a variable that is not set.
privileged	off	When this option is off, the real UID and GID are used. When this option is on, the UID and GID are set to the values that were in effect when you started the shell.
restricted	off	Sets a restricted shell.
trackall	off	Makes command tracked aliases when they are first encountered.
verbose	off	Displays the input as it is read.
vi	off	Sets vi as the in-line editor.
viraw	off	Specifies character-at-a-time input from vi.
xtrace	off	Displays commands and arguments as they are executed.

Customarily, these options are set in the .*<ksh-env>* file.

To enable an option, type **set -o *<option-name>*** and press Return. To disable an option, type **set +o *<option-name>*** and press Return.

For example, entering this line in the user's .*<ksh-env>* file will set the in-line editor to vi:

```
set -o vi
```

This turns off vi as the in-line editor:

```
set +o vi
```

You can also set these options from a command line using the same syntax.

Creating Korn Shell Aliases

The syntax for creating aliases for the Korn shell is alias *<name>*=*<value>*. This creates an alias for the alias command:

```
$ alias a=alias
$
```

This example aliases the history command to the letter *h*:

```
$ a h=history
$
```

The Korn shell comes with a default set of predefined aliases. To display the list, type **alias** and press Return.

```
$ alias
autoload=typeset -fu
false=let 0
functions=typeset -f
hash=alias -t -
history=fc -l
integer=typeset -i
nohup=nohup
r=fc -e -
stop=kill -STOP
suspend=kill -STOP $$
true=:
type=whence -v
$
```

The default aliases are described in Table 8.3.

Table 8.3 Korn Shell Preset Aliases

Alias	Value	Definition
autoload	typeset -fu	Define an autoloading function.
false	let -0	Return a nonzero status. Often used to generate infinite until loops.
functions	typeset -f	Display list of functions.
hash	alias -t -	Display list of tracked aliases.
history	fc -l	List commands from the history file.
integer	typeset -i	Declare integer variable.
nohup	nohup	Keep jobs running even if you log out.
r	fc -e -	Execute the previous command again.
stop	kill -STOP	Suspend job.
suspend	kill -STOP $$	Suspend job.
true	:	Return a zero exit status.
type	whence -v	Display information about commands.

Editing Commands with the Korn Shell In-Line Editor

You can edit the current command before you execute it using the Korn shell in-line editor. You can choose one of three in-line editors: emacs, gmacs, or vi. The in-line editor is specified using the set -o <*editor*> option, or by setting either the EDITOR or VISUAL environment variable. This section describes how to use the vi in-line editor to edit commands.

The vi in-line editor is a modified subset of the vi program; it lacks some of the features of vi. The vi in-line editor is automatically in insert mode. You can type commands and execute them by pressing Return without using the vi in-line editor. If you want to edit a command, press Escape to enter command mode. You can move along the command line using the standard cursor movement commands, and use standard vi editing commands to edit the contents of the line. When the command is edited, press Return to execute it, or press Escape to return to input mode.

If you want to edit the command line in a vi file, type **v** to open a vi file containing the contents of the command line. When you leave vi, the command is executed. See Chapter 2 for a quick-reference table of common vi commands.

Setting History for the Korn Shell

The Korn shell stores history commands in a file specified by the HISTFILE variable. If the variable is not set, the files are stored in $HOME/.sh_history. You can specify the number of commands stored using the HISTSIZE variable. If the variable is not set, the most recent 128 commands are saved. When the history list contains the maximum number of commands, as new commands are entered, the oldest commands become unavailable.

To set a different history size, type **HISTSIZE=<*n*>;export HISTSIZE** and press Return. History is set to the number of lines you specify.

In this example, the history size is set to 200:

```
$ HISTSIZE=200;export HISTSIZE
$
```

You can set the history temporarily for a shell window or set it "permanently" by entering the command as a line in the user's .profile or .<*ksh-env*> file.

Displaying Korn Shell History Commands

You can use two commands to show the commands from the history list: fc and history. Because history is aliased to fc -l as one of the default aliases, you can use the commands interchangeably.

To display the last 16 commands in the history list, type **history** and press Return. The last 16 commands in the history list are displayed:

```
$ history
    16  pwd
    17  ps -el
    18  ps -el | grep openwin
    19  cd
    20  more questionnaire
    21  su
    22  lp /etc/passwd
    23  lpstat -t
    24  man ksh
    25  du
    26  maker &
    27  tip -2400 5551212
    28  alias h=history
    29  find / -name ksh -print
    30  df -k
    31  history
$
```

An alternative way to display the same information is to type **fc -l** and press Return.

The history and fc commands take additional arguments that let you specify a range, display the last <*n*> number of commands, and display the commands in reverse order. See the ksh(1) manual page for more information.

Using Korn Shell History Commands

To use a command from the history list, type **r <*n*>** to reuse a command by number. This example would reuse command 27:

```
$ r 27
tip -2400 5551212
(Connection messages are displayed)
```

To repeat the last command in the history list, type **r** and press Return.

Editing Korn Shell History Commands

You can display individual history commands and edit them using the fc command, with this syntax:

```
fc [-e <editor>] [-r] [<range>]
```

or

```
fc -e - [<old>=<new>] [command]
```

You use the -e option to specify an editor. If no editor is specified, the FCEDIT environment variable value is used. If no value is set, the default editor is /bin/ed. The -r option reverses the order of the commands, displaying the most recent commands at the top of the list. If no range is given, the last command is edited.

For example, to use vi to edit the last command in a history list, type **fc -e vi** and press Return. A vi file is created containing the last entry from the history list. When you edit the command and save the changes, the command is executed.

CHAPTER

Administering Systems

Displaying System-Specific Information

Configuring Additional Swap Space (mkfile, swap)

Creating a Local Mail Alias (/etc/mail/aliases)

HIS CHAPTER DESCRIBES COMMANDS THAT ARE SPECIFIC TO INDIVIDUAL systems, and shows how to configure additional swap space and how to create a local mail alias.

Displaying System-Specific Information

Use the commands in this section to find system-specific information such as the host ID number, hardware type, processor type, OS release level, system configuration, how long the system has been up, and the system date and time. The following sections also describe how to set the system date and time and change the time zone for a system.

Determining the Host ID Number (sysdef -h)

New with SVR4.

To find a system's host ID number, type **sysdef -h** and press Return. The host ID for the system is displayed. This command replaces the SunOS 4.*x* hostid command.

```
oak% sysdef -h
*
* Hostid
*
  554095cc
oak%
```

Determining the Hardware Type (uname -m)

To find the hardware type of a system, type **uname -m** and press Return. The hardware type (architecture) for the system is displayed. The SunOS 4.*x* arch command, which provided similar information, is not available in SunOS 5.*x*.

```
oak% uname -m
sun4c
oak%
```

Determining the Processor Type (uname -p)

New with SVR4.

To find the processor type for a system, type **uname -p** and press Return. The processor type for the system is displayed. This command replaces the SunOS 4.*x* mach command.

```
oak% uname -p
sparc
oak%
```

Determining the OS Release (uname -r)

To find the OS release level for a system, type **uname -r** and press Return. The OS (kernel) release is displayed.

```
oak% uname -r
5.0
oak%
```

Displaying System Configuration Information (prtconf)

New with SVR4.

To display the configuration information for a system, type **prtconf** and press Return. The system configuration information is displayed.

```
oak% prtconf
System Configuration: Sun Microsystems sun4c
Memory size: 16 Megabytes
System Peripherals (Software Nodes):

Sun 4/65, unit #0
        options, unit #0
        zs, unit #0
        zs, unit #1
        fd, unit #0 (No driver.)
        audio, unit #0 (No driver.)
        sbus, unit #0
                dma, unit #0
                esp, unit #0
                        scsibus, unit #0
                                sd, unit #0
                                sd, unit #1
                le, unit #0
                cgsix, unit #0
        auxiliary-io, unit #0 (No driver.)
(More information not shown in this example)
oak%
```

An alternative way to display system configuration information and show the state of tunable parameters is to type **sysdef** and press Return. System configuration information is displayed.

```
oak% sysdef
*
* Hostid
*
```

```
530080d2
*
* sun4c Configuration
*
*
* Devices
*
options, unit #-1
zs, unit #0
zs, unit #1
fd, unit #-1
audio, unit #-1
sbus, unit #0
 dma, unit #0
 esp, unit #0
 scsibus, unit #0
 sd, unit #0
 sd, unit #1
 le, unit #0
 cgsix, unit #0
auxiliary-io, unit #-1
interrupt-enable, unit #-1
memory-error, unit #-1
counter-timer, unit #-1
eeprom, unit #-1
pseudo, unit #0
 lo, unit #0
 tidg, unit #0
 tivc, unit #0
(More information not shown in this example)
oak%
```

Determining How Long a System Has Been Up (uptime)

To find out how long a system has been up, type **uptime** and press Return. The time, number of users, and load average are displayed for the local system.

```
oak% uptime
11:18am  up 5 day(s), 16:12,  2 users,  load average: 16.46, 15. 92, 15.55
oak%
```

New with SVR4.

To find out when a system was booted, type **who -b** and press Return. The month, day, and time of the last boot are displayed.

```
oak% who -b
 . system boot Jul 14 08:49
oak%
```

Determining the System Date and Time (date)

To display the system date and time, type **date** and press Return. The system date and time are displayed.

```
oak% date
Tue Jul 14 19:40:47 PST 1992
oak%
```

Setting the System Date and Time (date)

Follow these steps to reset the system date and time:

1. Become superuser.
2. Type **date** ***<mmddhhmmyy>*** and press Return, where *mm* is the month, *dd* is the day, *hh* is the hour, *mm* is the minute, and *yy* is the year. The system date and time are reset using the month, day, hour, minute, and year that you specify.

```
# su
Password:
# date
Tue Jul 14 16:07:01 PST 1992
# date 07141552
Tue Jul 14 15:52:00 PST 1992
#
```

Changing the System Time Zone (/etc/TIMEZONE)

New with SVR4.

The time zone is set in the /etc/TIMEZONE file. The available U.S. time zone variables are shown below. Look in the /usr/share/lib/zoneinfo directory for a complete list of time zone variables.

US/Arizona

US/Central

US/East-Indiana

US/Hawaii

US/Mountain

US/Pacific

US/Pacific-New

US/Yukon

Follow these steps to change the system time zone:

1. Become superuser.
2. Edit the /etc/TIMEZONE file, change the TZ=<*time-zone*> variable, and save the changes. The time zone is reset.
3. Reboot the system.

Here is an example of the /etc/TIMEZONE file for a system set to Pacific Standard/Pacific Daylight Time:

```
oak% more /etc/TIMEZONE
#ident  "@(#)TIMEZONE   1.3     89/12/12 SMI"   /* SVr4.0
1.1   */
#       Set timezone environment to default for the machine
TZ=US/Pacific;export TZ
```

Here is an example of how to change the time zone from Pacific to Eastern:

```
oak% su
Password:
# vi /etc/TIMEZONE
TZ=US/East-Indiana;export TZ
:w!
# reboot
oak% date
Tue Jul 14 14:24:52 EST 1992
oak%
```

NOTE. *You may need to make your text editor do a confirmed write of the file. For example, in vi use the command :w! to write the changes even if the permissions normally would not allow it.*

Configuring Additional Swap Space (mkfile, swap)

New with SVR4.

To create and add additional swap space without reformatting a disk, first you create a swap file using the mkfile command. You can specify the size of the swap file in kilobytes (the default) or in blocks or megabytes by using the b and m suffixes, respectively. The swap file can either be on a local disk or be NFS-mounted. Then you add the swap space using the swap command.

To list available swap files, type **swap -l** and press Return. A list of available swap files is displayed. The swap command replaces the SunOS 4.*x* swapon command.

```
drusilla% swap -l
swapfile             dev   swaplo blocks   free
swapfs                -         0  94520  93512
/dev/dsk/c0t3d0s1   32,25       8  65512  45048
drusilla%
```

Follow these steps to create a swap file:

1. Become superuser. You can create a swap file without root permissions, but it is a good idea to have root be the owner of the swap file so that other processes cannot access it.
2. Type **mkfile <*nnn*>[k|b|m] <*filename*>** and press Return. The letter following the number you specify indicates kilobytes, blocks, or megabytes. The swap file of the size and file name you specify is created. In this example, you create a 1Mb swap file named SWAP:

```
oak% su
Password:
# mkfile 1m /files1/SWAP
#
```

Follow these steps to add the swap file:

1. Become superuser.
2. Type **swap -a <*pathname*>** and press Return. You must use the absolute path name to specify the swap file. The swap file is added and available.
3. Type **swap -l** to verify that the swap file is added.

```
# swap -a /files1/SWAP
# swap -l
swapfile             dev   swaplo blocks   free
swapfs                -         0  94520  93512

/dev/dsk/c0t3d0s1   32,25       8  65512  45048

/files1/SWAP  -  8   2040   2040
#
```

Follow these steps to remove a specified swap file from use:

1. Become superuser.
2. Type **swap -d <*pathname*>** and press Return. When the swap file is no longer in use, it is removed from the list so that it is no longer available for swapping. The file itself is not deleted.

```
oak% su
Password:
# swap -d /files1/SWAP
# swap -l
swapfile             dev  swaplo
blocks   free
swapfs                -        0
94520  93512

/dev/dsk/c0t3d0s1   32,25      8
65512  45048
# ls -l /files1/SWAP
-rw-------   1 root   root     1048576 Jan 31 13:56 SWAP
#
```

When you create additional swap space, if you want the swap space to remain available when the system is rebooted, you must add the entry to the /etc/vfstab file. Follow these steps to add a swap file entry to the /etc/vfstab file:

1. Become superuser.
2. Edit the /etc/vfstab file and add this line: **<*pathname*> - - swap - no -**. Be sure the line follows the entry for the partition where the swap file was created.

The next time the system is rebooted, the swap file is added automatically.

The following example adds the swap file /files1/SWAP to the /etc/vfstab file after the entry that mounts the file system /files1:

```
/files1/SWAP - - swap - no -
```

Creating a Local Mail Alias (/etc/mail/aliases)

In a network environment, you probably have a central way to administer mail aliases. In addition, users frequently want to set up local aliases for use from their systems. Follow these steps to create mail aliases on a local system:

1. Become superuser.

2. Edit the /etc/mail/aliases file.
3. At the end of the file, under the Local Aliases category, type ***<alias-name>:<username1>,<username2>,...*** and press Return after the last *<username>*.
4. Save the changes.

For example, if you want to create an alias called friends, edit the /etc/mail/aliases file and add an entry like this:

```
friends:dexter@elm,ogden@willow,mary@maple
```

CHAPTER

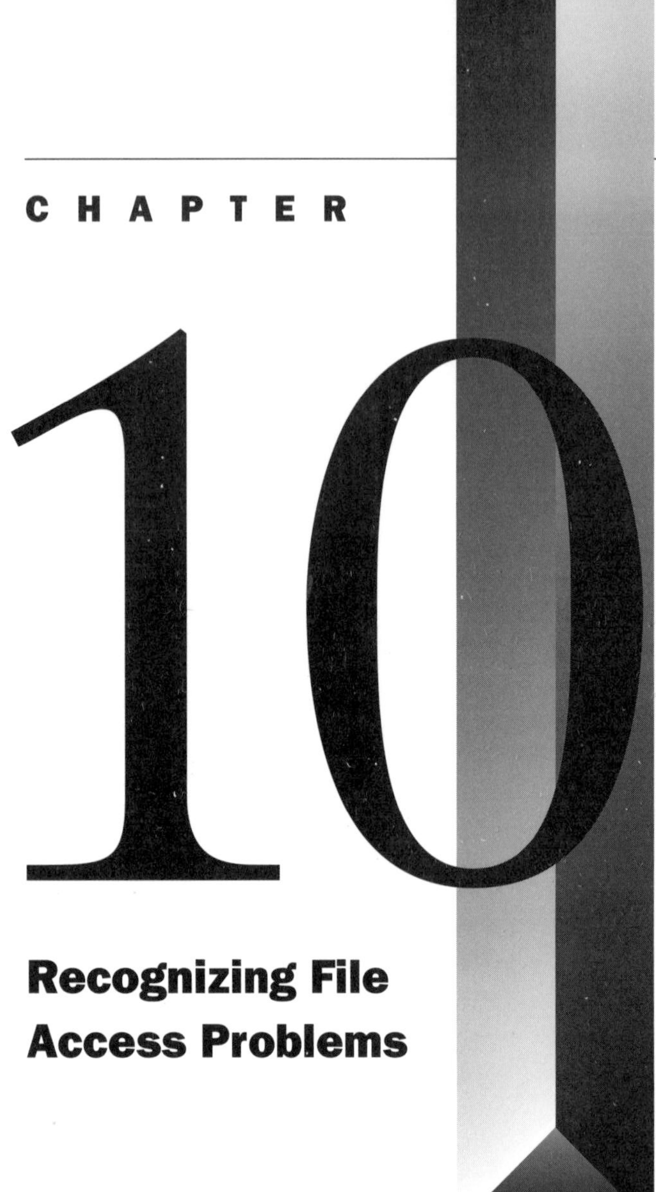

Recognizing File Access Problems

Recognizing Problems with Search Paths

Recognizing Problems with Permissions and Ownership

THIS CHAPTER DESCRIBES HOW TO RECOGNIZE PROBLEMS WITH SEARCH paths, permissions, and ownership.

Users frequently experience problems—and call on a system administrator for help—because they cannot access a program, a file, or a directory that they used to be able to access. Whenever you encounter such a problem, investigate one of two areas:

- The user's search path may have been changed, or the directories in the search path may not be in the proper order.
- The file or directory may not have the proper permissions or ownership.

This chapter briefly describes how to recognize problems in each of these areas and suggests possible solutions.

Recognizing Problems with Search Paths

If a user types a command that is not in the search path, the message "Command not found" is displayed. The command may not be found because the command is not available on the system or the command directory is not in the search path.

If the wrong version of the command is found, a directory with a command of the same name is in the search path. In this case, the proper directory may be later in the search path or may not be present at all.

To diagnose and troubleshoot problems with search paths, follow this procedure:

1. Display the current search path.
2. Edit the file where the user's path is set (.cshrc or .login for the C shell; .profile for the Bourne and Korn shells). Add the directory, or rearrange the order of the path.

NOTE. *For the C shell, always check both the .cshrc and .login files to make sure the path information is set all in one place. Duplicate entries can make the search path hard to troubleshoot and make search times less efficient for the user.*

3. Source the file to activate the changes.
4. Verify that the command is found in the right place.
5. Execute the command.

The tasks you use to follow this procedure are described below.

Displaying the Current Search Path

To display the current search path, type **echo $PATH** and press Return. The current search path is displayed.

```
cinderella% echo $PATH
/sbin:/usr/sbin:/usr/bin:/etc
cinderella%
```

Setting the Path for Bourne and Korn Shells

The path for the Bourne and Korn shells is specified in the user's $HOME/.profile file in this way:

```
PATH=/usr/bin:/$HOME/bin:.;export PATH
```

The dot (.) at the beginning of the path specifies that the current directory is always searched first.

Sourcing Bourne and Korn Shell Dot Files

When you have changed information in the .profile file, you must source the file to make the new information available to the shell. To source the .profile file, type **. .profile** and press Return.

Setting the Path for the C Shell

The path for the C shell is specified in the user's $HOME/.cshrc or .login file (with the set path environment variable) in this way:

```
set path =  (/usr/bin $home/bin .)
```

The dot (.) at the beginning of the path specifies that the current directory is always searched first.

Sourcing C Shell Dot Files

When you have changed information in the .cshrc or .login file, you must source the file to make the new information available to the shell. To source the .cshrc file, type **source .cshrc** and press Return. To source the .login file, type **source .login** and press Return.

Verifying the Search Path

When you have changed a user's path, use the which command to verify that the shell is finding the proper command. The which command looks in the

.cshrc file for information. The which command may give misleading results if you execute it from the Bourne or Korn shell and the user has a .cshrc file that contains aliases for the which command. To ensure accurate results, use the which command in a C shell. Alternatively, you can use the whence command instead of the which command from the Korn shell.

To verify the search path, type **which *<command-name>*** and press Return. If the command is found in the path, the path and the name of the command are displayed.

This example shows that the OpenWindows executable is not in any of the directories in the search path:

```
oak% which openwin
no openwin in . /home/ignatz /sbin /usr/sbin /usr/bin /etc
/home/ignatz/bin /bin /home/bin /usr/etc
oak%
```

This example shows that the executable for OpenWindows is found among the directories in the search path:

```
oak% which openwin
/usr/openwin
oak%
```

If you cannot find a command, look at the manual page. For example, if you cannot find the lpsched command (the lp printer daemon), the lpsched(1M) manual page tells you the path is /usr/lib/lp/lpsched.

Executing a Command

To execute a command, type ***<command-name>*** and press Return. The command is executed if it is in the search path. You can always execute a command that is not in the search path by typing the full path name for the command.

Recognizing Problems with Permissions and Ownership

When users cannot access files or directories that they used to be able to access, the most likely problem is that permissions or ownership on the files or directories has changed.

Frequently, file and directory ownerships change because someone edited the files as root. When you create home directories for new users, be especially careful to make the user the owner of the dot (.) file in the home directory. When users do not own the dot (.) files, they cannot create files in their own home directory.

Another way access problems can arise is when the group ownership changes or when a group that a user is a member of is deleted from the /etc/groups database.

Changing File Ownership

NOTE. *You must own a file or directory (or have root permission) to be able to change its ownership.*

Follow these steps to change file ownership:

1. Type **ls -l <*filename*>** and press Return. The owner of the file is displayed in the third column.
2. Become superuser.
3. Type **chown <*new-owner*> <*filename*>** and press Return. Ownership is assigned to the new owner you specify.

```
oak% ls -l quest
-rw-r--r--   1 fred    staff    6023 Aug  5 12:06 quest
oak% su
Password:
# chown ignatz quest
# ls -l quest
-rw-r--r--   1 ignatz   staff    6023 Aug  5 12:06 quest
#
```

Changing File Permissions

You use the chmod command to change file permissions. You can change permissions in two ways. If you use letters, use this syntax:

```
chmod [who]<operator>[permission(s)] <filename>
```

For who, you can specify u, g, or o (for user, group, or other). You can specify a to change all operators. If you do not specify who permissions are for, permissions are changed for all three groups. The operator is either + to add permission or – to take away permission. The permissions are r, w, or x, for read, write, or execute. See the chmod(1) manual page for more permissions.

For example, to grant read, write, and execute permissions to everyone, type **chmod +wrx <*filename*>** and press Return:

```
oak% chmod +wrx dog
oak% ls -l dog
-rwxrwxrwx  1    janice    staff    54  Jul 7  11:33  dog
oak%
```

To grant read and execute permissions to everyone, type **chmod +rx *<filename>*** and press Return:

```
oak% chmod +rx dog
oak% ls -l dog
-r-xr-xr-x  1    janice    staff    54  Jul 7  11:34  dog
oak%
```

Another way to change the permissions to read and execute only would be to deny write permission to everyone. Type **chmod –w *<filename>*** and press Return:

```
oak% chmod -w dog
oak% ls -l dog
-r-xr-xr-x  1    janice    staff    54  Jul 7  11:35  dog
oak%
```

To change ownership for a specific group, type the letter for the group followed by the operator and the permission. In the following example, read, write, and execute permissions have been granted for the owner to the file dog:

```
oak% chmod u+wrx dog
oak% ls -l dog
-rwxr-xr-x  1    janice    staff    54  Jul 7  11:36  dog
oak%
```

To deny execute permissions to group and other, type **chmod go-x *<filename>*** and press Return.

```
oak% chmod go-x dog
oak% ls -l dog
-rwxr--r--  1    janice    staff    54  Jul 7  11:37  dog
oak%
```

You can also use a numeric argument with the chmod command that describes the user class and permission to change as a sequence of bits. Table 10.1 shows the octal values for setting file permissions. You use these numbers in sets of three to set permissions for owner, group, and other. For example, the value 644 sets read/write permissions for owner, and read-only permissions for group and other.

1. Type **ls -l *<filename>*** and press Return. The long listing shows the current permissions for the file.
2. Type **chmod *<nnn>* *<filename>*** and press Return. Permissions are changed using the numbers you specify.

Table 10.1 Octal Values for File Permissions

Value	Description
0	No permissions
1	Execute-only
2	Write-only
3	Write, execute
4	Read-only
5	Read, execute
6	Read, write
7	Read, write, execute

NOTE. *You can change permissions on groups of files or on all files in a directory using metacharacters such as (* ?) in place of file names or in combination with them.*

This example changes the permissions of a file from 666 (read/write, read/write, read/write) to 644 (read/write, read-only, read-only):

```
oak% ls -l quest
-rw-rw-rw-   1 ignatz   staff    6023 Aug  5 12:06 quest
oak% chmod 644 quest
oak% ls -l quest
-rw-r--r--   1 ignatz   staff    6023 Aug  5 12:06 quest
oak%
```

Changing File Group Ownership

If a file has an incorrect group owner, users of the group will not be able to make changes to the file. To change file group ownership, you must either be a member of the group, own the file, or change it as root.

To change the group ID for a file, type **chgrp *<gid>* *<filename>*** and press Return. The group ID for the file you specify is changed. With Solaris 2.*x,* the ls -l command shows the owner and the group for the file. You can display only the group owner using the ls -lg command.

```
$ ls -lg junk
-rw-r--r-- 1 other 0 Oct 31 14:49 junk
$ chgrp 10 junk
```

```
$ ls -lg junk
-rw-r--r-- 1 staff Ø Oct 31 14:49 junk
$
```

The group ID is found in the Group database or the local /etc/group file. You can use the Administration Tool's Database Manager to look at and modify the members of groups.

Major Differences: SunOS 4.*x* versus SunOS 5.*x* Operating Systems

This appendix summarizes the major differences between the SunOS 4.*x* and SunOS 5.*x* operating systems in these areas:

- Installation and configuration
- Startup and shutdown
- File systems
- Printers, terminals, and modems
- Naming services
- TCP/IP
- UUCP
- Document tool differences
- Security

The last section in this appendix contains an alphabetical list of SunOS 4.*x* commands and shows the equivalent SunOS 5.*x* command, if one is available.

Installation and Configuration

Solaris 2.*x* software is distributed on compact disc (CD-ROM) only. You must have access to a CD drive before you can install the software. However, because you can set up a system to act as a remote server when installing the software on systems without local CD drives, you need access to only one CD drive on the network.

Solaris 2.*x* software is bundled into modules called packages. You can select packages that are relevant to your system and control the amount of space each installation requires. Sometimes packages are grouped into clusters so that you can install a set of packages for typical users, developers, or system administrators without selecting each package separately.

SunOS 5.*x* software includes architecture-specific kernels, rather than the generic kernel configuration provided in earlier SunOS software releases. You will find the installed kernel in /kernel/unix instead of /vmunix.

You no longer need to manually configure and build new kernels. When you install new device drivers and boot the system using the boot -r command, the kernel dynamically reconfigures itself.

The Administration Tool has a Host Manager application that you can use to add information about a new workstation to your network databases.

You can then configure the system so the workstation boots and installs from a remote-installation CD.

When you boot the installation CD, a utility called sysidtool checks network databases for system configuration information. The sysidtool utility uses the information it finds and prompts you to enter other required information.

What Is Installed on a SunOS 5.*x* System

The /var/sadm/install/contents file lists every file that installation puts onto the system. To find out if a specific file was installed, look through /var/sadm/install/contents to see if the file is listed. The file contains the complete path, the ownership and protection of the file, and the package from which the file was installed. For example, to display information about the printf file, type **# grep printf /var/sadm/install/contents**. Your screen will look like this:

```
# grep printf /var/sadm/install/contents
/usr/bin/printf f none 0555 bin 3716 31738 699928138 SUNWloc
#
```

NOTE. *When you complete system installation, you may need to boot -r to reconfigure the device names and modules so that they work with Solaris 2.*x.

Start-Up and Shutdown

SunOS 5.*x* system software has eight initialization states (init states or run levels). The default init state is defined in the /etc/inittab file. See Chapter 1 for a description of the initialization states.

The shutdown command works differently than in the SunOS 4.*x* version. The SunOS 4.*x* fastboot and fasthalt commands are available only on SunOS 5.*x* systems with BSD source compatibility package installed.

The halt and reboot commands (not found in AT&T SVR4 systems) have shutdown and init equivalents. We recommend that you use them because halt and reboot do not run the rc scripts properly.

The init command uses a different script for each run level instead of grouping all of the run levels together in the /etc/rc, /etc/rc.boot, and /etc/rc.local files. The files, named by run level, are located in the /sbin directory.

Here is a list of the default run control scripts in the /sbin directory:

```
drusilla% ls -l /sbin/rc*
-rwxr--r--   3 root    sys         2315 Jan  1  1970 /sbin/rc0
-rwxr--r--   1 root    sys         1018 Jan  1  1970 /sbin/rc1
-rwxr--r--   1 root    sys         1374 Jan  1  1970 /sbin/rc2
-rwxr--r--   1 root    sys          713 Jan  1  1970 /sbin/rc3
-rwxr--r--   3 root    sys         2315 Jan  1  1970 /sbin/rc5
-rwxr--r--   3 root    sys         2315 Jan  1  1970 /sbin/rc6
drusilla%
```

Run control files are located in the /etc/init.d directory. These files are linked to corresponding run control files in the /etc/rc/etc and /etc/rc*.d directories. The files in the /etc directory define the sequence in which the scripts are performed within each run level. For example, /etc/rc2.d contains files used to start and stop processes for run level 2.

```
cinderella% ls /etc/rc2.d
K20lp          K65nfs.client  S20sysetup     S71sysid.sys   S89bdconfig
K30fumounts    K70nis         S21perf        S72inetsvc     S91gsconfig
K40rumounts    S01MOUNTFSYS   S30sysid.net   S73nfs.client
K50rfs         S02PRESERVE    S69inet        S75cron
K55syslog      S05RMTMPFILES  S70uucp        S80lp
K60nfs.server  S10disks       S71rpc         S88sendmail
cinderella%
```

The scripts are always run in ASCII sort order. The names of the scripts are names of the forms: [K,S][0–9][A–Z][0–99]. Files beginning with *K* are run to terminate (kill) some system process. Files beginning with S are run to start up a system process. The actions of each run control level script are summarized in the following sections.

The rc0 Script

- Stops system services and daemons
- Terminates all running processes
- Unmounts all file systems

The rc1 Script

- Runs the /etc/rc1.d scripts
- Stops system services and daemons
- Terminates all running processes
- Unmounts all file systems
- Brings the system up in single-user mode

```
drusilla% ls /etc/rc1.d
K00ANNOUNCE   K60rumounts    K66nis    K80nfs.client
K50fumounts   K64rfs         K67rpc    S01MOUNTFSYS
K55syslog     K65nfs.server  K70cron
drusilla%
```

The rc2 Script

- Sets the TIMEZONE variable
- Runs the /etc/rc2.d scripts
- Mounts all file systems
- Saves editing files in /usr/preserve
- Removes any files in the /tmp directory
- Creates device entries in /dev for new disks (only if boot -r is run)
- Updates device.tab device table
- Prints system configuration (The default is not to save core.)
- Configures system accounting
- Configures default router
- Sets NIS domain
- Sets ifconfig netmask
- Starts inetd
- Starts named, if appropriate
- Starts rpcbind
- Starts Kerberos client-side daemon, kerbd
- Starts NIS daemons (ypbind) and NIS+ daemons (rpcnisd), depending on whether the system is configured for NIS or NIS+, and as a client or a server
- Starts keyserv
- Starts statd, lockd
- Mounts all NFS entries
- Starts automount
- Starts cron
- Starts the LP daemons

- Starts the sendmail daemon

```
cinderella% ls /etc/rc2.d
K201p          K60nfs.server  S05RMTMPFILES  S69inet        S73nfs.client
K30fumounts    K65nfs.client  S10disks       S70uucp        S75cron
K40rumounts    K70nis         S20sysetup     S71rpc         S801p
K50rfs         S01MOUNTFSYS   S21perf        S71sysid.sys   S88sendmail
K55syslog      S02PRESERVE    S30sysid.net   S72inetsvc     S89bdconfig
                                                            S91gsconfig
cinderella%
```

The rc3 Script

- Runs the /etc/rc3.d scripts
- Starts syslogd
- Cleans up sharetab
- Starts nfsds
- Starts mountd
- If boot server, starts rarpd and rpc.bootparamd
- Starts nis_cachemanager
- Starts rpc.nisd
- Starts RFS services, if configured

The rc5 Script

- Runs the /etc/rc0.d scripts
- Kills the printer daemons
- Unmounts local file systems
- Kills the syslog daemon
- Unmounts remote file systems
- Stops RFS services
- Stops NFS services
- Stops NIS services
- Stops rpc services
- Stops cron services

- Stops NFS client services
- Kills all active processes
- Initiates an interactive boot (boot -a)

```
drusilla% ls /etc/rcØ.d
KØØANNOUNCE    K55syslog      K66nfs.server  K7Øcron
K2Ø1p          K6Ørumounts    K67nis         K75nfs.client
K5Øfumounts    K65rfs         K68rpc
drusilla%
```

The rc6 Script

- Executes /etc/rc0.d/K*
- Kills all active processes
- Unmounts the file systems
- Executes the initdefault entries in /etc/inittab

File Systems

The following sections describe changes to the file systems.

NFS and RFS

Solaris 2.*x* software includes a common set of commands and files to administer both Network File System (NFS) and Remote File Sharing (RFS) resources. This set of commands is called Distributed File System (DFS) administration. The common DFS commands replace the separate NFS and RFS commands required in SunOS 4.*x* systems, and simplify NFS and RFS resource sharing because it is necessary to remember only one set of commands. See Chapter 4 for more information about file system commands.

Directory Changes

The directory structure is changed. The following sections provide an overview of file and directory information. If you cannot locate a familiar file or directory, it may not be available or its contents may be relocated.

Addition of the /opt Directory

The /opt directory contains optional add-on application software packages. These packages were installed in /usr on SunOS 4.*x* systems. Keeping them in /opt leaves the /usr directory stable as packages are installed and removed.

Addition of the /proc Directory

The /proc directory contains a numerical list of processes. Information in the /proc directory is used by commands like ps. Debuggers and other development tools can also access the address space of the processes using file system calls.

Addition of the /devices directory

The /devices directory contains character and block special device files. Here is an example of the contents of the /devices directory:

```
oak% ls -l /devices
total 12
crw-rw-rw-   1 root    sys      28,128 Aug  3 15:10 audio@1,f7201000:audioctl,0

crw-------   1 root    sys      68, 11 Aug  3 13:56 eeprom@1,f2000000:eeprom
brw-rw-rw-   1 root    sys      36,  0 Aug  3 13:56 fd@1,f7200000:a
crw-rw-rw-   1 root    sys      36,  0 Aug  3 13:56 fd@1,f7200000:a,raw
brw-rw-rw-   1 root    sys      36,  1 Aug  3 13:56 fd@1,f7200000:b
crw-rw-rw-   1 root    sys      36,  1 Aug  3 13:56 fd@1,f7200000:b,raw
brw-rw-rw-   1 root    sys      36,  2 Aug  3 13:56 fd@1,f7200000:c
crw-rw-rw-   1 root    sys      36,  2 Aug  3 13:56 fd@1,f7200000:c,raw
drwxrwxrwx   2 root    sys        4608 Aug  3 15:10 pseudo
drwxrwxrwx   3 root    sys         512 Aug  3 13:56 sbus@1,f8000000
crw-rw-rw-   1 root    sys      29,  0 Aug  3 13:56 zs@1,f1000000:a
crw-rw-rw-   1 root    sys      29,131072 Aug  3 13:56 zs@1,f1000000:a,cu
crw-rw-rw-   1 root    sys      29,  1 Aug  3 13:56 zs@1,f1000000:b
crw-rw-rw-   1 root    sys      29,131073 Aug  3 13:56 zs@1,f1000000:b,cu
oak%
```

Addition of the /kernel Directory

The /kernel directory contains the UNIX kernel and kernel-level object modules. Table A.1 describes the subdirectories that have been added to the /kernel directory.

Table A.1 Contents of the /kernel Directory

Directory	Description
/kernel/*<modules>*	Contains loadable kernel modules
/kernel/unix	Contains the UNIX kernel

Changes in the /dev Directory

The /dev directory is changed from a flat directory to a hierarchical one. Table A.2 shows the added subdirectories.

Table A.2 **Additions to the /dev Directory**

Directory	Description
/dev/dsk	Block disk devices
/dev/pts	Pseudo terminal (pty) slave devices
/dev/rdsk	Raw disk devices
/dev/rmt	Raw tape devices
/dev/sad	Entry points for the STREAMS Administrative Driver
/dev/term	Terminal devices

Changes in the /etc Directory

The /etc directory contains system-specific configuration information. Several files and subdirectories are added, removed, or changed from the SunOS 4.*x* /etc directory.

- File system–specific commands, such as mount_rfs, are moved to the /usr/lib/fs directory.
- The /etc/fstab file is replaced with /etc/vfstab.
- Initialization scripts, such as rc, rc.boot, rc.local, and rc.single, are not available in the SunOS 5.*x* release.
- Mail commands that used to be in the /etc directory are moved into the new /etc/mail directory.

Table A.3 describes the subdirectories that have been added to the /etc directory.

Changes in the /sbin Directory

The /sbin directory contains the rc* scripts used to alter system run levels and the bcheckrc script used to initialize the system prior to mounting file systems.

Changes in the /sys Directory

The /sys directory has been retired. The files used to build the kernel that were stored in this directory are no longer needed because of the dynamic kernel.

Changes in the /usr Directory

The /usr directory contains sharable files and executables provided by the system. Table A.4 shows the added subdirectories.

Table A.3 **Additions to the /etc Directory**

Directory	Description
/etc/default	Default system configuration
/etc/inet	Internet services configuration
/etc/lp	LP system configuration
/etc/mail	Mail files (aliases, sendmail, *.rc files)
/etc/opt	Installed optional software
/etc/rcn.d	Run-state transition operations
/etc/saf	Service Access Facility (SAF) configuration

Table A.4 **Additions to the /usr Directory**

Directory	Description
/usr/ccs	Compiler support systems
/usr/snadm	Administration Tool executables

Table A.5 shows files that have been moved from the /usr directory.

Changes in the /var Directory

The /var directory contains files whose sizes change during normal operation. Several files and subdirectories in the /var directory are added, removed, or changed.

- The /var/opt/<*packagename*> directory contains software package objects whose sizes change, such as log and spool files.
- The /var/sadm directory contains databases that are maintained by the software package management utilities.
- The /var/saf directory contains Service Access Facility (SAF) logging and accounting files.
- The /var/spool/mail directory has been moved to /var/mail.

Table A.5 Files Moved from the /usr Directory

SunOS 4.*x* Location	SunOS 5.*x* Location
/usr/5bin	/usr/bin
/usr/5include	/usr/include
/usr/5lib	/usr/lib
/usr/etc	/usr/sbin
/usr/rfs	/etc/rfs
/usr/old	Contents removed
/usr/xpg2bin	/usr/bin
/usr/xpg2lib	/usr/lib
/usr/xpg2include	/usr/include

Device-Naming Conventions

The SunOS 5.*x* release uses device-naming conventions that make it easier to infer certain characteristics of a device from its device name. The SunOS 5.*x* conventions are slightly different from AT&T SVR4 device names, because the SunOS 5.*x* release only allows eight partitions on a disk.

You must use SunOS 5.*x* device-naming conventions with SunOS 5.*x* commands. However, if the binary compatibility package is installed, it creates links from the old device-naming conventions to the new ones, and you can continue to use SunOS 4.*x* device names. See Chapter 3 for a description of device-naming conventions.

Table A.6 shows some examples that compare the SunOS 4.*x* and SunOS 5.*x* device-naming conventions.

Printers, Terminals, and Modems

Solaris 2.*x* software includes the Service Access Facility (SAF), which is used to manage access to local and network system services (such as printers, modems, and terminals) in a similar way, whether they are on the network or attached only to local systems. SAF uses Service Access Control (SAC) commands to set up and manage services.

Table A.6 **SunOS 4.*x* and SunOS 5.*x* Device Names**

Device Description	SunOS 4.*x*	SunOS 5.*x*
Disk devices	/dev/sd0g	/dev/dsk/c0t3d0s6
	/dev/rsd3b	/dev/rdsk/c0t0d0s1
	/dev/rsd3a	/dev/rdsk/c0t0d0s0
Tape devices	/dev/nrmt8	/dev/rmt/8hn
	/dev/rst0	/dev/rmt/0h
CD-ROM device	/dev/sr0	/dev/dsk/c0t6d0s2

Terminal and Modem Differences

The SAF controls access to system and network resources. It provides a common interface for managing a range of services, including the ability to:

- Log in (either locally or remotely)
- Access printers across the network
- Access files across the network

SAF provides two major commands: sacadm and pmadm. The sacadm command controls daemons called port monitors. The pmadm command controls the services associated with the port monitors. The SAF replaces /usr/etc/getty for controlling logins.

Printing Differences

The LP print service replaces the lpd daemon and lpr, lpq, lprm, and lpc commands. The services provided by the /etc/printcap file are handled by the terminfo database and by the files in the /etc/lp directory. SunOS 4.*x* printing commands are provided as part of the BSD compatibility package. However, the compatibility package provides only SunOS 4.*x* command names, which are actually an interface to the underlying LP print services.

The LP print service provides additional functionality not available in SunOS 4.*x* systems. This functionality allows you to control forms, printwheels, and interface programs, and to set up network print services.

Even though some SunOS 4.*x* printing commands are available, encourage users to learn the SunOS 5.*x* versions. Convert your own administration environments as soon as possible because support for compatibility mode may not be available in future releases.

Naming Services

A new naming service, NIS+, replaces NIS on previous SunOS releases. NIS+ supports the following combinations of systems:

- SunOS 5.*x* software installed on all servers and workstations
- SunOS 5.*x* software installed on one server, but combined with some SunOS 4.*x* servers
- SunOS 5.*x* software installed on some workstations, running with SunOS 4.*x* servers

NIS+ information is stored in tables instead of in NIS maps. You use NIS+ shell commands to set up an NIS+ service. To administer the service, you can use either NIS+ shell commands or the Administration Tool's Database Manager.

NIS+ responds to requests from NIS. SunOS 5.*x* clients can run either NIS or NIS+.

TCP/IP

The user interface for TCP/IP is the same, but you administer NIS+ tables using the Administration Tool. The NIS+ tables administered by Administration Tool include:

- hosts
- services
- rpc
- ethers

UUCP

The UNIX-to-UNIX Copy (UUCP) is the same as the HoneyDanBer UUCP available with SunOS 4.*x* systems. It uses the same set of configuration files, scripts, and commands, so any changes you made in SunOS 4.*x* files and scripts should work with this release.

Table A.7 describes new files and commands that were not part of the SunOS 4.*x* implementation.

Table A.7 New SunOS 5.*x* UUCP Files and Commands

Command or File	Function
D. data files P. data files	These data files are created when a UUCP command line specifies copying the source file to a spool directory. All data files have the format *<systmxxxxyyy>*. The *<systm>* is the first five characters in the name of the destination system, *<xxxx>* is a four-digit job sequence number, and *<yyy>* distinguishes between several data files created for one job.
/etc/uucp/Grades	Maps text grade names to system names.
/etc/uucp/Limits	Specifies the number of concurrent UUCP sessions that can occur. Replaces Maxuuscheds and Maxuuxqts files in previous versions.
/etc/uucp/Config	Contains information to override tunable parameters in UUCP. The only tunable parameter currently available is Protocol, so system administrators normally will not have to modify this file.
uuglist	Sets service grade permissions available.

UUCP includes a few additional features that can affect system administration.

- Checkpoint-restart facilities
- Job grades that control UUCP transmission
- Two new configuration files to limit the number of concurrent UUCP sessions that the system can run, and to override tunable UUCP parameters

Document Tool Differences

NOTE. *SunOS 5.*x *systems provide a set of PostScript filters and device-independent fonts. However, some SunOS 4.*x *TranScript filters have SunOS 5.*x *equivalents, and others do not. In SunOS 5.*x *systems, there is no TEX filter, no pscat (C/A/T) filter, and no raster image filter.*

The SunOS 5.0 system provides device-independent troff, with these changes:

- SunOS 4.*x* troff input files work with SunOS 5.*x* troff.
- The troff default output goes to stdout instead of the printer. Therefore, you must specify a printer when you use troff formatting or scripts to print the output.

Security

Security combines a number of features from SunOS 4.1 and AT&T SVR4 with functionality added specifically for the Solaris 2.*x* releases. Some of the SunOS 4.*x* security programs are packaged differently.

The following sections describe major security differences and highlight how those changes may affect system administration procedures. The security features are:

- SunOS 4.*x* security features available with SunOS 5.*x* software
- SunOS 5.*x* security features
- The Automated Security Enhancement Tool (ASET)
- Kerberos security
- Administration Tool (admintool) security

SunOS 4.*x* Security

Most of the security features from SunOS 4.*x* systems are available. These include:

- Internet security
- .rhosts and hosts.equiv files
- Secure RPC, NFS, and RFS

SunOS 5.*x* Local Security

Security for local systems includes storing encrypted passwords in a separate file, controlling login defaults, and providing restricted shells. Equivalent NIS+ security controls network-wide access to systems. The following sections summarize security features under local system control.

The /etc/passwd and /etc/shadow Files

The SunOS 5.*x* password command stores encrypted versions of passwords in a separate file, /etc/shadow, and allows root access to the shadow file only. General access to the encrypted passwords is thus restricted. The /etc/shadow file also includes entries that force password aging for individual user login accounts.

The /etc/default Files

Several files that control default system access are stored in the /etc/default directory. These files limit access to specific systems on a network. Table A.8 summarizes the files in the /etc/default directory.

Table A.8 Files in /etc/default Directory

File	Function
/etc/default/login	Controls system login policies, including root access. The default is to limit root logins to the console.
/etc/default/passwd	Controls default policy on password aging.
/etc/default/su	Controls what root (su) access to system will be logged and where it is displayed.

Restricted Shells

System administrators can use restricted versions of the Korn shell (rksh) and Bourne shell (rsh) to limit the operations allowed for a particular user account. Restricted shells do not allow these operations:

- Changing directories
- Setting the $PATH variable
- Specifying path or command names containing /
- Redirecting output

Note that the restricted shell and the remote shell have the same command name, with different path names:

Restricted shell	/usr/lib/rsh
Remote shell	/usr/bin/rsh

ASET Security

The Automated Security Enhancement Tool (ASET) is included with the Solaris 2.*x* system. It was available as an unbundled option with SunOS 4.*x* systems. ASET allows you to specify an overall system security level (low, medium, or high) and automatically maintain systems at those levels. It can be set up to run on a server and all of its clients or on individual clients.

ASET performs these tasks:

- Verifies system file permissions
- Verifies system file contents
- Checks integrity of group file entries
- Checks system configuration files
- Checks environment files (.profile, .login, and.cshrc)
- Verifies EEPROM settings to restrict console login access
- Allows establishment of a firewall or gateway system

Kerberos Security

The Solaris 2.*x* system introduces support for Kerberos authentication for secure RPC. Kerberos source code and administrative utilities are available from MIT.

Solaris 2.*x* Kerberos support includes:

- Client applications library that can use Kerberos
- Kerberos option to secure RPC
- NFS application with Kerberos
- Commands to administer user tickets on the client

Everything else is available in the MIT Kerberos release.

Administration Tool Security

The security of Administration Tool introduces the concept of setting up a group of nonroot users who have permission to administer systems. Any authorized user can access Administration Tool functionality to display the information it controls. However, the ability to make system administrative changes depends on other security decisions. Users who are a member of the sysadmin group (GID 14) can use Administration Tool to make administrative changes. NIS+ also has security mechanisms that work with Administration Tool. In addition to being a member of the sysadmin group, administrators must have appropriate permissions to make changes to specific NIS+ tables.

Table of Command Equivalents

Table A.9 lists SunOS 4.*x* commands and files in alphabetical order and describes the new SunOS 5.*x* command, equivalent, or unavailability. Commands that are not listed in this table are completely compatible with previous releases.

Table A.9 System Administration File and Command Equivalents

SunOS 4.*x*	SunOS 5.*x*	Comments
ac	sar	The System Accounting Resource package (SAR) provides most of the accounting functionality available in ac.
add_services	pkgadd	
analyze	adb	Use adb on core files to analyze crashes.
arch	uname -m	SunOS 4.*x* shell scripts used the arch command to determine system architecture. Use uname -m as a replacement in SunOS 5.*x* scripts.
at, atq, atrm	at, atq, atrm	The at, atq, and atrm commands behave slightly differently than they do in SunOS 4.*x* systems. Security for nonprivileged users is more restricted on SunOS 5.*x* systems.
audit, audit_warn, auditd	Not available	See your system vendor for information on this product.
automount	automount	The auto.master and auto.home files are renamed auto_master and auto_home. The default home directory path is /export/home/<*username*>. The -m option is not available. The SunOS 5.*x* automount program searches for Auto_master and Auto_home as the default. If these files are not found, it looks for Auto.master and Auto.home files. You do not need to rename these files on SunOS 4.*x* systems.
bar	Not available	Use the tar command to replace bar for most uses. You can use cpio -H bar to restore existing SunOS 4.*x* bar backups.
batch	batch	The c, s, and m options are not in the batch command. By default, the batch job <*queuename*> is not specified.
biff -y biff -n	chmod o+x /dev/tty chmod o-x /dev/tty	When users log on, start-up shell scripts often use the biff command to set default file protection for the user. Replace those commands to make SunOS 5.*x* scripts work correctly.
/bin/mail	mail	

Table A.9 System Administration File and Command Equivalents (Continued)

SunOS 4.*x*	SunOS 5.*x*	Comments
biod	Not available	
C2conv	Not available	See your system vendor for information on this product.
C2unconv	Not available	See your system vendor for information on this product.
cc	Not available	The C compiler is available only as an unbundled product.
change_login	Not available	
check4	Not available	
chgrp	Changed	The -f option to suppress error reporting is not available.
chmod	Changed	
chown	Changed	The default behavior of symbolic links is changed. SunOS 4.*x* chown changed ownership of the symbolic link. SunOS 5.*x* chown follows the link. To change the ownership of the link, use chown -h. SunOS 5.*x* chown does not allow the group ID of a file to be changed.
client	Not available	
colldef	colltbl	
crash	Changed	The default file name in SunOS 5.*x* software is /kernel/unix instead of /vmunix.
date	Changed	
dbxtool	debugger	See your system vendor for information on this product.
dcheck	Not available	
dd	Changed	The Sun OS 4.1 dd command uses 4-byte words. The SunOS 5.*x* dd command uses 2-byte words.
devinfo	Changed	
devnm	Changed	The *<name>* argument is required for SunOS 5.*x* devnm. The output format has also changed.
df	df -k	Output of the df command is changed. The SunOS 4.*x* df -t *<fstype>* command reports on files of the specified type. The SunOS 5.*x* df -t command prints full listings with totals.
dkctl	Not available	
dkinfo	prtvtoc	

Table A.9 System Administration File and Command Equivalents (Continued)

SunOS 4.*x*	SunOS 5.*x*	Comments
dorfs	rfstart	
	rfstop	
du	du -k	The SunOS 4.*x* version of du reports disk usage in kilobytes, but the SunOS 5.*x* du command reports disk usage in 512-byte blocks (by default).
dump	ufsdump	The -a option dumps the archive header of each member of an archive. The -D option dumps debugging information. The -v option dumps information in symbolic form.
dumpfs	Not available	
etherfind	Not available	Similar functionality is available in the SunOS 5.*x* snoop command.
exportfs	share	
extract_files	Not available	
extract_patch	Not available	
extract_unbundled	pkgadd	
fastboot	init 6	
fasthalt	init 0	
file	Changed	The file command does not have the -L option.
find	Changed	The find command does not have the -n cpio option.
fmt_mail	Not available	
fsck	Changed	fsck specifies most options after the file system type. fsck -m does a quick file system check. The -w option is not available. New options include -f, -v, and -o.
fsirand	Not available	
hostid	sysdef -h	
hostname	uname -n	
init	Changed	See Chapter 1 for more information on init.
installtxt	msgfmt	

Table A.9 System Administration File and Command Equivalents (Continued)

SunOS 4.*x*	SunOS 5.*x*	Comments
intr	Not available	
iostat	Changed	The -x and -c options are added: -x to provide disk statistics, and -c to report the time the system spends in user mode, system mode, and idle.
keyenvoy	Not available	
ldconfig	Not available	
leave	Not available	Functionality in cron and at replace the leave command.
lint	Not available	Available with unbundled C compiler for SunOS 5.*x* systems.
load		
loadc	pkgadd	Provides part of the functionality of the SunOS 4.*x* load command.
load_package	Not Available	
lpc	lpsched	
lpd	lpadmin	
lpq	lpstat	
lpr	lp	
lprm	cancel	
lptest	Not available	
ls	Changed	Default output for the ls command is changed. The ls -l command displays both user and group ownership.
mach	uname -p	
makekey	Not available	
man	Changed	The organization of man pages is changed. All system administration man pages are now located in section 1M. The man command now allows you to set an environment variable to specify a default order of directories and sections for man to search.
mkfs	Changed	mkfs supports different file system types.
mknod	Changed	Users other than root can now create character and block special files.

Table A.9 System Administration File and Command Equivalents (Continued)

SunOS 4.*x*	SunOS 5.*x*	Comments
modstat	modinfo	
mount	Changed	Options must be specified after the file system is specified (unless the file system is in /etc/vfstab).
mount_tfs	mount -F *<fstype>*	Options to the mount command (instead of separate mount commands) are used to specify file system types.
ncheck	Changed	Allows use of specific file system types.
ndbootd	Not available	The -m option is not available. The -l option changes *<addr>* immediately. The variable *<addr>* cannot be specified in hexadecimal format.
nlsadmin		
nulladm	Not available	
pac	Not available	
passwd	Changed	The -F *<filename>* option is not available. The -f and -s options have different meanings. The -f option forces the user to change the password at the next login. The -s option displays the password attributes for the user's login name.
pax	cpio	
paxcpio	cpio	
portmap	rpcbind	
praudit	Not available	Will be available when the unbundled C2 security product is released.
printenv	env	
ps	Changed	Many of the 4.*x* options to ps are not available or the meanings have changed. Instead of ps -aux, use ps -el for SunOS 5.*x* systems. See the ps(1) manual page for more information.
pstat	sar	
pstat -s	swap -s	Shows the total amount of swap space available on the system.
rc	Not available	The organization of rc files is changed. They are now divided into subdirectories by run levels.
rc.boot	Not available	
rc.local	Not available	

Table A.9 System Administration File and Command Equivalents (Continued)

SunOS 4.*x*	SunOS 5.*x*	Comments
rdump	ufsdump	
reset -s	Not available	
restore	ufsrestore	
rmail	Changed	The rmail command in the SunOS 4.*x* system handles remote mail. The rmail command in the SunOS 5.*x* system is a link to mail and is used to read mail.
rm_client	Not available	Functionality of admintool replaces this command.
rm_services	Not available	
rpc.etherd	Not available	
rpc.lockd	lockd	
rpc.mountd	mountd	
rpc.rexd	Not available	
rpc.rquotad	Not available	
rpc.showfhd	showfhd	
rpc.statd	statd	
rpc.user_agentd	Not available	
rpc.yppasswdd	Not available	
rpc.ypupdated	ypupdated	
rrestore	ufsrestore	
rusage	Not available	
rwall	Changed	The -f and -n options are not available.
setsid	Not available	
shutdown	Changed	See Chapter 1 for more information on shutdown.
startup	Not available	
stty	Changed	
suninstall	Changed	Although the command name is the same, the installation procedure is changed completely.

Table A.9 System Administration File and Command Equivalents (Continued)

SunOS 4.*x*	SunOS 5.*x*	Comments
swapon	swap -a	In general, options to the swap command replace functionality of individual swap-related commands, such as swapon, in SunOS 4.*x* systems.
sys-config	Not available	Functionality of admintool replaces this command.
tfsd	Not available	
trpt	Not available	
tset	Changed	The -S option is not available.
ttysoftcar	Not available	
tvconfig	Not available	
tzsetup	Not available	
umount	Changed	File-specific options may be required.
umount_tfs	umount -F *<fstype>*	
unlink	Changed	Any user can unlink a directory.
unload	pkgrm	
unset4	Not available	
update	fsflush	
uptime	Unchanged	You can also use who -b to display the system boot time.
users	who -q	
uulog	Changed	The -u option, used to print information sorted by user, is not available.
uusend	Not available	
vipw	Not available	
vmstat	Changed	The -f option is not available.
vswap	Not available	
wall	Not available	
whereis	Not available	

Table A.9 System Administration File and Command Equivalents (Continued)

SunOS 4.*x*	SunOS 5.*x*	Comments
whoami	id	The id command prints the user name and user and group IDs, instead of just the user name.
ypbatchupd	Not available	
yppasswd	nispasswd	The yppasswd command is still available to access the password information on NIS servers. The equivalent command for NIS+ databases is nispasswd, and the equivalent command for systems with no name service is passwd.
ypserv	Not available	

New Administration Tools with Solaris 2.1

This appendix describes changes to Administration Tool and introduces two new applications that are available with the Solaris 2.1 Administration Tool: Printer Manager and User Account Manager. The Database Manager has one additional database: the Aliases database.

The Printer Manager provides a graphical user interface that you can use to set up the Service Access Facility for printing, to configure print servers and print clients, and to modify and delete printers.

The User Account Manager provides a graphical user interface that you can use to add user accounts to the Passwd, Group, Auto_home, and Cred databases; create home directories; set password security; and set up the user's mail server. You can also modify and delete user accounts with the User Account Manager.

Changes to the Administration Tool User Interface

The Solaris 2.1 Administration Tool has some user interface changes and provides two new tools: Printer Manager and User Account Manager. Administration Tool also has a help button that you can use to display information about each of the applications. Figure B.1 shows the Solaris 2.1 Administration Tool window.

Figure B.1 Solaris 2.1 Administration Tool window

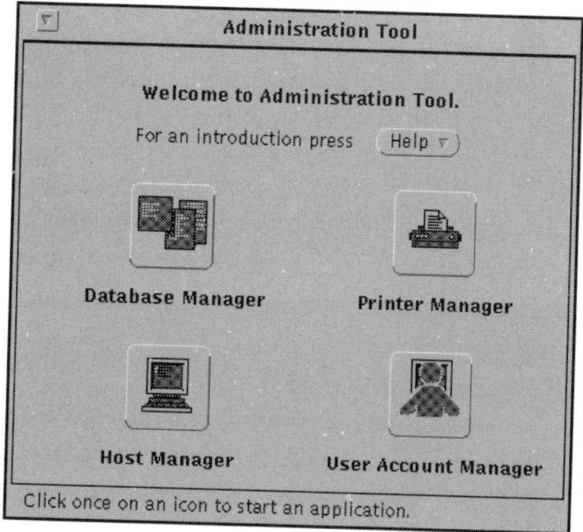

Database Manager

With Solaris 2.1 system software, you can use the Database Manager to edit the NIS+ Aliases database and local /etc/aliases files. Because the databases are listed alphabetically, and the Aliases database is the first database on the list, it is automatically selected when you open the Database Manager. Figure B.2 shows the Aliases database window.

Figure B.2 The Aliases Database window

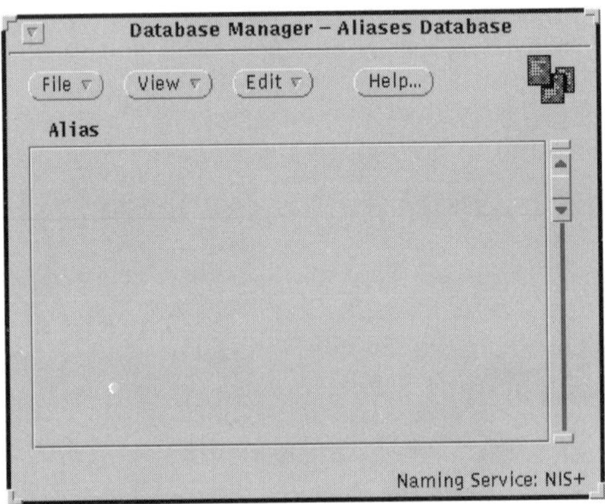

When you use the Aliases database to add entries for NIS+, the Add Entry window has the text fields shown in Figure B.3. The fields in the NIS+ Aliases window match the four columns in NIS+ aliases table, as described in Table B.1.

Figure B.3 The Add Entry window for the NIS+ Aliases database

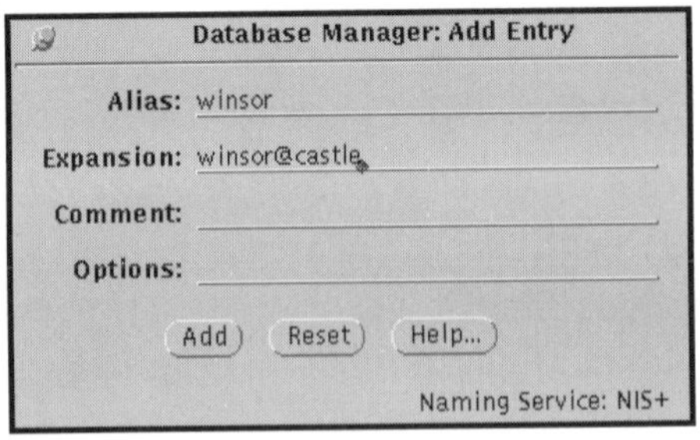

Table B.1 **Fields in the NIS+ Aliases Database**

Column	Description
Alias	The name of the alias
Expansion	The value of the alias as it would appear in a sendmail /etc/aliases file
Options	Reserved for future use
Comments	Can be used to add specific comments about an individual alias

When you use the Aliases database to add entries to local /etc/aliases files, the Add Entry window has text fields for the alias and its expansion, as shown in Figure B.4. The Options and Comments fields are not needed.

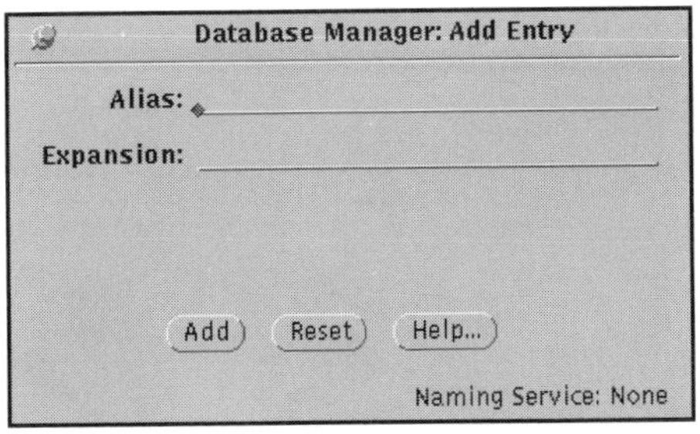

Figure B.4 The Add Entry window for local /etc/aliases files

Database Manager: Add Entry

Alias:

Expansion:

Add | Reset | Help...

Naming Service: None

Printer Manager

You can use the Printer Manager to set up Solaris 2.1 printer server and printer client systems. The Printer Manager automatically configures the port monitors for the Service Access Facility and updates the LP print service files using the information that you enter into the Printer Manager windows.

Setting Up a Print Client (Solaris 2.1)

If Solaris 2.1 is installed on the print client system, you can use the Printer Manager to set up printing. The Printer Manager automatically sets up the port monitors for Solaris 2.*x* print servers and print clients and updates the LP print service files.

This section describes how to use the Printer Manager to set up a print client to print on either a BSD (SunOS 4.*x*) or SVR4 (Solaris 2.*x*) print server.

To use the Administration Tool Printer Manager to set up print clients, you must be a member of the UNIX sysadmin group (GID 14).

NOTE. *The print client you want to set up must be running the Printer Manager. The Printer Manager is available with SunOS 5.1 system software. Alternatively, the print client can be a SunOS 5.0 system with the Printer Manager installed.*

To set up a print client, you need this information:

- Printer name
- Print server name
- Type of operating system the print server is running (BSD or System V)
- Whether this is the default printer for the print client system

Follow these steps to set up a print client:

1. If Administration Tool is not running, type **admintool &** and press Return. The Administration Tool window is displayed.
2. Click SELECT on the Printer Manager icon. The Printer Manager window is displayed, as shown in Figure B.5.

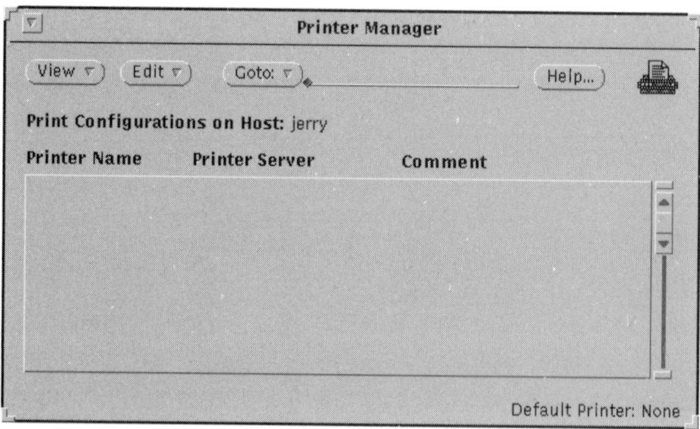

Figure B.5 The Printer Manager window

3. If you are running the Printer Manager from the print client system, you can skip this step. If you are running the Printer Manager from a remote system, type the name of the print client system in the Goto text field and click SELECT on the Goto button.

4. Choose Add Access to Remote Printer from the Add Printer menu, as shown in Figure B.6. The Access to Remote Printer window is displayed, as shown in Figure B.7.

Figure B.6
The Add Printer menu

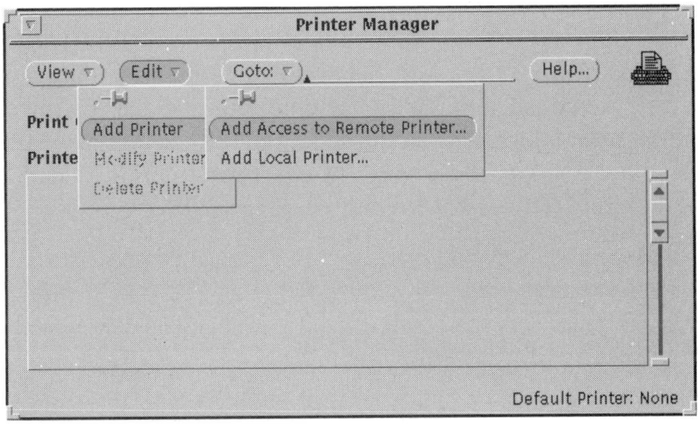

Figure B.7
The Access to Remote Printer window

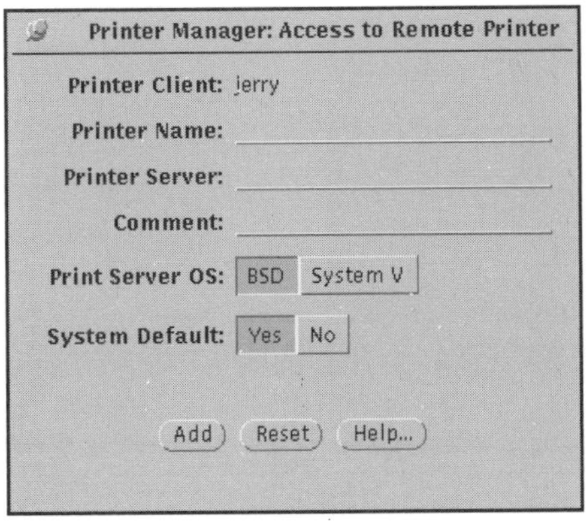

5. Type the name of the printer in the Printer Name text field.
6. Type the name of the print server in the Printer Server text field.
7. Type comments in the Comment field (optional). Include useful information such as the location of the printer or the name of the person responsible for administering it.

8. If the print server is a BSD system, go to the next step. If the print server is running SunOS 5.*x*, click SELECT on System V. You have specified the version of the operating system running on the print server.
9. The default is to use this printer as the default printer for the printer client system. If you do not want this printer to be the default printer, click SELECT on No.
10. Click SELECT on Add. The information defined in the Add Client window is recorded in the /etc/lp configuration files on the selected system, the print client, and on the specified print server system. If you make some mistakes and want to re-enter information, click SELECT on Reset to reset all the fields to their original values.

To add more clients to a print server, repeat this procedure.

The example shown in Figure B.8 adds a remote printer named carvel on an SVR4 print server named carvel, and specifies carvel as the default printer for the print client system named jerry.

Figure B.8
Example, adding a remote printer

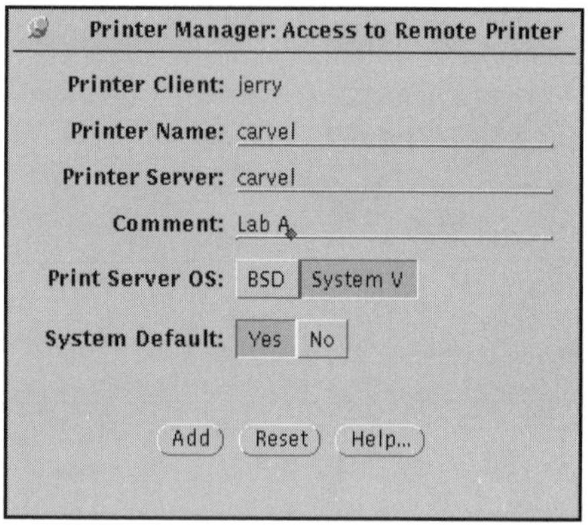

Printer Manager: Access to Remote Printer
Printer Client: jerry
Printer Name: carvel
Printer Server: carvel
Comment: Lab A
Print Server OS: BSD System V
System Default: Yes No
Add Reset Help...

Setting Up a Print Server (Solaris 2.*x*)

You can use the Printer Manager to automatically configure the port monitors and set up a Solaris 2.*x* print server.

To use the Administration Tool Printer Manager to set up print servers, you must be a member of the UNIX sysadmin group (GID 14).

NOTE. *The print server you want to set up must be running the Printer Manager. The Printer Manager is available with SunOS 5.1 system software. Alternatively, the print client can be a SunOS 5.0 system software with the Printer Manager installed.*

You need this information to set up a Solaris 2.*x* print server:

- Printer name.
- Server name.
- Device name of port to which printer is connected.
- Printer type. (The default is PostScript.)
- File content type. (The default is PostScript.)
- Fault notification policy for this print server. (The default is Write to superuser.)
- Whether this printer is the default printer for the print server. (The default is yes.)
- Whether a banner is printed before each print job. (The default is to print a banner.)
- Whether you want to register this printer with the NIS+ service. (The default is no.) If your network is running NIS+, you can add the printer to the table of printers that are available on the network.
- Whether you want to create a specific list of users who can access this printer. (The default is to permit access to all users.) If you create a user list, only users who are on the list can use this printer.

Follow these steps to set up a print server:

1. If Administration Tool is not running, type **admintool&** and press Return. The Administration Tool window is displayed.
2. Click SELECT on the Printer Manager icon. The Printer Manager window is displayed, as shown in Figure B.9. The printers already available to the current system are listed.
3. If you are running Printer Manager from the print server, skip this step. If you are running Printer Manager from another system, type the system name in the Goto field and click SELECT on the Goto button.
4. Choose Add Printer from the Edit menu, then Add Local Printer as shown in Figure B.10. The Local Printer window (Figure B.11) is displayed.

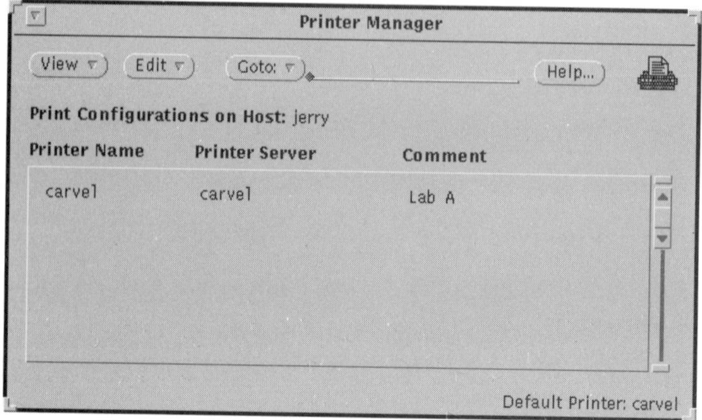

Figure B.9
The Printer Manager window shows current printers

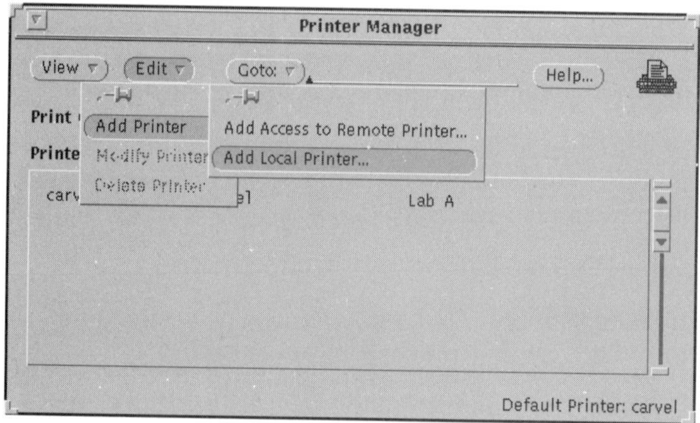

Figure B.10
The Edit menu

5. Type the printer name in the Printer Name text field. Choose a name unique to the network or to your administrative domain within the network.

6. Type a comment in the Comment text field. Any comment you type in this field is displayed when users request printer status.

7. Choose the appropriate printer port. If the printer port is not /dev/term/a, choose an item from the Printer Port menu. The Printer Manager sets the ownership and permissions on the device file to grant access to the special user lp.

Figure B.11
The Local Printer window

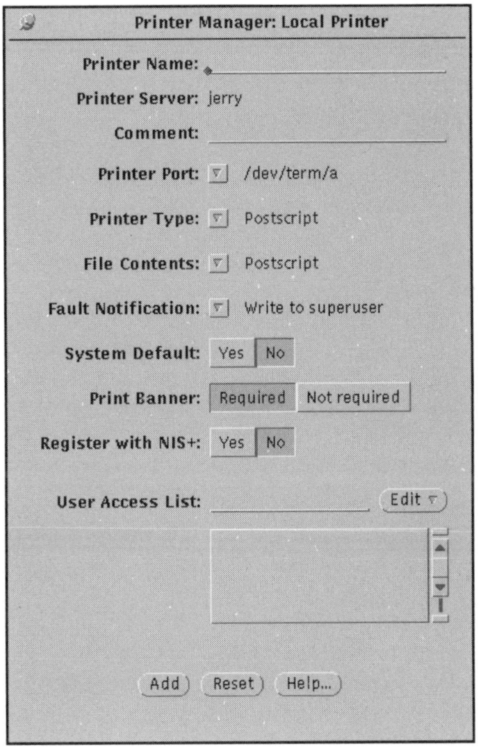

Printer Manager: Local Printer
Printer Name:
Printer Server: jerry
Comment:
Printer Port: /dev/term/a
Printer Type: Postscript
File Contents: Postscript
Fault Notification: Write to superuser
System Default: Yes No
Print Banner: Required Not required
Register with NIS+: Yes No
User Access List: Edit
Add Reset Help...

8. Choose the printer type. If the printer type is not PostScript, choose a printer type from the Printer Type menu. A list of available printer types is constructed from the terminfo database. If your printer type is not included, choose Other and type the name in the pop-up window that is displayed. If you specify printer type Postscript (PS) and find that pages print in reverse order, use the Modify option under the Edit menu to change the printer type to Postscript Reverse (PSR).

9. Choose the file contents type. If the printer is not a PostScript printer, choose a file contents type from File Contents menu. The file contents type indicates the type of file that can be printed directly on the printer without any filtering.

10. Choose the fault notification policy. If you do not want fault messages to be written to the superuser's (root) terminal, choose another option from the Fault Notification menu. The only other choices are to have fault messages sent by e-mail to the superuser's (root's) mailbox, or to have no fault messages delivered at all (none).

11. Specify whether or not the printer is the default printer for this system. If you do not want the printer to be the default printer for the system to which it is being added, click SELECT on No in the System Default field.

12. Choose a banner page policy. If you do not want banner pages to be required, click SELECT on Not Required.

13. Choose whether or not to register the printer with NIS+. If you want to register the printer with NIS+, click SELECT on Yes.

14. Decide whether or not you want to restrict user access to the printer. If you want to restrict user access, type the login name of each user in the User Access List text field and click SELECT on the Edit button. Any user not in the list is denied access to the printer. If you do not create a list, all users have access to the printer.

15. Click SELECT on Add. The port monitors are configured and the information defined in the Local Printer window is recorded in the /etc/lp configuration files on the selected system.

User Account Manager

The User Account Manager edits the Passwd, Group, Auto_home, and Cred databases; sets password security; and creates the user's home directory. When you use the User Account Manager, you do not need to edit the appropriate databases or create the user's home directory manually. If you create more than one user with the same user profile, you can clone information from an existing user account to create a new user account.

Always run Administration Tool using your own UID, not as root. You must be a member of the sysadmin group (GID 14). If the network is running NIS+, you also need create and delete permissions on the NIS+ databases.

Follow these steps to add a user account with the User Account Manager:

1. Click SELECT on the User Manager icon. The Select Naming Service window is displayed, as shown in Figure B.12.

2. Choose either the NIS+ naming service or None (local /etc/files) just as you did with the Solaris 2.0 Administration Tool. The NIS+ naming service is chosen by default and the current domain name is displayed. If you are adding a user to a different domain, type the name of the domain in the Domain Name text field. If you are adding a user to a local system, click SELECT on None and type the system name in the text field. If you select NIS, you can view information about user accounts but cannot add or modify them because the User Account Manager does not provide methods for updating NIS maps.

Figure B.12
The Select Naming Service window

3. Choose the amount of information you want displayed in the User Account Manager window using the Show menu, illustrated in Figure B.13. By default, all users in a domain are shown in the User Account Manager window. Because it can take a while to display all of the user accounts in a domain, you can choose how much information will be displayed when you open the User Account Manager.

Figure B.13
The Show menu

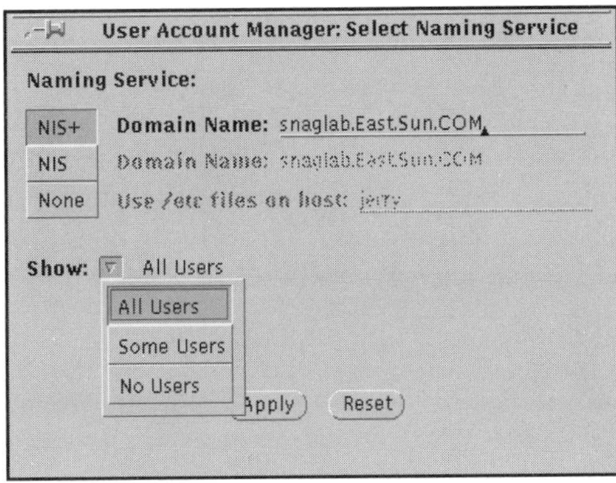

4. If you choose Some Users from the Show menu, a text field is displayed in the window, as shown in Figure B.14. Type a user name or a search pattern in the text field. You can use the wildcard characters *, ?, !, and [ ] in the text field to match entries.

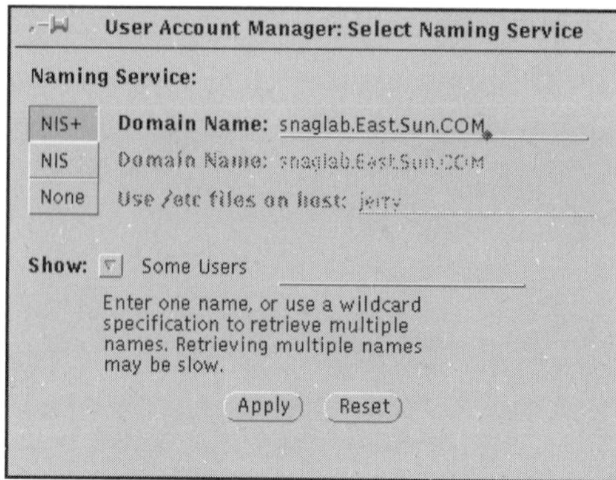

Figure B.14
The Some Users text field

5. When you have chosen the naming service and the amount of information you want displayed, click SELECT on Apply. The User Account Manager window is displayed, as shown in Figure B.15.

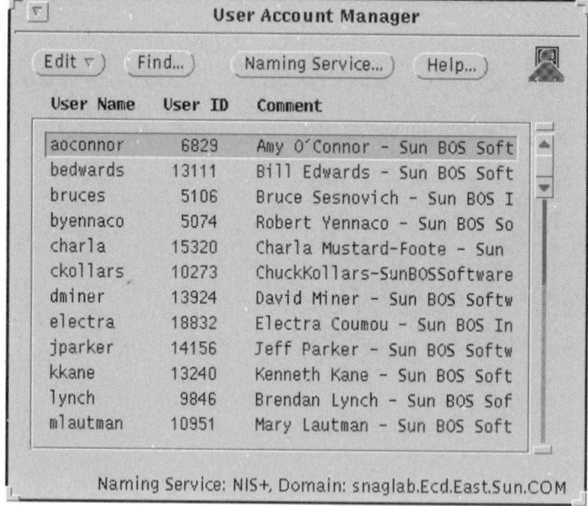

Figure B.15
The User Account Manager window

NOTE. *If you want to change the domain or the naming service after the User Account Manager window is opened, click SELECT on the Naming Service button. The Naming Service window is displayed, and you can use it to change the information displayed in the User Account Manager window.*

6. Choose Add User from the Edit menu, as shown in Figure B.16. The Add User window is displayed, as shown in Figure B.17. If you are copying user

information, choose Copy User from the Edit menu. The Copy User window fills in all information from the existing user except the User Name and User ID text fields.

Figure B.16
The Edit menu

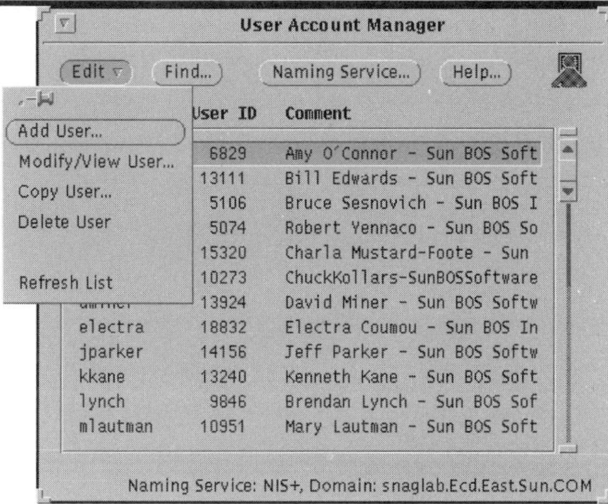

7. Type the user's login name in the User Name text field. Choose a login name unique to your organization with two to eight lowercase characters and digits (excluding colons).

8. Type the UID number in the User ID text field. Choose a number between 100 and 60000 that is unique to your organization.

9. Type the user's group name or group number in the Primary Group field.

10. If the user is assigned to any secondary groups, type the names or numbers of the additional groups in the Secondary Groups text field.

11. Type identifying information about the user in the Comment text field.

12. Choose a default login shell for the user from the Login Shell menu.

13. Choose a password status from the Password menu.

14. If you want additional password aging information, set it in the appropriate text fields.

15. If you want to automatically create the user's home directory, click SELECT on the Create Home Dir checkbox. The Skeleton Path text field is activated.

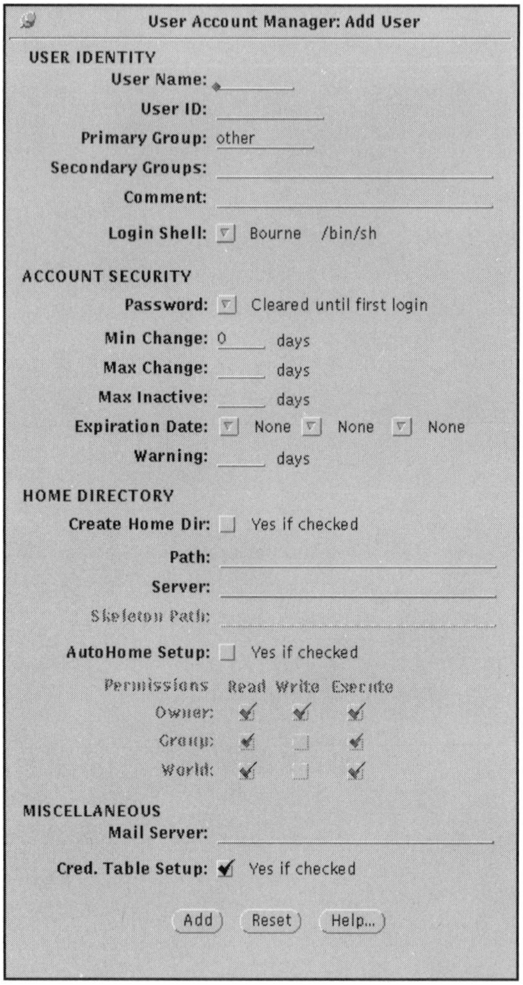

Figure B.17
The Add User window

User Account Manager: Add User
USER IDENTITY
User Name:
User ID:
Primary Group: other
Secondary Groups:
Comment:
Login Shell: Bourne /bin/sh
ACCOUNT SECURITY
Password: Cleared until first login
Min Change: 0 days
Max Change: days
Max Inactive: days
Expiration Date: None None None
Warning: days
HOME DIRECTORY
Create Home Dir: Yes if checked
Path:
Server:
Skeleton Path:
AutoHome Setup: Yes if checked
Permissions Read Write Execute
Owner:
Group:
World:
MISCELLANEOUS
Mail Server:
Cred. Table Setup: Yes if checked
Add Reset Help...

16. Type the path of the home directory to be entered in the Passwd database in the Path text field. If you checked the Create Home Dir box, the home directory is also created on a server.

17. Type the name of the server for the home directory in the Server text field. If you checked the Create Home Dir box, the home directory is created on a server.

18. Type the path to the directory that stores the initialization (skeleton) files that will be copied into the user's home directory in the Skeleton Path text field. Note that the initialization files and home directory must be on the same (server) system.

19. Choose whether or not you want the user's home directory to be automounted. If you choose AutoHome Setup (checkbox checked), an entry is created for the user in the Auto_home database. If you do not want the user's home directory to be automounted (checkbox unchecked), an entry is not created in the Auto_home database.

20. Click SELECT on the Permissions checkboxes to set the Read, Write, and Execute permissions for the user's home directory.

21. If you want to set up a mail account, type the name of the system that will hold the user's mail in the Mail Server text field.

22. If you want the user to be added to the NIS+ cred table, make sure the Cred. Table Setup checkbox is checked.

23. When you have filled in all the information, click SELECT on Add. The information is added to the Passwd database, the Group database, the Auto_home database (if specified), the Cred database (if specified), and the Aliases database (if a mail server is specified). If specified, the user's home directory is created with the proper ownership and the permissions you set, and the default initialization files are copied into the user's home directory.

Modifying a User Account

To modify a user account, you must be a member of the sysadmin group (GID 14). If the network is running NIS+, you also need to create and delete permissions on the NIS+ databases. If you want to change a user's home directory, create the directory (mkdir) before making changes with the User Account Manager.

Follow these steps to modify a user account:

1. From Administration Tool, click SELECT on User Account Manager. The Select Naming Service window is displayed.

2. Choose the naming service. If you know the name(s) of the users you want to modify, choose Some Users from the Show menu and type the names of the users in the text field.

3. Click SELECT on Apply. The User Account Manager window is displayed.

4. If you want to search through the list of user names, click SELECT on Find. The Find User window is displayed, as shown in Figure B.18.

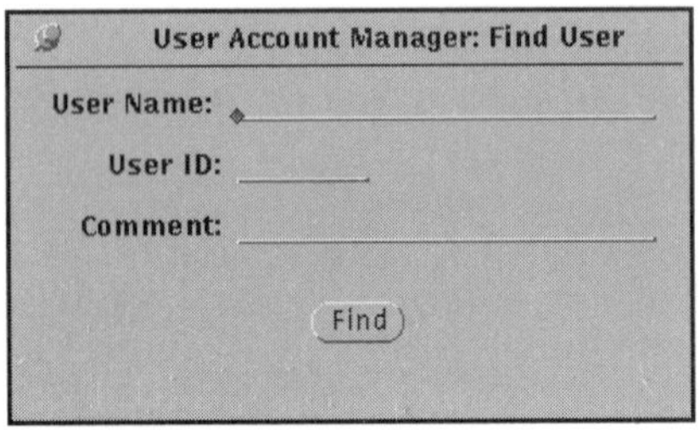

Figure B.18
The Find User window

5. Type the patterns you want to match in the text fields. The search looks for the first entry (in the set of entries currently displayed) that matches all of the fields. You can use wildcard characters in the search patterns.
6. Click SELECT on Find.
7. When you have found the entry you want to modify, double click SELECT on the entry in the User Account Manager window to display the Modify/View User window. Alternatively, choose Modify User from the Edit menu. The Modify User window is displayed, as shown in Figure B.19.
8. Change the information in fields, as desired.
9. Click SELECT on Apply. The user account is modified using the new information.

Deleting a User Account

To delete a user account, you must be a member of the sysadmin group (GID 14). If the network is running NIS+, you also need to create and delete permissions on the NIS+ databases.

Follow these steps to delete a user account:

1. From Administration Tool, click SELECT on User Account Manager. The Naming Service window is displayed.
2. Choose the naming service. If you know the name(s) of the users you want to delete, choose Some Users from the Show menu and type the names of the users in the text field.

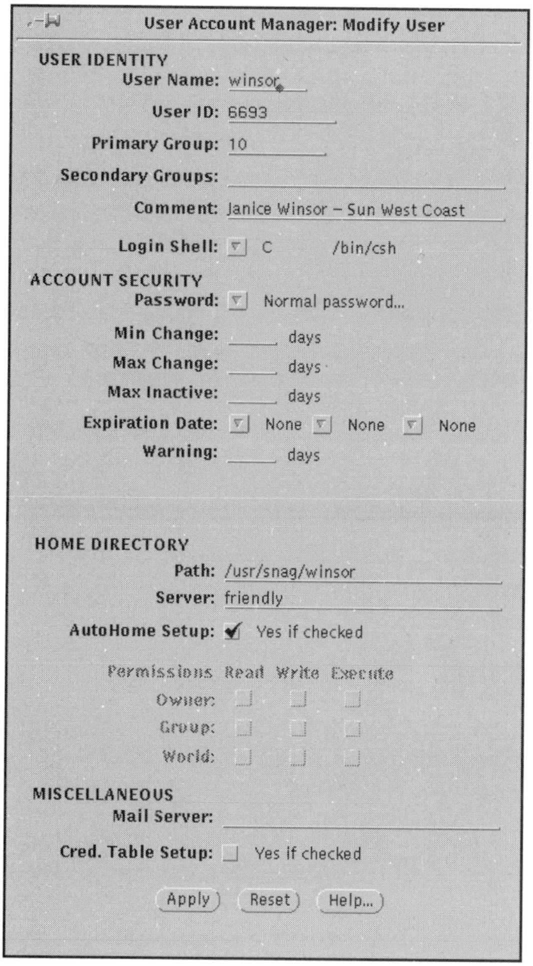

Figure B.19
The Modify User window

User Account Manager: Modify User

USER IDENTITY
User Name: winsor
User ID: 6693
Primary Group: 10
Secondary Groups:
Comment: Janice Winsor – Sun West Coast
Login Shell: C /bin/csh

ACCOUNT SECURITY
Password: Normal password...
Min Change: days
Max Change: days
Max Inactive: days
Expiration Date: None None None
Warning: days

HOME DIRECTORY
Path: /usr/snag/winsor
Server: friendly
AutoHome Setup: Yes if checked
Permissions Read Write Execute
Owner:
Group:
World:

MISCELLANEOUS
Mail Server:
Cred. Table Setup: Yes if checked

Apply Reset Help...

3. Click SELECT on Apply. The User Account Manager window is displayed.
4. Click SELECT on the entry you want to delete. The entry is highlighted.
5. Choose Delete User from the Edit menu. The Delete User window is displayed, as shown in Figure B.20.
6. If you want to delete the user's home directory and its contents, click SELECT on the checkbox.

Figure B.20
The Delete User window

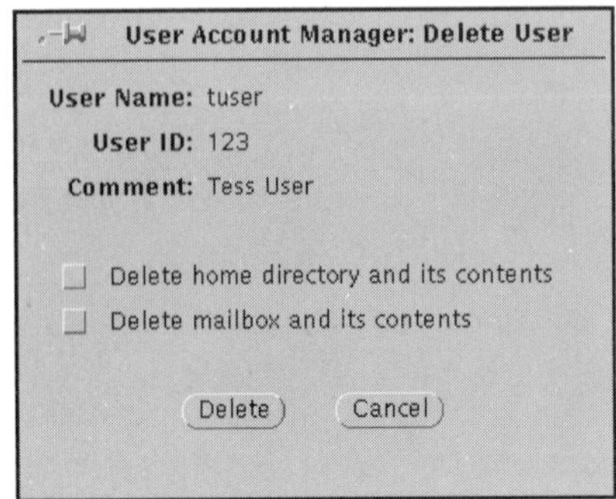

7. If you want to delete the user's mailbox and its contents, click SELECT on the checkbox.
8. Click SELECT on Delete. The user's entry is removed from the Passwd database and the user is automatically removed from all groups. If specified, the home directory and its contents are deleted, as are the mailbox and its contents.

GLOSSARY

Administration Tool An OpenWindows tool from which you can access Host Manager and Database Manager applications. With the Solaris 2.1 environment, Printer Manager and User Manager applications are also available. See also **Database Manager**.

archive A copy of files on secondary media, which have been removed from the system because they are no longer active.

Auto_home database The database that you use to add home directories to the automounter. You access the Auto_home database using the Database Manager. In SunOS 4.*x* releases, this database is a file named auto.home.

automounter Software that automatically mounts a directory when a user changes into it and unmounts the directory when it is no longer in use.

backup schedule The schedule you establish for a site that determines when you run the ufsdump command on a regular basis at different levels to back up user files and essential file systems.

bang An exclamation point (!) that acts as a single-character UNIX command or as a separator between the routes of a route-based e-mail address.

boot block An 8k disk block that contains information used during booting: Block numbers point to the location of the /boot program on that disk. The boot block directly follows the disk label.

booting The process of powering up a system, testing to determine which attached hardware devices are running, and bringing the operating system kernel into memory and operation at the run level specified by the boot command.

cache A small, fast memory area that holds the most active part of a larger and slower memory.

core file An image of the state of the software when it failed, used for troubleshooting. The core files can be created by any software, including the operating system kernel.

crash See **hang**.

crash dump A core file image of the operating system kernel that is saved in the swap partition when a system crashes. If crash dumps are enabled, the core image is written from the swap partition to a file.

cylinder group One or more consecutive disk cylinders that include inode slots for files.

cylinder group map A bit map in a ufs file system that stores information about block use and availability within each cylinder. The cylinder group replaces the traditional free list.

daemon A special type of program that, once activated, starts itself and carries out a specific task without any need for user input. Daemons typically are used to handle jobs that have been queued such as printing, mail, and communication.

Database Manager An OpenWindows tool accessed from the Administration Tool, which is used to administer NIS+ tables and ufs files in the /etc directory. You can also use the Database Manager to look at (but not edit) the contents of NIS maps.

diskette A nonvolatile storage medium used to store and access data magnetically. SunOS 5.*x* system software supports 3.5-inch double-sided high-density (DS, HD) diskettes.

diskless client A system with no local disk drive that relies on an NFS server for the operating system, swap space, file storage, and other basic services.

disk quotas A mechanism for controlling how much of a file system's resources any individual user can access. Disk quotas are optional and must be configured and administered to be used.

domain A directory structure for electronic mail addressing and network address naming. Within the United States, top-level domains include *com* for commercial organizations, *edu* for educational organizations, *gov* for governments, *mil* for the military, *net* for networking organizations, and *org* for other organizations. Outside of the United States, top-level domains designate the country. Subdomains designate the organization and the individual system.

domain addressing Using a domain address to specify the destination of an electronic mail message.

DS, HD Double-sided, high-density. The type of 3.5-inch diskettes supported by the SunOS 5.*x* system software.

dump The process of copying directories onto media (usually tape) for off-line storage using the ufsdump command. The ufsdump command is an enhanced version of the SunOS 4.*x* dump command.

electronic mail A set of programs that transmit mail messages from one system to another, usually over communications lines. Electronic mail frequently is referred to as *e-mail*.

e-mail See **electronic mail**.

environment variable A system- or user-defined variable that provides information about the operating environment to the shell.

file system A hierarchical arrangement of directories and files.

floppy diskette See **diskette**.

free list See **cylinder group map**.

full backup A complete, level 0 backup of a file system done using the ufsdump command.

fully qualified domain name A domain name that contains all of the elements needed to specify where an electronic mail message should be delivered. See also **domain**.

gateway A system that handles electronic mail traffic between different communications networks.

GID The group identification number used by the system to control access to accounts owned by other users.

Group database The database that you use to create new group accounts or to modify existing group accounts. You access the Group database from the Database Manager.

hang A condition where a system does not respond to input from the keyboard or mouse.

home directory The part of the file system that is allocated to an individual user for private files.

Hosts database The database that you use to control network security. You access the Hosts database from the Database Manager.

incremental backup A partial backup of a file system using the ufsdump command that includes only those files in the specified file system that have changed since a previous backup at a lower level.

initialization files The dot files (files prefixed with ".") in a user's home directory that set the path, environment variables, windowing environment, and other characteristics to get users up and functioning.

init states One of the seven initialization states, or run levels, a system can be running in. A system can run in only one init state at a time.

inode An entry in a predesignated area of a disk that describes where a file is located on that disk, the size of the file, when it was last used, and other identification information.

IP address A unique internet protocol number that identifies each system in a network.

kernel The master program set of SunOS software that manages all the physical resources of the computer, including file system management, virtual memory, reading and writing files to disks and tapes, scheduling of processes, printing, and communicating over a network.

login name The name assigned to an individual user that controls access to a system.

monitor The program in the PROM that provides a limited set of commands that can be used before the kernel is available.

mount point A directory in the file system hierarchy where another file system is attached to the hierarchy.

NFS The default SunOS 5.*x* distributed file system that provides file sharing among systems. NFS servers can also provide kernels and swap files to diskless clients.

NIS The SunOS 4.*x* network information service.

NIS+ The SunOS 5.*x* network information service.

OpenWindows A windowing system based on the OPEN LOOK graphical user interface.

parse To resolve a string of characters or a series of words into component parts to determine their collective meaning. Virtually every program that accepts command input must do some sort of parsing before the commands can be acted upon. For example, the sendmail program divides an e-mail address into its component parts to decide where to send the message.

partition A discrete portion of a disk, configured using the format program.

Passwd database The database that you use to add, modify, or delete user accounts. You access the Passwd database from the Database Manager.

path The list of directories that are searched to find an executable command.

path name A list of directory names, separated with slashes (/), that specifies the location of a particular file.

port A physical connection between a peripheral device (such as a terminal, printer, or modem) and the device controller.

port monitor A program that continuously watches for requests to log in or requests to access printers or files. The ttymon and listen port monitors are part of the Service Access Facility.

power cycling Turning the power to a system off and then on again.

preen To run fsck with the -o p option, which automatically fixes any basic file system inconsistencies normally found when a system halts abruptly without trying to repair more serious errors.

Printer Manager An OpenWindows tool accessed from the Solaris 2.1 version of Administration Tool, which is used to add printers to both print servers and print clients. The Printer Manager automatically updates the LP system files and the Service Access Facility files required to configure port monitors for printing.

process A program in operation.

PROM Programmable read-only memory. A chip containing permanent, nonvolatile memory and a limited set of commands used to test the system and start the boot process.

run level See **init states.**

SAF See Service Access Facility.

server A system that provides network service such as disk storage and file transfer, or a program that provides such a service.

Service Access Facility (SAF) The part of the system software that is used to register and monitor port activity for modems, terminals, and printers. SAF replaces /etc/getty as a way to control logins.

shell The command interpreter for a user, specified in the Passwd database. The SunOS 5.*x* system software supports the Bourne (default), C, and Korn shells.

slice An alternate name for a partition. See also **partition**.

spooling directory A directory where files are stored until they are processed.

spooling space The amount of space that is allocated on a print server for storing requests in the printer queue.

stand-alone system A system that has a local disk and can boot without relying on a server.

state flag A flag in the superblock that the fsck file system check program updates to record the condition of a file system. If a file system state flag is clean, the fsck program is not run on that file system.

superuser A user who is granted special privileges if the correct password is supplied when logging in as root or using the su command. For example, only the superuser can edit major administrative files in the /etc directory.

swap file A disk partition or file used to temporarily hold the contents of a memory area until it can be loaded back into memory.

symbolic link A file that contains a pointer to the name of another file.

system A computer with a keyboard and terminal. A system can have either local or remote disks, and may have additional peripheral devices such as CD-ROM players, tape drives, diskette drives, and printers.

ufs UNIX file system. The default disk-based file system for the SunOS 5.*x* operating system.

UID number The user identification number assigned to each login name. UID numbers are used by the system to identify, by number, the owners of files and directories.

user account An account set up for an individual user in the Passwd database that specifies the user's login name, UID, GID, login directory, and login shell.

User Manager An OpenWindows tool that is accessed from the Solaris 2.1 version of Administration Tool, which is used to add users to an NIS+ environment or to a local system.

user mask The setting that controls default file permissions that are assigned when a file or directory is created. The umask command controls the user mask settings.

virtual memory A memory management technique that is used by the operating system for programs that require more space in memory than can be allotted to them. The kernel moves only pages of the program currently needed into memory; unneeded pages remain on the disk.

zombie A process that has terminated but remains in the process table because its parent process has not sent the proper exit code. Zombie processes do not consume any system resources and are removed from the process table when a system is rebooted.

B

C

INDEX

B

C

G

H

I

K

L

Q

R

S

U

SunOS 4.x to SunOS 5.x Transition Information

This card lists commonly used SunOS™ 4.x commands and files in alphabetical order and describes the new SunOS 5.x command, equivalent, or unavailability. See Appendix A for a complete list of command changes.

SunOS 4.x Command	SunOS 5.x Equivalent
ac	sar
add_services	pkgadd
arch	uname -m
bar	Not available. Use cpio -H bar to retrieve
biff -y	chmod o+x /dev/tty
biff -n	chmod o-x /dev/tty
cc	Not available
dbxtool	debugger
df	df -k
dkctl	Not available
dkinfo	prtvtoc
du	du -k
dump	ufsdump
dumpfs	Not available
etherfind	snoop
exportfs	share
extract_files	Not available
extract_patch	Not available
extract_unbundled	pkgadd
fastboot	reboot or init 6
fasthalt	init 0
hostid	sysdef -h
hostname	uname -n
intr	Not available
leave	Use cron and at
lint	Not available

SunOS 4.x Command	SunOS 5.x Equivalent
load	pkgadd
loadc	pkgadd
load_package	Not available
lpc	lpadmin
lpd	lpsched
lpq	lpstat
lpr	lp
lprm	cancel
lptest	Not available
mach	uname -p
modstat	modinfo
mount	mount -F <*fstype*> [options]
mountall	mount -a
mount_tfs	mount -F <*fstype*>
pax	cpio
paxcpio	cpio
portmap	rpcbind
printenv	env
ps -a	ps -e
ps -aux	ps -el
pstat	sar
pstat -s	swap -s
rdump	ufsdump
restore	ufsrestore
rm_client	admintool
rm_services	Not available
rpc.etherd	Not available

SunOS 4.*x* Command	SunOS 5.*x* Equivalent
rpc.lockd	lockd
rpc.mountd	mountd
rpc.rexd	Not available
rpc.rquotad	Not available
rpc.showfhd	showfhd
rpc.statd	statd
rpc.user_agentd	Not available
rpc.yppasswdd	Not available
rpc.ypupdated	ypupdated
rrestore	ufsrestore
rusage	Not available
showmount	dfmounts
startup	Not available
swapon	swap -a
sys-config	admintool
umountall	umount -a
umount_tfs	umount -F <*fstype*>
unload	pkgrm
update	fsflush
uptime	who -b
users	who -q
vipw	Not available
wall	Not available
whereis	Not available
whoami	id
ypbatchupd	Not available
yppasswd	Use nispasswd for NIS+
ypserv	Not available